JAMES BOND

THE SECRET HISTORY

SEAN EGAN

JOHN BLAKE

Published by John Blake Publishing Ltd,
3 Bramber Court, 2 Bramber Road,
London W14 9PB, England

www.johnblakebooks.com

www.facebook.com/johnblakebooks
twitter.com/jblakebooks

This edition published in 2016

ISBN: 978 1 78606 020 4

British Library Cataloguing-in-Publication Data:

A catalogue record for this book is available from the British Library.

Design by www.envydesign.co.uk

Printed in Great Britain by CPI Group (UK) Ltd

1 3 5 7 9 10 8 6 4 2

Papers used by John Blake Publishing are natural, recyclable products made from
wood grown in sustainable forests. The manufacturing processes conform to the
environmental regulations of the country of origin.

Every attempt has been made to contact the relevant copyright-holders,
but some were unobtainable. We would be grateful if the
appropriate people could contact us.

To my Dad
FRANK EGAN
who allowed my mother to name me after Mr Connery
and whose copy of *Live and Let Die* was life-changing

CONTENTS

FOREWORD

Books about James Bond appear with the tedious inevitability of an unloved season, but I can't think of any that have either the range or tenor of *James Bond: The Secret History*.

When one knows a lot about a subject, it's easy to miss the forest for the trees, and, while this book offers an excellent overview of the history of the Bond phenomenon for casual fans, it also provides a lot of information and insights that cast the familiar in surprising new angles. Covering Ian Fleming's books and short stories, the continuation authors, the comics, the video games and of course the film series, Sean Egan charts the passage of 007 from 1952, when Fleming first sat down to write a Bond story, to the present day, and does so in prose both fluid and studded with astute and often amusing opinions (even if I don't agree with all of them). He has interviewed Fleming intimates, Bond scholars and movie cast and crew to give us an insider's view of the development of the icon, debunking several myths along the way.

'You forgot the first rule of mass media,' Bond screams into the ears of media mogul Elliot Carver in the closing act of *Tomorrow Never Dies*. 'Give the people what they want!' Egan demonstrates in this very fast and highly enjoyable read that, through all the ups and downs, Bond producers Eon haven't ever forgotten that rule – and show no sign of doing so any time soon.

Jeremy Duns
Author,
The Dark Chronicles
Diamonds In The Rough: Investigations into the
Worlds of Ian Fleming and James Bond
Duns on Bond
Rogue Royale: The Lost Bond Film by
the 'Shakespeare of Hollywood'
Mariehamn, October 2015

INTRODUCTION

James Bond first made an appearance in 1953 with the novel *Casino Royale*.

The writing of his creator Ian Fleming provided a new paradigm for action heroes. By blending existing thriller ingredients with his own innovations, he ramped up the power, sophistication and reach of the genre.

His protagonist stood square against Soviet evil even as it was acknowledged that his moral landscape had been complicated by the real-life treachery of the Cambridge spy ring; he was unapologetically depicted as having a full and non-marital sex life, where such behaviour was usually the preserve of villains; instead of engaging in clean, consequence-free fisticuffs, he received and dealt violence that was often untidy, grisly and a matter for regret; despite the manifold fantasy elements of his adventures, he made his way through a world recognisable as real from the brand names that Fleming took the uncommon step of sprinkling into his text. On top of all this was a newspaperman's evocative and sophisticated writing style that left Fleming's rough-hewn populist influences in the dust.

Despite his capturing the public imagination, the British secret-intelligence agent codenamed '007' should logically long have been consigned to the dustbin of history.

In 1953, the Cold War was still raging and Britain's Empire was sufficiently intact as to make plausible the idea that the UK could be an important player on the world espionage stage. More than half a century later, the Iron Curtain has long been torn down and Bond's home country has been reduced to a geopolitically insignificant island. Meanwhile, sexual intercourse – casual or committed – has been turned, by the advent of reliable contraception, from a taboo into an unremarkable part of everyday life. Depictions of violence – whether celebratory or regretful – are no longer noteworthy. Even the fact that Fleming saw Bond as a 'blunt instrument' of state is a dated concept in a world that has long switched its affections from notions of duty to ones of personal liberty.

Yet instead of disappearing into the vault reserved for the once audacious, now merely embarrassing – see Harold Robbins – the man with a 'Licence to Kill' is more popular than ever. Simplify the character as they may have, the Bond films adapted from Fleming's prose constitute the most successful franchise in cinema history. Meanwhile, the original, grittier books still hold such sway with more intellectual palates that renowned literary novelists such as Sebastian Faulks and William Boyd have been persuaded by the Fleming estate to write Bond continuation novels. Underlining Bond's media and generation-straddling allure, N64's *GoldenEye 007* from 1997 was the most successful video game of all time. Bond film catchphrases such as 'Bond, James Bond' and 'Shaken, not stirred' have embedded themselves in society's lexicon. Bond's modus operandi, weaponry and jargon have become the template for all secret-agent stories. Even the glossy, gargantuan Bond-movie theme songs have created an instantly recognisable archetype.

The Bond industry has not been without hiccups. Fleming quickly began to resent writing the Bond books he tapped out at his Jamaican holiday home. He repeatedly made weary noises to his editor about his current manuscript being the last 007 novel. His shrivelling inspiration eventually led to his co-opting for a book the plot of a dormant collaborative Bond screenplay, which resulted in an unholy legal tangle and severe stress that may have hastened his own death.

The Bond films have periodically been struck by existential crises. While the public lapped up any Bond featuring the original cinema 007, the recasting process necessitated by Sean Connery's 1967 departure raised doubts about whether the series had a future without him. His successor, George Lazenby, made only one film; Roger Moore took time to settle in and was always hated by sections of the Bond fanbase; Timothy Dalton was a Bond actor to whom the public never really took; Daniel Craig's casting initially provoked a tsunami of contempt. The traumatic mid-seventies rupture of the production partnership of Cubby Broccoli and Harry Saltzman – who originated the series – threw a huge spanner in the works. This, though, was as nothing compared with legal battles in the 1990s that almost destroyed the franchise.

Yet Bond has ultimately proven impervious to any obstacle thrown in his path, whether it be by one of his larger-than-life adversaries such as Rosa Klebb, Oddjob or Ernst Stavro Blofeld or by the waxings and wanings of public affection and the changes in political trends. He has persevered where his real-life prototypes have passed away, and has retained a massive cultural presence where other fictional action heroes such as Sherlock Holmes, Tarzan and the Saint have been severely reduced in significance. He has also outlasted his countless imitators, from Danger Man to The Man from U.N.C.L.E. Even the mocking by the likes of Austin Powers and Johnny English of the shapes thrown by him and his antagonists could not dent Bond's appeal. *Skyfall* (2012) took more money at cinemas than any of the previous twenty-two official Bond films, even allowing for inflation.

James Bond: The Secret History seeks to explain the reason for Bond's longevity. By exploring all aspects of the billion-dollar 007 phenomenon, from books to television to radio to films to music to comics to video games to merchandise, it tries to unravel the reasons why what began in the mind of a rather melancholy newspaperman as a niche product for a select class turned into a globe-straddling icon like none before or since.

A CONVOLUTED
CREATOR

When in the mid-1960s the James Bond motion-picture franchise began taking the world by storm, a curious aspect of the craze was that it was perceived as part of a modernistic and classless *zeitgeist*. The swaggering, rule-bucking, increasingly gadget-wielding secret agent of the Bond films was felt to be implicitly in tune with the same reformist trend as the Beatles, Swinging London, the contraceptive pill and civil-rights demonstrations. As the *News of the World* put it in 1964, Bond was 'as typical of the age as Beatlemania, juvenile delinquency or teenagers in boots'.

It was curious because Ian Fleming, the creator of James Bond, was a man who simply could not have been more Establishment. In fact, Fleming's biographer and onetime colleague John Pearson agrees that he would probably have even hated the term 'franchise'. Pearson states of Fleming, 'He was very much what you'd expect from his background.' That background was quintessentially upper-class.

Ian Lancaster Fleming was born on 28 May 1908. He had an older brother, two younger brothers and a younger half-sister. His father Valentine was a Member of Parliament at a time when that was largely a gentleman's profession. When his father was killed in action during World War I, his *Times* obituary was written by no less a figure than Winston Churchill. Ian Fleming attended Eton College, the quintessential English 'public school' (by which is meant, private boarding school steeped in arcane tradition) and Sandhurst, the nation's premium military academy. He also attended Munich University and the University of Geneva. Fleming excelled in languages, being proficient in German, French and Russian. His career in banking thereafter is also part of an archetypal 'toff' trajectory of the period, underlined by the fact that his grandfather founded the bank Robert Fleming and Company.

Yet at the same time Fleming was not a clichéd product of his privileged upbringing. His mother pulled him out of both Eton and Sandhurst for his 'fast' ways. His stint as a stockbroker was not a success. 'I must do something that entertains me,' he told the BBC of the fact that 'I didn't get on very well there.' He was hedonistic in the manner one would expect of someone with far fewer prospects in life, indulging his vices to such a degree that he was cut down shockingly young. Moreover, when, in August 1963, he appeared on the BBC's *Desert Island Discs* radio programme, his choice of favourite pieces of music contained no classical works but instead was comprised exclusively of offerings by Édith Piaf, The Ink Spots, Rosemary Clooney and other examples of what most of his class would have dismissed as low culture.

Prior to his stint in banking, Fleming worked for Reuters. He didn't stay with the famous international news agency longer than three years, but his dissatisfaction was with the money, not the job.

He said, 'I had a wonderful time in Reuters, was a correspondent in Moscow and Berlin and all over the place. And of course I learnt there the straightforward writing style that everybody wants to have if they're going to write books.' Fleming eventually returned to journalism, beginning in 1945 a long-term relationship with *The Sunday Times*. In the half-decade preceding that, he – like so many men of his generation – had found his life and career taking a detour into the service of King and Country.

There have been a hilarious number of docudramas positing Fleming as a man of action during World War II, among them *Goldeneye* and *Spymaker*, both subtitled *The Secret Life of Ian Fleming*. In point of fact, Fleming's war was axiomatically unheroic and sedentary. He was assistant to the Director of Naval Intelligence, John Godfrey. He worked his way up the Royal Naval Volunteer Reserve from lieutenant to commander, but never stepped off dry land in that capacity. He would later give James Bond the same rank and background, his creation conceding in the book *Thunderball* that he had been 'supercargo' and 'a chocolate sailor'. It's quite true that in his work in Room 39 of the Admiralty – the fabled nerve centre of the Naval Intelligence Division – Fleming was involved in numerous important operations and schemes involving intrigue and cunning. One was a plan that was an accidental precursor to Operation Mincemeat, the famous Allied plot to mislead the enemy with bogus documents planted on a corpse. In 1941, he even wrote the original charter of the Office of Strategic Services, precursor to the Central Intelligence Agency. However, he was almost never allowed to participate in the field, not least because it ran the risk of capture and valuable information being extracted from him by torture.

Nonetheless, Fleming adored his work in Room 39. Pearson

says of the Navy, 'That was one thing he really did worship. That was the only organisation he belonged to which he really enjoyed and respected.'

After the war, Fleming became foreign manager of the Kemsley newspaper group, owned by *The Sunday Times*. It was a job for which he was qualified on more than one level. Pearson explains, 'He ran this press agency, a foreign news service called Mercury which he built up in the war as part of the British secret service effort within America with a lot of old secret service friends and so on.' Some might observe that this sounds as though Fleming was playing a dual role as newspaper employee and intelligence operative. Pearson: 'There was certainly an element of that.'

Pearson also says, 'Ultimately it didn't work because the competition with Reuters was all too tough and Mercury faded. That's when, to keep him happy, he was given a job at [the gossip column] "Atticus".' Fleming would also be given other tasks by the paper, including foreign assignments. In fact, for six years after his first published Bond novel, Fleming continued to work full-time for *The Sunday Times*.

Not that that day job was particularly onerous. Pearson says Fleming 'had a very cushy time at *The Sunday Times*' because proprietor Lord Kemsley and his wife 'were extremely fond of him'. Moreover, the fact that Fleming married the ex-wife of Lord Rothermere, proprietor of the *Daily Mail*, served, says Pearson, to grant Fleming 'a sort of *ex-facie* role as almost a member of the newspaper aristocracy within *The Sunday Times*. He was treated much better than most journalists were. He had longer holidays and so forth.' Indeed. Fleming negotiated a contract that allowed him to avoid the bitter English winters. He spent his annual two-month leave in Jamaica. He had fallen in love with the Caribbean island – then still a British colony – when he had occasion to visit it during the war. He bought a patch of land with its own private cove and there built a three-bedroom house, which he named Goldeneye, either after one of his wartime operations from 1940 or Carson McCullers's novel *Reflections in a Golden Eye* (1941), depending on which story he felt like telling.

Little has been written about Fleming's journalism down the years, and his newspaper writing has not been the subject of any mainstream anthology. (An omnibus volume titled *Talk of the Devil* appeared in 2008 but only as part of a deluxe centenary box set of his corpus retailing at a wallet-straining minimum of £2,000.) His travelogue *Thrilling Cities* (1963) was enjoyable enough, if hardly substantial, while *The Diamond Smugglers* (1957) was an arid affair, rather like his James Bond books minus the excitement and glamour. Yet Fleming was a highly skilled newspaperman. Pearson would be something of a protégé of Fleming's at *The Sunday Times*, at which Fleming secured him a job in the mid-1950s. He describes himself as 'a sort of leg man' for Fleming in putting together 'Atticus'. Fleming – who overhauled a feature that had traded in high-society talk – would suggest stories to Pearson and then deftly hone his submitted copy. Pearson says, 'I was always amazed at the speed and skill with which he would turn the raw material which I presented him with into very polished journalese.'

The visual image of Fleming that the wider world would come to have was the one created by the photographs on the flyleaves and back covers of his Bond books. By the time of the appearance of the first of them, he was well past forty. That he would not live to see sixty indicates the life of excess that was made evident in these pictures by his puffy jawline and drooping eyelids. There was a slight air of the ridiculous – even a campness – about the accoutrements with which he usually posed: a bow tie and a cigarette holder. Yet Fleming as a young man was handsome. His oval face was peculiar, but at the same time striking and sensuous. It's little surprise that he was a ladies' man.

In 1952, though, he settled down, marrying Ann Charteris. Their relationship long preceded their nuptials. Charteris had been Fleming's lover during her marriages to both the 3rd Baron O'Neill and 2nd Viscount Rothermere. She had given birth to Fleming's stillborn daughter during the latter marriage, and it was over her adultery that Rothermere divorced her in 1951. Fleming married her more out of duty than love: she was already pregnant by him again when they wed. Sometimes the viciousness of their relationship was played out on the safe ground of sadomasochistic sex. Other times it was enacted mentally and left deep scars.

This added to Fleming's pre-existing mental scars, numerous and multi-origined. His melancholy and fatalism was deep-seated. Raymond Benson investigated Fleming's past and, by extension, psyche when writing *The James Bond Bedside Companion* (1984). He recalls, 'Ivar Bryce was his absolutely closest friend – they shared everything – and Ernest Cuneo was his closest American friend. They both would say that Fleming was always just unsatisfied. That he felt like there was something he needed to accomplish that was eluding him.' Acquaintance Barbara Muir once remarked that 'Ian always was a death-wish Charlie.' This suggests far deeper roots for dissatisfaction than living with someone about whom he was ambivalent – namely that during his formative years Fleming felt neither valued nor wanted.

When it is suggested to him that Ian Fleming was a very convoluted person, John Pearson says, 'You can say that again.

He had his demons, as they say . . . Ian was a classic case of a problematic second son in the shadow of a very, very successful older brother, who was Peter Fleming. Now almost entirely forgotten, very unjustly, but he was a very good prewar travel writer. He was a man of action, very glamorous fellow, highly successful and adored by his racy old mother, Mrs Val Fleming, whereas Ian was always the odd one out and the reprobate and all the rest of it.'

Mrs Val Fleming forced Ian to break off an engagement when he was at university in Geneva, implicitly holding over him the power of disinheritance provided by her late husband's will. Her hard-heartedness did not stop there. Although Fleming had not excelled academically and had brought a minor level of shame on the family, with his literary creation he outflanked his brother Peter to become by far the most successful of Val Fleming's brood, yet she would not seem to have been placated by this. Asked if his mother began to respect Ian as he became one of the world's most successful authors, Pearson says, 'Don't think so. I think she became more reconciled to him, but I don't think that success really impinged upon Mrs Fleming.'

Also unimpressed by Bond was his supposed nearest and dearest. Ann looked down on James Bond novels, jokily dismissing them as 'pornography'. 'Annie had this desire to be a bluestocking saloniste,' says Pearson. 'She was an intellectual snob and she had a lot of smart followers around her, some of whom were lovers – Hugh Gaitskell was one. A whole group of rather smart intellectuals, writers and so forth, and I think Annie always thought that Ian couldn't possibly come up to that sort of standard.'

'That hurt him the most of anything,' says Benson of Fleming's wife's failure to take seriously his literary achievements. 'One evening he came home and she and some of her literary friends were in the living room and they were reading from his latest Bond novel aloud and laughing.'

In both public and in private correspondence, Fleming would come out with self-deprecating remarks about his work: 'I'm not in the Shakespeare stakes'; 'My books tremble on the brink of corn'; Bond was a 'cardboard booby'. Yet this strikes one as being not so much a genuinely held feeling but an example of getting his retaliation in first, the position automatically lunged for by someone in a lifelong cringe at the expectation of reproach.

Both Fleming's American agent Naomi Burton and his friend and fellow writer Noël Coward felt he had it in him to write a non-thriller, i.e. literary fiction. From Burton's point of view, the only reason Fleming did not was that he was afraid of being ridiculed by his wife and her friends.

No fewer than three characters in Fleming's fiction are afflicted by 'accidie', defined by the *Oxford English Dictionary* as 'Spiritual or mental sloth; apathy'. It seems reasonable to conclude that in fact Fleming had this malaise, and that the malaise was the consequence of a deflated spirit engendered by a lifelong lack of validation.

Pearson recalls of Fleming, 'He really gave very little of himself away. Although when I worked for him I had three children, including two sons, I don't think I ever discussed the fact that he had a son too. There was never any interplay of family relations or anything very much.' Although Pearson suggests this circumspection is partly attributable to his old profession ('I always felt that he had absorbed an awful lot of spymaster's mentality from his time in Room 39'), the fact that Fleming did not readily proffer the information of the existence of Caspar – born in 1952 – seems yet another measure of his lack of conviction that anything about him might be of interest to anyone else.

Yet his spiritual flatness was by no means perpetual. Cubby Broccoli, co-producer of the Bond movies, recalled Fleming as a man curious about everything, always anxious to glean knowledge about people and their lives. This hardly chimes with the notion of a man weary of existence, notwithstanding the natural inquisitiveness of writers. Benson offers, 'He was very melancholic by nature, although he had a very dry wit and a dark humour about him. When he was out and about with his buddies, he was a barrel of laughs and a lot of fun.'

Nor did Fleming exhibit the unpleasantness that is the usual giveaway of self-loathing. 'Oh, no, not at all,' says Pearson. 'I never saw any sign of it whatsoever.' Politesse comes naturally to the upper classes but Fleming's civility was not a thin veneer. Pearson: 'He was in fact very, very kind to me. He got me my first commission to write a book. That was very much typical of Ian.' Someone who was on far more intimate terms with Fleming was his stepdaughter Fionn Morgan (née O'Neill), daughter of Ann and her first husband Shane. Aged sixteen when her mother married Fleming, she has described him as 'as much a father to me as a stepfather' and bristles at criticism of him.

James Bond, though, ultimately seems to be born of Fleming's unhappiness. He said he wrote the first Bond book to 'take my mind off the shock of getting married at the age of forty-three'. Although the point he was making was about the upending of what had seemed the natural course of his life – bachelorhood – it's still a peculiar thing indeed to say about what is usually a cause of great joy and anticipation.

For Pearson, James Bond stemmed from his creator's fantasy of a happier life. 'It was very much an essay in the autobiography of dreams,' he says. 'I think he used the books, or used Bond, as an alter ego to enjoy himself in ways that he couldn't in reality.'

BIRTH
OF BOND

Journalism aside, writing had long featured in Fleming's life.
At Eton, he produced a magazine called *The Wyvern*, which published his first piece of fiction ('a shameless crib of Michael Arlen'). In 1926, Fleming attended a finishing school in Kitzbühel, Austria, run by Ernan Forbes Dennis (an ex-spy) and Phyllis Bottome. When he was around nineteen, Bottome encouraged Fleming to write. One result was a short story entitled 'A Poor Man Escapes', another a story called 'Death, On Two Occasions'. Not long after leaving Reuters, Fleming wrote and privately published a collection of poetry called *The Black Daffodil*, although shortly became so embarrassed by it that he burned all copies.

Fleming toyed with the idea of authoring an espionage novel from at least summer 1944, when he told war colleague Robert Harling that, once demobilised, he would 'write the spy story to end all spy stories'. What is remarkable about Fleming's idle boast is that it was accurate: the espionage template was changed for all time by *Casino Royale* and its sequels. Before he thus changed the landscape, though, Fleming was – like any other writer – merely the sum of his influences.

Asked in 1963 by *Counterpoint* which writers had influenced him, Fleming offered, 'I suppose, if I were to examine the problem in depth, I'd go back to my childhood and find some roots of interest in E. Phillips Oppenheim and Sax Rohmer.' Oppenheim wrote thrillers laced with vignettes of high living, convincing psychology and Edwardian morality. His famous works included *The Great Impersonation* (1920) and *The Spy Paramount* (1935). Rohmer was the creator of Fu Manchu, a Chinese criminal mastermind nicknamed the Yellow Peril on whom Bond villain Dr No seems to be heavily based.

Fleming gave a couple of notable quotes about Bulldog Drummond and his creator, Sapper (H.C. McNeile). When asked to describe Bond, he said, 'Sapper from the waist up and Mickey Spillane below.' In a posthumously published December 1964 *Playboy* interview, Fleming said, 'I didn't believe in the heroic Bulldog Drummond types. I mean, rather, I didn't believe they could any longer exist in literature.' Both quotes invoke Drummond/Sapper in a negative, or at least ambiguous, sense. The impression that might be gleaned from this is that Fleming had never liked Sapper, but, as John Pearson discovered, he had been partial to his writings when as a young boy they had been read to him by his headmaster's wife at boarding school. Drummond was an ex-army man whose rough-hewn features created his nickname. Bored with life, he advertised in *The Times* for adventure. Fleming's later conviction that Drummond's escapades belonged to the past was probably not due to Bulldog's oft-stated contempt for Jews, Germans, 'wops', 'dagos', 'frogs', 'niggers' and 'greasers': such racism would be pretty much matched by Fleming, whose hero detested Koreans and Germans, and almost all of whose adversaries would be foreigners. As alluded to in Fleming's comments above, it was more likely due to the complete absence of the carnal in Sapper's prose, plus Drummond's unlikely preternatural abilities in physical combat. Moreover, Sapper had 'no literary pretensions', to use the peculiar phrase employed to describe those who can't write very well – as though their lack of ability is both voluntary and a defiant statement of integrity.

Pearson found John Buchan to be another action author who featured in Fleming's reading history. Buchan's most famous protagonist was Richard Hannay, whose best-known adventure is *The Thirty-Nine Steps* (1915). Hannay was a departure from previous action-adventure protagonists in being vulnerable and flawed, and this was something that Fleming would bring to his own hero.

The character the Saint was introduced to the world by author Leslie Charteris in 1928 with *Meet the Tiger*. Many novels and short stories followed. He was brought to a wider public by movies and television. 'It's surprising that very little comparison is made between the Saint and James Bond,' says Jeremy Duns, a Bond fan and scholar, as well as an espionage novelist himself. 'It must be that Ian Fleming was aware of the Saint. He was a hugely successful character and there are an enormous number of similarities between the Saint and James Bond.' Simon Templar – whose initials gave rise to his sobriquet – was a handsome, charming, dapper, hedonistic Englishman of action, as knowledgeable about gourmet meals as martial arts and weaponry. He was also catnip to the ladies, and his premarital sex life was explored in a relatively frank manner. Although there was a certain Robin Hood element to his persona, he was darker than Bond. Duns: 'If you ever watch parodies of Bond, they actually tend to be more like the Saint. The Saint is a ruthless, devil-may-care rogue, whereas Fleming's character was a much more straightforward sort.'

Somerset Maugham may have been an influence on Bond via *Ashenden: or the British Agent*, a 1928 volume of spy stories set in World War I. That Ashenden's superior is known by an initial, like Bond's boss M, may be coincidence, but indisputable is the fact that Maugham was a friend of Fleming and that Fleming's 007 short story 'Quantum of Solace' is – uncharacteristic though it is of the literary Bond canon – modelled on Maugham's stories of colonial domestic drama.

When Fleming submitted his first Bond novel, he was told by William Plomer – his friend and subsequent copy editor – that it needed revision. Fleming wrote back, 'It remains to be seen whether I can get a bit closer to Eric Ambler and exorcise the blabbering ghost of Cheyney.' Ambler was a writer much admired for his devising in the 1930s a new model for the thriller. We can infer from Fleming's comment that he shared that admiration, although probably more for Ambler's realism, deftness and literary bent than an unusually leftish perspective, which was for many a refreshing change from the elitism and/or racism of Sapper, Buchan, et al. Ambler became best-known for *The Mask of Dimitrios*, which had an Istanbul background. Fleming – who was acquainted with him – picked Ambler's brains about that city and Byzantium in general when writing *From Russia with Love* (in that book Bond is to be found reading an Ambler).

Fleming's putdown of Peter Cheyney wasn't his only one. Despite being British, the crime writer popular since the late thirties devised Americanised titles such as *Dames Don't Care* and *Your Deal, My Lovely* and gave protagonists handles such as Lemmy Caution and Slim Callaghan. Strangely, though, reviews of Fleming's books often compared them to Cheyney's. The one such comparison that really delighted Fleming was the occasion W. H. Smith's *Trade News* columnist Whitefriar, reviewing *Casino Royale*, called him the 'Peter Cheyney of the carriage trade'. Fleming made sure that Whitefriar received inscribed copies of his books from that point on.

The end of that *Playboy* 'I didn't believe in the heroic Bulldog Drummond types' quote was, 'I wanted this man more or less to follow the pattern of Raymond Chandler's or Dashiell Hammett's heroes – believable people, believable heroes.'

Fleming was referring to purveyors of American 'hard-boiled' fiction (of whom Mickey Spillane was also an example, if a less refined one). They were the sorts of writers whose low-life vignettes and wise-guy argot Cheyney attempted to imitate from the distance and incongruous surroundings of drizzly, low-key Britain. The private-detective heroes of these writers were cynics and loners, low-waged characters hired by wealthy clients to discreetly solve shameful mysteries and who faced the dangers that resulted therefrom with alternate muscularity and wryness. The writers concerned tended to be very good on colloquial dialogue, albeit with a suspicion of its being souped up with witticisms and street poetry beyond the average denizen of a back alley. Unlike Cheyney, Fleming ensured that, whatever trappings he co-opted from the hard-boiled genre, his protagonist was quintessentially English.

Jeremy Duns has alighted on what he feels is a clear but little-known inspiration for James Bond. At the end of his life, Dennis Wheatley was notorious for the likes of *The Devil Rides Out* and *To the Devil a Daughter*. However, before that tumble into the *outré*, he was known as a writer of thrillers. His protagonist, Gregory

Sallust, and the adventures in which he became entangled were, for Duns, prototypically 007.

Duns says of Sallust, 'He has a scar on his face. He's a cynical, hedonistic British secret agent. He's a freelance secret agent, so he doesn't have quite the organisational, bureaucratic power behind him, but he has this M figure in Sir Pellinore, who he's got a very similar, paternal relationship to, although it's perhaps more friendly. The character is womanising, drinking, gambling – quite unusual for a hero.' Moreover: 'There is a surprising amount of sex in the Dennis Wheatley books. There's lots of spanking in it. Sallust seems to be absolutely obsessed with spanking women. And so was Fleming.' Sallust made his debut in *Contraband*, published in 1936. Duns: 'That whole first chapter. Hang on a bloody minute: this is a British secret agent with a scar on his face in a casino in northern France . . . A beautiful woman comes in on the arm of a villainous aristocrat who also happens to be a dwarf . . . It feels like you're reading *Casino Royale*. *Come into My Parlour* is the one that I would really single out. That very much feels like a prototype of *From Russia with Love*.'

Yet, while Fleming acknowledged other influences in interviews and journalism, he never mentioned Wheatley. Duns thinks that this is because he wanted to look cool in terms of his inspirations: 'Wheatley is a very below-stairs writer.'

Fleming had the advantage of not having to draw his inspiration only from fellow writers. He had worked alongside – even directed the missions of – real-life action heroes. Asked about 007 on *Desert Island Discs*, he said, 'He's a mixture of commandos and secret-service agents that I met during the war, but of course entirely fictionalised.' Merlin Minshall, Michael Mason, Commander Wilfred 'Biffy' Dunderdale and Commander Alexander 'Sandy'

Glen are all names that will be meaningless to most, but there is circumstantial evidence that the personalities and/or exploits of these intelligence colleagues and acquaintances of Fleming contributed to the character of James Bond. William Stephenson *is* fairly well known to the public – if only by his codename: Intrepid – and seems one of the strongest candidates of all. An operation engaged in by the MI6 employee in New York with Fleming by his side involved a break-in at the office of a Japanese cypher expert. It later became – in a heightened version – a mission that helped earn Bond his double-O status. Moreover, in 1941 Fleming participated in the exercises undertaken by students at a type of training school for saboteurs run by Stephenson in Canada. One of the tasks – attaching a limpet mine to the underside of a ship – turns up in *Live and Let Die* in a scene containing considerable verisimilitude. It seems logical that other techniques Fleming learned there also pepper the Bond canon.

Fleming's 'spy novel' would not take place in World War II, however, nor any of the other conflicts around which twentieth-century spy fiction had so far revolved. Novels with a backdrop of World War I, World War II and early-twentieth-century anti-Bolshevism became, as soon as those conflicts were concluded, period pieces (if, in some cases, enduringly readable ones). The war of attrition and ideology that developed after World War II between Communist, totalitarian East and capitalist, democratic West was, however, a novelist's gift that kept on giving. Although it was a war of low-level intensity, for several decades it genuinely seemed one without end and it was into that conflict – rife with fictional possibilities – that Fleming dropped his new character.

What, though, should he call him? 'I wanted the simplest, dullest plainest-sounding name I could find,' Fleming told the

Manchester Guardian in 1958. '"James Bond" was much better than something more interesting like "Peregrine Carruthers". Exotic things would happen to and around him, but he would be a neutral figure – an anonymous, blunt instrument wielded by a government department.'

It was long assumed Fleming got the name for his hero from the American author of *Birds of the West Indies*, a book on his shelves at Goldeneye. However, another Fleming biographer, Andrew Lycett, proffers a different story. When during the war Fleming spoke of his literary ambitions to C.H. Forster of the Ministry of Aircraft Production, the latter asked him how he would choose names. Fleming replied that he would think of the first couple of names in his house at school and change – by which it seems he meant 'transpose' – their first names. Replied Forster, 'In my case, the first names were James Aitken and Harry Bond. So you could have Harry Aitken and James Bond.' Of course, the two stories don't necessarily contradict each other.

Fleming met the 'real' James Bond in 1964 when he was writing his final 007 story, *The Man with the Golden Gun*. It was a convivial affair in which the ornithologist and his wife amusedly explained how their lives were now punctuated by ribbing from people in minor officialdom such as porters and airport staff to whom they had cause to reveal their names. In a letter to Mary Wickham Bond – Mrs James Bond – Fleming said the name was just what he needed because it was 'brief, unromantic, Anglo-Saxon and yet very masculine'. The name, though, was less prosaic and more in the poetical literary tradition than Fleming might have thought: 'bond' – another word for promise or pledge – was ideal for a character of patriotic duty and iron purpose.

Armed with his influences, his first-hand insight into intelligence matters, a facility with the written word and a name for his protagonist, Fleming set about amalgamating them. In devising his own angle on the espionage genre, he became known for several specific plot and style characteristics. Many assumed he invented all of them. This was partly because Bond's phenomenal success took such characteristics from the ghettoes of pulp into the mainstream. It was also partly because no previous purveyor of this type of material had Fleming's breeding or his personal contacts in the literary world. He was able to get his books reviewed in the 'posh papers' and the likes of *The Times Literary Supplement*. To reviewers in such outlets – who would never sully their hands with a Dennis Wheatley – his type of writing *was* new.

The trademarks he became known for were:

1. SEXUAL FRANKNESS: Public discussion of sex – particularly sex outside marriage – was largely taboo at the time Fleming began writing Bond books in the early 1950s. This state of affairs was due to the absence of reliable contraception, a situation that never really changed during Fleming's lifetime. Those who depicted or discussed in art non-marital sex were often accused of encouraging immorality and undermining the cause of preventing single-motherhood. Fleming's participation in the disregard of this taboo was therefore shocking. It was also thrilling. His matter-of-fact acknowledgement of sexual desire and depiction of, if not its mechanics, its preamble and aftermath were, on a base level, titillating. This was not least because he was clearly kinky: spanking is mentioned in half a dozen Bond novels, with the secret agent's first thought of it occurring towards the end of earliest book *Casino Royale*, and his actually first threatening to take across his lap a wilful female in fifth book *From Russia with*

Love. However, his frankness was also refreshing in a pure sense for people fed up with the circumspection then surrounding this most everyday and pleasurable of human functions, one groan-making manifestation of which was heroes in thrillers making their excuses and leaving when sex looked like raising its supposedly shameful head.

2. THE UNOBTAINABLE: The dreary austerity of an already pitilessly class-bound country provided a ready-made audience for Fleming's semi-posh, jet-setting, casino-haunting creation. There was a notable authenticity to Fleming's travelogues that added another dimension to their exoticness. 'I rarely write about places I have not seen,' he noted. Gambling was illegal in the UK except in private clubs, and even those forms of it that were legal were not allowed to be advertised or encouraged. Even the statement in *Diamonds are Forever* that Bond is taking his fourth shower of the day fits into this syndrome: hygiene in mid-fifties Britain was commonly a matter of a weekly bath, with showers virtually unknown even in well-to-do households.

3. BRAND NAMES: Fleming's fascination with the non-generic was unusual. The mythical 'ACME' was usually posited as the universal manufacturer of the products that appeared in fiction, or else false names were substituted for familiar ones. Fleming once observed, 'I see no point in changing the name of the Dorchester to the Porchester, or a Rolls-Royce to an Hirondelle.' Fleming claimed that he inserted such references as a sort of mooring as his settings and plots took off into the sphere of the fantastical – a way to make the reader feel 'that he and the writer have still got their feet on the ground'. However, he must have been aware of their function as product porn: his references to the likes of Chanel and Fleurs des Alpes served to provide

a window on another world as much as did Bond's games of *chemin de fer*.

4. CLASSY VILLAINS: Fleming's baddies were not Nazi caricatures or belligerent cockneys. Rather, they were larger-than-life personalities with an etiquette incongruous in the context of their murderousness. A set-piece confrontation between Bond and baddie – over a dinner table or similar calm tableaux – became a staple of the part of the narrative just prior to the final, bloody showdown.

5. ANTI-HEROISM: Any English professor will tell you that the lead character in a book is a protagonist, not a hero, but James Bond didn't even fit that neutral term. Fleming would make more than one interview comment down the years indicating that the reader was not expected to like his creation. In a 1958 BBC radio duologue with fellow writer Raymond Chandler, for instance, he observed, '. . . he's always referred to as my hero. I don't see him as a hero myself. On the whole I think he's a rather unattractive man . . . ' In 1964, Fleming told journalist Ken Purdy, 'I never intended him to be a particularly likeable person, which makes me wonder a bit about the real motives behind the people who treat him like a cult.' Fleming told Michael Howard of his publishers Cape that he wrote tenth 007 book, *The Spy Who Loved Me*, as a 'cautionary tale' because 'young people were making a hero out of James Bond'.

Tied into this is the changed world in which Bond was operating. Fleming began work on *Casino Royale* just six months after the disappearance of British spies Guy Burgess and Donald Maclean. The two men would not be publicly confirmed as having defected to the Union of Soviet Socialist Republics until 1956, but it was immediately widely assumed that they had been double agents, something that engendered national humiliation and anger. The members of the Cambridge Spy Ring, as it became known, were not the square-jawed types of espionage fiction but turncoats allied to one of the most monstrous regimes in modern history. With the changes created by this occurrence to public assumptions about heroism and the upper classes, Fleming would seem to have concluded that Bond could not be depicted as operating in a black-and-white world. Ethical ambivalence was now the order of the day. Bond had a clear morality about right and wrong in geopolitical terms – he hated the cruelties of Communism – but on a personal level made what many would consider transgressions, whether it be sleeping with married women or cold-bloodedly dispatching defenceless enemies.

This in turn fed into a sense of modernity. That Bond was not a practitioner of the Queensberry Rules or an un-nuanced yes-man made him both an antidote to the stiff, Establishment figures of many previous spy books and attractive to a wider demographic. Even working-class people sceptical of values that they felt benefited only people in a higher income bracket could relate to a fornicating rule-bucker.

While with the above ingredients Fleming may have just been updating or refining already existing – if not necessarily commonplace – espionage elements, there are some things about his work that genuinely were revolutionary:

1. PROCEDURAL: Fleming's naval espionage knowledge, though not always directly transferable and though not acquired from working in the field, provided a verisimilitude of protocol,

mentality, terminology and backdrop. Moreover, where he needed more land-based expertise, he could rely on his brother Peter, who had worked in military intelligence during the war. Where Fleming had no direct knowledge or handy source to tap, he did his research, having meetings with, and sending out letters to, experts on relevant subjects and even allowing them to read through early drafts of his manuscripts.

2. TEXTURE: Because Fleming intended Bond as a cypher, he gave his character almost none of his own aesthetic bent, the type of which led to his amassing a culturally significant collection of first-edition books. However, that Fleming was a sensualist was written all over his Bond texts. Where previous writers would, in order to keep the action going and the cliffhangers coming, gloss over or even dispense with specifics of clothes, food, drink, travel and surroundings, Fleming would explore his hero's observations and experiences in rich, leisurely and even digressive detail. Action and setup took an incongruous back seat.

3. VULNERABILITY: Despite occasional ruthlessness, Bond does not exult in violence in the manner of the likes of Templar or Drummond. He often ruefully reflects on having had to engage in it. Additionally, although good at his job, he is by no means a preternaturally poised operative, cheating death through serendipity as often as by ingenuity or bravery. He is also in the habit of availing himself of Benzedrine to sharpen his reflexes.

4. SALARY MAN: Perhaps Fleming's most interesting departure from the espionage genre is the fact that his protagonist was not a freelancer. Bulldog Drummond and the Saint were adventurers of independent means, the American 'gumshoes' were self-employed, the protagonists of the works of Buchan

and Ambler were often hapless ordinary people caught up by chance in forces beyond their understanding. There had, of course, always been salaried policemen and government spies in thrillers. However, rarely, if ever, had there been a man like 007. Bond got entangled in the most outrageous adventures, but they resulted from his job as a civil servant and, like anybody who answers to an employer, he was subject to rules, process and routine. For a society that universal education and decreasing deference had made more knowing and less credulous, this placing of the hero within the same exigencies of existence with which the average mortal had to contend was an intriguing and pleasing step forward. Moreover, Bond's government job raised the stakes: his missions involved not some common-or-garden delinquency but risk to the world order.

Despite his background knowledge, Fleming's depiction of espionage work was in no way the most authentic. Even the convincing procedural detail that often led up to his fantastical developments and denouements were sometimes nonsensical. For instance, Duns observes, 'In real-life espionage, you already have your intelligence officer or officers in the city involved and have a network of people all over the world. When there's a crisis in Paris, then the person who speaks fluent French who's been in Paris for three years deals with it. The idea that you send in this one guy into all these places all over the world – that's a fantasy premise.'

However, the espionage paradigm Fleming created was the one to which the world took more than any other. From a point within around half a dozen years after Bond's entrée, every espionage story would be compared to Fleming's tales and, later, the films derived from them. It therefore came to feel the most natural paradigm even if it wasn't the most authentic. The shadow it cast over the genre was so huge that spy novelists and filmmakers to this day fight off accusations of imitation when they adhere to it, and are perceived to be almost comically self-conscious when they deviate from it.

That was then. Today, sex is ubiquitous, gambling is legal, global travel and brand names affordable and lack of deferentialism pretty much the norm. If published for the first time today, the values of the Bond books would not inspire the wonder they once did.

But, then, the mantle of the James Bond paradigm for espionage tales was long ago passed from the books to the films, which – as well as distributing it more widely – heightened it, stylised it, sanitised it and continuously updated it. One could even make the claim that Fleming deserves little credit for the James Bond cinema construct, which was already largely out of his hands even before his death and which has been expanded, traduced, refined and toyed with ever since. Nonetheless, the essential idea of Bond purveyed by his creator – a preternaturally able, unusually handsome, sexually voracious, epicurean British secret agent granted a licence to kill by his employer – has survived all the upheavals and redrawings of approach necessitated by box-office returns, alterations in actors and changes in cultural standards across the course of half a century. This must count for something in terms of Fleming's legacy, to say the least.

As must one thing missing from the above list of ingredients in Fleming's Bond books: high-grade writing. The genre wasn't necessarily bereft of such before Bond. Joseph Conrad's *The Secret Agent* (1907), G.K. Chesterton's *The Man Who Was Thursday* (1908) and several post-World War II novels by Graham Greene are espionage tomes few intellectuals would be ashamed to have on their bookshelves. In an unusually non-self-deprecating comment, Fleming stated that his objective was 'thrillers designed to be read as literature'. He would never have been so immodest as to state whether he felt he had been successful in this object, but he assuredly was. He managed to weld the outlandish plots of pulpier writers to the smooth-flowing, economical, evocative and often exquisite prose style of the type of novelists who won literary awards.

While Fleming's skill may be irrelevant to the millions who continue to flock to Bond films – most of whom have probably never read a Bond novel – it's to be doubted that Bond would have become a filmable proposition without the springboard to mass public attention provided by the author's classy template.

Moreover, the original literary incarnation of Bond has a purity and legitimacy no film – however well made – can ever claim. Not for nothing did, post-Roger Moore, 'I went back to the books' become a mantra for actors taking on the role of 007. This was not just an implicit repudiation of the way the film franchise had sagged into softness over the course of the seventies and eighties but an acknowledgement of the power and lodestar status of the source material.

ENTER: THE
SECRET AGENT

G oldeneye was the location of the writing of the first drafts
of all of Fleming's Bond stories, starting on 15 January
1952 with *Casino Royale*.

While the poise of his prose might suggest long, even agonised,
deliberation, an inspection of Fleming's modus operandi reveals
anything but. *Casino Royale*'s 62,000-word manuscript was
completed in no more than eight weeks. This was actually a slow
rate for Fleming: he would later so refine the process that he was
able to produce 2,000 words a day, which equated to completion
of a draft in six weeks. Of course, that was not the end of the
process. Or indeed the start of it: Fleming's mind percolated
ideas over a long period, during which he conducted research and
jotted down ideas in notebooks. However, writing a manuscript
quickly made commensurately easier the revising and enriching
subsequently executed in Jamaica or back in Britain.

Fleming explained his technique in a May 1963 *Books and*

Bookmen article called 'How To Write a Thriller': 'By following my formula, you write 2,000 words a day and you aren't disgusted with them until the book is finished . . .' He disclosed that he didn't even pause to choose the right word or to verify spelling or a fact. 'When my book is completed I spend about a week going through it and correcting the most glaring errors and rewriting passages. I then have it properly typed with chapter headings and all the rest of the trimmings.'

Despite what would be an increasing boredom with his creation, Fleming's productivity for the next dozen years was utterly dependable. His disciplined routine at Goldeneye – the 2,000-word target reached via three hours' work in the morning and another hour in the evening – ensured that a new James Bond book would be published in his native country in either March or April each year.

James Bond, we learn during the course of the narrative of *Casino Royale*, lives in a flat in Chelsea (in later books revealed to be in an unnamed square off the King's Road, where he is tended to by his 'treasure' of a housekeeper, May), smokes at least seventy cigarettes a day of a Balkan and Turkish mixture custom-made by Morlands of Grosvenor Street and decorated with a triple gold band (not mentioned by Fleming at any time is that the bands would seem to refer to Bond's/Fleming's naval rank of commander) and, as a consequence of his bachelorhood and his attention to detail, takes 'a ridiculous' pleasure in food and drink. His only hobby is his supercharged 4.5-litre circa 1933 vintage Bentley (although it occurs to the reader that his stated love of gambling would also surely fall into the hobby category). He has invented his own elaborate dry martini drink, which he intends one day to patent (three measures of Gordon's, one of vodka, half a measure of Kina Lillet, shake it very well until it's ice-cold, then add a large thin slice of lemon peel – all served in a deep champagne goblet). He is a deductive man, for example instantly clocking some elderly inn-keepers as a childless couple whose frustrated affection is lavished on their guests and pets. At some point in the hazy future, Bond intends to resign and travel the world.

When Bond sleeps, his face is ironical, brutal and cold, although this is offset when he is awake by his eyes' warmth and humour. That face – at least according to supporting character Vesper in conversation with French agent René Mathis – is both very good-looking and resembles that of famous songwriter Hoagy Carmichael. Bond disagrees with this comparison when gazing into a mirror (although – in an example of the frequent continuity clumsiness in Fleming's canon – we are not told how he came to know of Vesper's remark). He finds himself looking at a face into which are set a pair of ironically inquiring grey-blue eyes, over the right of which hangs a comma of hair that will never stay in place. Together with the thin vertical scar down his right cheek, the effect is 'faintly piratical'. (In future books we will learn his height is an even six feet.)

Professionally we discover that Bond works for the 'Secret Service', an adjunct to the British Defence Ministries, and has done so since before the war, as World War II was usually referred to then. 'The Service' is located on the ninth floor of a tall, grey building overlooking Regent's Park in Central London. There, he answers to a chief of staff known as M, whom Bond worships even despite his harrumphing crustiness. Psychologists will be interested to learn that as a boy Fleming called his mother 'M'. (Later in the series we will learn that M is an admiral and a knight named Miles Messervy.)

When Bond's cigarette lighter is mentioned herein, where most authors of the time would have made no comment on it further than its function, Fleming takes great care to specify it to be a black, oxidised Ronson. Yet the one major exception Fleming made to his preference for using names and brands from real life was Bond's employer. There was, and is, no organisation with the title the Secret Service, even if it is obvious what is its real-life counterpart: the Secret Intelligence Service, also known as MI6. Lightly disguising an existing organisation is, of course, a literary tradition employed for the same sorts of reasons as giving one's hero a name different from the person or persons on whom he is based. Those reasons range from discretion to convenience to fear of libel writs to a disinclination to distract the reader. In addition to all or any of those things, Fleming was to some extent hamstrung by the Official Secrets Act and the interrelated fact that SIS/MI6 did not officially exist. As late as 1966, the British Government barred the usage in print of even the generalised phrase 'British Secret Service'. Although this was a King Canute mandate, Fleming was an ex-intelligence man and therefore presumably bound by loyalty where he wasn't the law. Moreover, as someone who picked up titbits of information at MI6 dinners, he would also have been conscious of the need to keep valuable sources on-side.

The name that Fleming chose as a substitute is rather peculiar. The Secret Service Bureau was formed in 1909 and during World War I was split into two. The Security Service – or Military Intelligence, Section 5 (MI5) – covers domestic intelligence matters. The Secret Intelligence Service (SIS) – Military Intelligence, Section 6 (MI6) – gathers foreign intelligence. The British government began acknowledging the existence of MI5 only in 1989 and MI6 in 1994. Fleming's term 'Secret Service' could be said to nod to the original unbifurcated organisation's name. It had also been used in many previous British espionage books as either a colloquial or umbrella term. However, by now it seemed American nomenclature: the Secret Service has the job of ensuring the physical safety of high-ranking members of the US government.

Whatever Fleming's reason, he ultimately lost interest in his disguise. Although he never employed the more common MI6, by the time of the ninth Bond book, *Thunderball* (1961), he was occasionally stating SIS to be Bond's employer.

Bond carries a .38 Colt Police Positive with a sawn barrel and a very flat .25 Beretta automatic with a skeleton grip. The fact that he carts around weapons is germane to his codename: 007. Fleming would later in the series change the meaning of the 'double-O' prefix to that of a licence to kill, but in *Casino Royale* it is stated as denoting an agent who has had to kill in cold blood in the course of a job. What never changed was that the double-O status is of no little prestige in the Service.

In either of its meanings, the double-O status has no counterpart in real life. There have been some suggestions from ex-SIS employees that executions occasionally happened, albeit carried out by contractors, but never any claim that this was commonplace. In 1953, however, society was far less open and governmental agencies far less answerable to the public, or indeed the executive. It would therefore have seemed possible – and, in the case of an organisation that didn't officially exist, un-disprovable – that secret agents went around surreptitiously dispensing death.

As to the actual nomenclature, Fleming told *Playboy*, 'I pinched the idea from the fact that, in the Admiralty, at the beginning of the War, all top-secret signals had the double-O prefix.' Although it is widely assumed – including by this text – that the phrase 'double-oh' means two zeros, it should be noted that nowhere in Fleming's corpus is it stated that this is the case.

Bond is not without a tender side, something hinted at by his terror of being brought to his knees by love or by luck, a fate he considers inevitable. He is also, if not afflicted by moral doubts, then certainly not prone to brainless my-country-right-or-wrong standpoints. He notes of the shifting definitions of villainy in a developing Welfare State, 'If I'd been alive fifty years ago, the brand of Conservatism we have today would have been damn near called Communism and we should have been told to go and fight that.' Additionally, he opines that the people whose killings had garnered him the double-O number were 'probably quite decent people' who were 'just caught up in the gale of the world . . .' Nonetheless, his attitude towards his antagonist in this book is never sympathetic.

Said antagonist is Le Chiffre, one of the Opposition's chief agents in France, in which role he acts as undercover paymaster for a fifth-column trade union. In one respect, this villain is what the world would come to consider quintessentially Bondian: 'Le Chiffre' is French for 'figure' or 'numeral' and has been adopted because this stateless, apparently amnesia-stricken ex-inmate of Dachau considers himself merely a number on a passport. That tinge of the outlandish aside, however, he is a fairly common-or-garden baddie. That he is a 'flagellant' and 'does not laugh' hardly distinguishes him from those touched with the banality of evil. Or indeed from the often grim, often spank-happy Bond himself.

Although he is a competent operative, Le Chiffre's financial difficulties have caused him to misappropriate monies entrusted to him by the Soviet Union ('Redland', in Secret Service nomenclature). He is therefore in a perilous position. Unknown to him, but known to the Secret Service, an operative of SMERSH is already heading his way with deadly intent.

SMERSH is, to quote a memo sent to M, an 'efficient organ of Soviet vengeance'. It would be Bond's nemesis until the ninth 007 book, when Fleming decided to make his character's main adversary SPECTRE. Although Fleming sets up an elaborate and ostensibly knowledgeable explanation for the title of the organisation – SMERSH is a conflation of Russian phrase '*smert shpionam*', which means 'Death to Spies' – it didn't actually exist. A Russian World War II counterintelligence agency of that name had long since been broken up. The organisation to which Fleming was alluding was clearly the KGB.

Le Chiffre has decided to make good his losses by gambling in the casino at Royale everything in his trade union's depleted coffers. For the purposes of inflicting a blow – financial and psychological – on the enemy, it is recommended to M that 'the finest gambler available to the service should be given the necessary funds and endeavour to out-gamble this man'. Guess who.

A showdown over a baccarat table hardly sounds exciting – or even Bondian – stuff, but the drama actually picks up at this point. Although *Casino Royale* has an arresting first line ('The scent and smoke and sweat of a casino are nauseating at three in the morning') and features in Chapter 6 a blood-splattered failed assassination attempt on Bond by means of a bomb, the book's opening is leisurely. No explosive 'pre-title sequence' here – or, really, in any of Fleming's books – but an opening six-dozen pages that merely pootle along.

Bond is assigned Vesper Lynd as his Number Two. 'What the hell do they want to send me a woman for?' he thunders. 'Do they think this is a bloody picnic?' He is, though, somewhat mollified when Vesper turns out as promised to be a black-haired, blue-eyed beauty with 'splendid . . . protuberances . . . back and front'.

The book's most exciting scene comes when Le Chiffre is facing potential ruination at the card table. One of the villain's henchmen discreetly tries to make Bond withdraw his bet by pressing into his coccyx a silent gun disguised as an umbrella. Faced with the alternatives of his spine being shattered and of letting Le Chiffre win his desired loot, Bond ingeniously creates a diversion by toppling backwards in his chair.

In an attempt to retrieve his money, Le Chiffre abducts Vesper. After an exciting and well-written car chase, 007 ends up in the clutches of Le Chiffre, who takes him to his villa and begins torturing him by swatting with a carpet beater what the mores of the time dictated be delicately referred to as 'the underpart of his body'. Bond determines not to talk and resigns himself to death, but he is saved from a grisly fate by the intervention of the SMERSH agent tasked with executing Le Chiffre. With no orders relating to Bond, the assassin simply carves a warning sign into his hand.

Bond is not just smitten enough by his new colleague to decide to name his proprietary Martini a 'Vesper' – he resolves to propose to her. However, her behaviour at the secluded inn at which they are staying becomes strange and disturbing. The next morning Bond is woken with the devastating news that Vesper has killed herself with a bottle of sleeping pills. Her suicide note piles on the devastation. She had been a double-agent for the Russians, blackmailed into the role by their torture of her Polish lover. She has been conspiring with Le Chiffre against Bond all along, if reluctantly. With SMERSH now on her trail, she had put herself and Bond beyond danger by her fatal action.

Bond weeps. The 'harsh obscenity' which he emits before he does is something to which we are not made privy. For all their reputation of raciness, Fleming's books would usually only allude to profanity or represent it with underlining. Only in the last few books of the series would the likes of 'arse', 'cock' and 'balls' rear their heads, and never the short version of what Fleming rendered in *You Only Live Twice* as 'Freddie Uncle Charlie Katie'.

Despite 007's callous statement to his handler, 'The bitch is dead now,' there is a hint that this woman to whom Bond had so frequently patronisingly thought of as 'the girl' was in fact cleverer than he: Bond acknowledges that, in contrast to his ostentatious actions, she had been working at his elbow for the other side quietly and without heroics. Bond was no feminist, but women would often be portrayed in Fleming's books in just such a proactive and positive light, something not at all common in the fifties and sixties, especially in thrillers.

Bond had been contemplating resigning from the Service, but the thought of helping to take on SMERSH – without whose terror methods people like Vesper would not engage in treachery for the Soviet Union – gives him a professional resolve. Although Fleming can't have known at this point that the Bond character would play out over a series, it almost feels as if this new attitude is intended as a long-term *raison d'être* for the hero – what is commonly known today as an origin story.

The narrative of *Casino Royale* consists of generally businesslike third-person prose but with touches of lyricism ('The moonlight shone through the half-closed shutters and lapped at the secret shadows in the snow of her body on the broad bed'). Most of it is from Bond's point of view but we are also occasionally given glimpses into the minds of other characters, including Vesper.

This would usually be the case in Fleming books and, as here, the non-Bond points of view, as well as the occasional passages of omniscience, really serve only to weaken and slacken the prose.

The salient details about espionage are dropped in casually enough to create verisimilitude, while the author is clearly on comfortable ground when describing the plush and upholstered terrains Bond traverses. However, Fleming – in one of the first of many examples across the series of his insufferably propounding on things he clearly knew little or nothing about – attributes psychopathic behaviour to ingestion of marijuana. (Even the way he spells it – 'marihuana' – seems gauche.)

As well as Mathis, the book features supporting characters who will be recurring in the series. We meet here Bill Tanner, M's chief of staff and Bond's best friend in the Service; Miss Moneypenny, Fleming's secretary and gatekeeper; and Felix Leiter, a good-humoured Texan CIA operative.

Casino Royale is a peculiar way to kick off the James Bond series. It's thin and sedate enough to carry the whiff of being a padded-out novella. Moreover, the hero of this volume of just 218 pages in its first edition is a man not with a mission to kill but a licence to bankrupt. However, it is only what succeeded *Casino Royale* that makes a slim book of dossiers, card games, travelogue, blundering and lovey-doveyness seem atypical Bond.

Additionally, we should remember that at the time *Casino Royale* was unusual and hard-hitting: frankness about non-marital sex, an allusion to masturbation ('Bond awoke in his own room at dawn and for a time he lay and stroked his memories') and a testicles-oriented torture scene were not mainstream stuff in 1953.

Fleming's first foray into novels was not without its difficulties. After his long-term friend William Plomer – an editor at Jonathan

Cape – had prised it out of his reluctant, self-deprecating hands, it was submitted to Mr Cape himself. While Plomer and his colleague Daniel George thought a lot of the manuscript, it would seem that Cape agreed to publish it only as a favour to Peter Fleming, a Cape author. Ian Fleming also had to agree to extensive revisions, which delayed its publication.

Once publication was imminent, Fleming set up Glidrose Productions, a company in which he and his wife owned all shares and to which he assigned his Bond literary rights, the type of manoeuvre common in a period marked by rising top-rate income-tax levels. In a gesture whose extravagance was worthy of some of the villains he would create for his character, Fleming also ordered a gold-plated typewriter.

Casino Royale was published on 13 April 1953, housed in a sedate jacket designed by Fleming himself, featuring an arrangement of valentine hearts dripping blood. It attracted some sparkling praise in the book-review sections. That *The Sunday Times* described Fleming as 'the best new English thriller-writer since Ambler' would have impressed no one aware of Fleming's connection to the paper, but the plaudits for the new book were widespread: 'a first-rate thriller' (*Manchester Guardian*); 'an extremely engaging affair' (*The Times Literary Supplement*); 'Fleming tells a good story with strength and distinction' (*The Listener*).

Fleming would continue to pick up garlands but not, for a while, spectacular sales. Yet *Casino Royale*'s print run of 4,750 would not, from Pearson's recollection, have dismayed the author. 'That was one of the oddities about the whole Bond phenomenon,' Pearson says. 'Jonathan Cape . . . was a very upmarket, rather smart publisher, not the sort of publisher who normally did thrillers, and he saw them at that time as very much upmarket thrillers.

Very much a private, closet activity which he indulged in largely for reasons of his own psychology and the rest of it. I worked for him for six months on *The Sunday Times* before somebody said, "Oh, Ian writes books, you see."

'I got *Live and Let Die*, which I thought was very good. I said to him, "Ian, I never realised you did this sort of thing. I think *Live and Let Die* is marvellous, it would make a marvellous film."

'"Film, dear boy? Let's not exaggerate," he said. "These books are caviar for the general, not for the hoi polloi." He didn't say "the hoi polloi", but that's what he meant – they wouldn't have a mass impact.'

This suggestion is borne out by a letter Fleming wrote in 1957 to CBS television in which he said, '. . . my books are written for and appeal principally to an "A" readership but . . . it appears that the "B" and "C" classes find them equally readable, although one might have thought that the sophistication of the background and detail would be outside their experience and in part incomprehensible.'

Pearson adds of his conversation with Fleming, 'I think already he was trying to film *Casino Royale* and he was very keen to make some money out of the books, but he never envisaged them being at that stage what they became.'

HEADWAY

Live and Let Die, published on 8 April 1954, would have made far more sense than *Casino Royale* as the inaugural James Bond novel. It is bigger, more exotic and more action-oriented than its predecessor and contains many of the elements that would come to be Bond hallmarks. Perhaps significantly, it marked the point where Fleming did not simply write from personal knowledge – as with *Casino Royale* – but immersed himself in research beforehand.

Universal Export – mentioned as a cover name for the Secret Service for the first time – dispatches Bond across the Atlantic because coins that look as if they may be the fabled treasure of the pirate Bloody Morgan are mysteriously finding their way to the United States from a small, isolated island within British colony Jamaica. Their passage has apparently been arranged by Buonaparte Ignace Gallia, whose initials give rise to the name by which he is commonly known: Mr Big. While Le Chiffre had been a fairly vanilla villain, the symbiotic physical and mental monstrousness of Mr Big would transpire to be the usual mould for Fleming's baddies. The author would almost always use ugliness or disfigurement as a shorthand for evil. Mr Big is an unsettlingly huge and grey-tinged man. He commands obedience by playing on the terror of voodoo in the American black community, allowing a rumour to thrive that he is the Zombie of Baron Samedi, the Prince of Darkness. The British government are particularly anxious to stop his distribution of the gold coins because it bankrolls Soviet activity: somewhat implausibly, Mr Big is an agent of SMERSH.

Bond is initially told by the American law-enforcement services not to go stirring up trouble and that their policy, until the time is appropriate to strike, is 'Live and let live'. Replies a quizzical Bond, '. . . I have another motto. It's "Live and let die".' This phrase has, via Bond's vast cultural popularity, become arguably more famous than the motto of tolerance of which it's a vengeful inversion.

Bond cuts off the source of the coins in Jamaica and rescues Solitaire, a beautiful and allegedly clairvoyant Haitian pet of Mr Big's. Through Bond's resourcefulness, the latter is subjected to the fate of being eaten alive by sharks Mr Big had intended for him.

On its first American printing the chapter 'Nigger Heaven' was renamed 'Seventh Avenue', but the modern-day reputation the book has for antiquated racism smacks of manufactured outrage. Racist though he − or at least his character − often was, Fleming is shown in *Live and Let Die* to be in possession of opinions about black people that these days would be described as politically correct. Jazz-loving Leiter proffers the a-few-rotten-apples argument when he says, 'In any half a million people of any race you'll get plenty of stinkeroos.' It is stated that Bond knows Jamaica well as a consequence of a long assignment there just after the war and had come to 'love the great green island and its staunch, humorous people'.

Despite the air of authenticity created by the likes of an opening three-dozen pages that read a little like a slow-burning police procedural, *Live and Let Die* is riddled with illogicalities and even comic-book occurrence. For instance, Bond's planting of a mine for the assault on Mr Big's fortress seems less logical than a raid that might glean Soviet-related information. Meanwhile, the credence Bond seems to give to Solitaire's supposed clairvoyance is odd when she never definitively demonstrates her power.

Continuity howlers include the fact that an escape from death sees Bond crying his 'first tears since his childhood' (in fact, he wept at Vesper's death in *Casino Royale* – and, one would assume, at the treatment of his testicles in the same text) and the statement that Bond has shared 'so many adventures' with Felix Leiter (he only met the American in the first book and has been on leave since).

As before – and as ever – there is a certain flatness of tone brought about by the fact that Bond is neither excitable nor warm. One doesn't love this character.

Stylistically, though, Fleming is sure-footed. Particularly lyrical are the passages that draw upon this keen snorkeller's deep knowledge of the sea, such as the depiction of the mysterious, creepy, multi-coloured, multi-tentacled aquatic life Bond has to negotiate on his way to plant the mine. The action sequences are consistently good. When Bond is discovered after breaking into the Floridian worm-and-bait shop that acts as a cover for Mr Big's activities, we feel we are right in the middle of the resultant gun battle ('a shot whammed between his legs into a pile of conchs, sending splinters of their hard china buzzing round him like wasps'). This same scene results in the book's most powerful passage: a Mr Big henchman begs Bond for mercy as he finds himself dangling over a shark tank and Bond – cognisant of the fact that it is this man who is responsible for Leiter's losing an arm and a leg in the same tank – coldly kicks him to a watery grave.

What completes the impression that *Live and Let Die* would have made more sense than *Casino Royale* as the opening novel in the franchise is Bond's skirmishes with Mr Big. Here, Fleming provides the ingredients for many classic Bond showdowns to come: the villain's menace tempered by ironic politeness (Mr Big addresses the hero as 'Mister James Bond'), Bond's calm defiance in the villain's clutches, the villain's incongruous eloquence, the notice given Bond of his death that grants him convenient thinking time – all are elements that would become lovably familiar in the Bond canon.

There was interest from an early stage in adapting Bond to the big screen. The UK's Associated British Pictures and Hollywood's MCA made enquiries about *Casino Royale*, but both overtures failed to make any progress because of squabbles over percentages between Cape and Fleming's US agent, Curtis Brown.

However, a television deal was struck for the property and, on 21 October 1954 at 8.30 p.m. EST, the American television network CBS broadcast an adaptation of *Casino Royale* as part of its *Climax!* drama strand.

Excluding commercials, CBS's adaptation of the first Bond novel ran to just under fifty-two minutes. As with all television of the era it was in monochrome and, as with much televised drama of that time, it was broadcast live. It was directed by William H. Brown and its script came from Antony Lewis and Charles Bennett.

Actor Barry Nelson was not Bond as we know him. Referred to as

'Jimmy' ('007' is nowhere mentioned), he works for the 'Combined Intelligence Agency' in Washington, has a bouffant of swept-back hair and uses his American accent to drawl unperturbed quips ('Still in one piece, but I wouldn't know how'). The redrawing of the character's nationality was typical of an era when there was no reason for the United States to dance to any other nation's tune, economic, political or cultural.

As in the book, Le Chiffre has a gambling vice that makes him vulnerable and Bond's objective is to clean him out. He is assisted by Clarence (*sic*) Leiter, played by Michael Pate, the show's token Brit.

Unlike in the book, Chiffre (as opposed to the affectation of Le Chiffre) is a real name. Naturally, on fifties prime-time TV, testicle torture to obtain the hidden cheque is out of the question, although the pliers-and-toes substitution has its own wince-making properties, even if not directly seen. A torture-racked Bond manages to shoot Chiffre dead as Chiffre is about to dispatch Valerie Mathis (Linda Christian), the production's substitute for Vesper Lynd.

Cut to host William Lundigan previewing the next week's episode. He also, on behalf of the network, salutes the 42nd National Safety Congress currently occurring in Chicago – an act that is the epitome of the sort of clean-cut gushing alien to Fleming, his creation and the rest of the British race.

Despite that grisly all-American kiss-off, *Casino Royale* is not a half-bad entrée for James Bond to the world of visual drama. Leaving aside the necessary truncation and dilution, the adaptation is fairly faithful and adroit, and actually quite sophisticated in the way it convincingly portrays the procedures and tempo of the baccarat table. Although Bond is not in full tuxedo, his bow tie in the casino scenes even provides a precursor to one of the trademarks of the cinema Bond, as does his snogging the girl as the closing music starts up. While Nelson might be a boringly identikit square-jawed type common to the time, Peter Lorre as Chiffre is indeed as repulsively 'toad-like' as Leiter describes him.

Fleming never saw the broadcast, having to content himself with a critique provided by old friend Clare Blanshard. In a video/DVD/Internet-less world, Fleming must have written it off as a shady buck-making little secret that wasn't likely to contaminate his literary series. If its being forgotten not long after he had banked his $1,000 fee was his desire, he got his wish, at least in his lifetime. The Americanisation of Bond remained merely the stuff of rumour and increasingly fading memories for several decades, giving rise to urban myths such as the one about Lorre getting up after he is killed because he doesn't realise he's still in shot. The show was long considered lost when a partial copy surfaced in 1981 followed by other, full, copies, and it has now graduated to commercially available DVDs.

The cultural heavy-handedness of the *Casino Royale* TV production also attended Bond's entrée on the American literary scene. *Casino Royale* was published in hardback by Macmillan in the States in March 1954. However, a paperback was initially passed over in favour of a soft-cover version of the third Bond novel, *Moonraker*, which appeared in 1955 through Permabooks. It reduced the title to a parenthesised subheading in favour of something one could more imagine coming out of the mouth of Humphrey Bogart than a British government agent: *Too Hot To Handle*. The text had been tweaked to make it more understandable to non-Britons, 'lifts' becoming 'elevators,' 'zebra crossings' changed to 'pedestrian crossings', etc. Whole paragraphs containing material thought inordinately English were excised and there were some explanatory footnotes from Fleming. When *Casino Royale* did make it into paperback in the States in 1955 via American Popular Library, its title was reduced to a bracketed subtitle beneath a gumshoe-y new name: *You Asked for It*. On the back, the hero was 'Jimmy Bond'.

Mercifully, this was the extent of American tampering. The US would, moreover, embrace Bond specifically because of his Englishness. In a short course of time, the success of the Bond books and, especially, movies would be one of the things mainly responsible for making America more open to the virtues of the 'Briddish'.

In 1954, Fleming sold to producer Gregory Ratoff a $600 option on a movie version of *Casino Royale*. Ratoff bought full rights for $6,000 in 1955. By the beginning of the following year, Ratoff was announcing that Twentieth Century Fox would distribute an adaptation he planned to start filming in the summer. (It was revealed that Fleming had written a screenplay but that it would not be used.)

A surviving *Casino Royale* script dating from 1957 is by an unknown hand. Like the CBS adaptation, it's fairly faithful to the book except for its disdain for the idea of the hero being British: Bond becomes American gangster and poker expert Lucky Fortunato. 'I did think it was good,' says Jeremy Duns. However, he adds, 'It's a draft script – it's not filmable. It felt quite old-fashioned. It felt much more like a Sinatra film.'

In what would become a pattern over the following years with putative Bond live-action projects, the Ratoff film failed to materialise.

Novelist Len Deighton – who first met him in 1963 – recalled that for Ian Fleming 'writing was a challenge and a test of his manly resilience to pain; he made no secret of the fact that he hated it.'

While it may not be the case that by the time of the third Bond book he was already detesting the process, it seems that what had started as a hobby for Fleming was already on the cusp of becoming a resented chore. After he had produced its first draft, he wrote to Cape to tell them that he might already be moving into self-parody. He said that 'the future of James Bond is going to require far more thought than I have so far devoted to him' and that the books seemed destined to follow 'more or less the same pattern, but losing freshness with each volume'. To Fleming's credit, little or none of this showed in *Moonraker*, published on 5 April 1955. The book lacks the exotic backdrops and sometimes hectic action of *Live and Let Die*, but is a smoother read than both that and *Casino Royale*.

This is despite the fact that there is remarkably little action in *Moonraker*: a kick up the backside, some mild torture and a high-speed car chase are about the extent of it. We do, though, get a positive landslide of insight into Bond's private and professional lives.

'It was only two or three times a year that an assignment came along requiring his particular abilities,' we are told of 007. The rest of the year he is more like an 'easy-going senior civil servant', laboriously reading through the endless dockets and files about anything that the Service thinks he may need to know.

Musing on the fact that the compulsory double-O retirement age is forty-five, Bond is glumly conscious of the potential for only two dozen tough assignments in the eight years he has left until he is given a staff job at headquarters. Thirty-seven is a fairly realistic age for an espionage agent and, interestingly, is the age Fleming was when his own intelligence career ended with the conclusion of World War II. One should also note that before youth culture (the dawn of which was then just around the corner), thirty-seven was not the quintessential 'middle-age' that it is to modern sensibilities. The mental definition herein of Bond as a 'young man' by female character Gala Brand would have been a common categorisation in 1955.

Bond's yearly salary of £1,500 (about £32k in today's money) is that of a principal officer in the Civil Service. He lives very well because he also has a yearly, tax-free private income of £1,000 and when on assignment can spend as much money as he likes. Despite his financial comfort, Bond hasn't much use for filthy lucre. In his depressed moments he is sure he will be killed before that forty-five cut-off and wants to have as little as possible in his bank account when that happens.

His private life – when not involving playing cards with a few close friends or high-stakes golf at weekends – revolves around three married women, to whom he makes love 'with rather cold passion'.

Plotwise, Bond is – courtesy of his fluency in German, expertise in sabotage and knowledge of geopolitical issues – assigned to be a government security man at the site of the Moonraker rocket. The Moonraker is funded, designed and staffed by wealthy industrialist Hugo Drax in lieu of Britain's ability to provide its own nuclear deterrent. (In real life, it would have one by the late fifties.) The Prime Minister has to give the authority for a Secret Service agent to become involved in what is technically a domestic affair. (This is in fact the only Fleming novel in which Bond doesn't go abroad.)

Drax is, like Le Chiffre, somebody who claims to have no idea who he is. He has distorted teeth and a face deformed by the same wartime accident that robbed him of his memory, something he tries to cover up with a big red moustache and the tufts of hair on his cheeks. Drax also has filthy manners. Worse than those shortcomings is the fact that he cheats at cards, something exposed by Bond at M's behest in a first section whose relationship to what follows is curiously superficial.

It transpires that Moonraker's test-flight coordinates have deliberately been changed so that it will land not in the Channel but the middle of London, which must naturally mean that its dummy weaponry has been replaced by a real warhead. Although Bond discovers some suspicious facts, the full nefarious plan is uncovered by Gala, a beautiful Special Branch policewoman.

'You don't know how I have longed to tell my story,' Drax informs Bond and Gala, who have been captured and bound. This is of course a precursor to a self-justifying backstory and gloating revelation of malevolent plan, interspersed with Bond's ejaculations of scorn. It's now known as the epitome of Bondian, but Jeremy Duns points out, 'The thing with the villain explaining to Bond what his plot is before he kills him – the supposedly amazingly clever villain actually stupidly tells Bond everything – this was already being parodied by Leslie Charteris twenty years earlier, it was so common.'

Drax is in fact a Nazi, as are all his German scientists. The Soviet Union has assisted him in his plans for its own ideological reasons. Drax intends that Bond and Gala be incinerated with the explosion of the warhead, but the two free themselves and alter the flight plan. That Bond and Gala then listen to the radio to find out whether their plan has succeeded is a damp squib of a climax to be sure, but is in the book's general spirit of realism. The interaction with what is nominally the 'Bond girl' also turns out to be a damp squib: Bond's presumptions about her are upended by the revelation that Gala is about to get married. In a melancholy ending, they decorously shake hands.

A glut of error, inconsistency and nonsense is by now to be expected in a Bond book, but it's difficult to overlook the fact that it is inconceivable, even at the height of the Cold War, that Moscow would have sanctioned a missile strike that would almost certainly have precipitated global nuclear combat. Yet such is the verisimilitude of Fleming's story – especially his research on rocket science and the way he conveys the Moonraker's awe-inspiring, gleaming giganticness – that this occurs to one only when mulling it over, and that this mulling process does not occur when the pages are being turned.

Moonraker aroused the interest of Hollywood. However, just as famed director Alexander Korda had failed to follow-up his interest after seeing an advance copy of *Live and Let Die*, John Payne and subsequently the Rank Organisation did not capitalise on the property on which they had taken out options. *Moonraker* rights transferred back to Fleming in 1959.

The book, though, did get adapted to another medium, even if Fleming may not have known about it. A South African radio broadcast of a *Moonraker* production by the Durban Repertory Theatre has variously been reported as occurring in 1955, 1956, 1957 and 1958 and to have been both an hour and ninety minutes long. There is a suspicion that it may not have been authorised by Fleming or his agents.

The second actor to portray James Bond was, like Barry Nelson, not British. Bob Holness spent most of his formative years in the UK but was born in South Africa and returned there as a young adult. Holness told one Bond fan that his performance as 007 was broadcast live and that no recording was made.

Some might suggest this to be for the best. The idea of Holness playing a blunt instrument is rather comical for Britain, where Holness eventually returned in his grey-haired, bespectacled late middle age and became known as quizmaster of iconic British teenage game show *Countdown*, remembered for its sniggering catchphrase, 'I'll 'ave a "P", please, Bob.' However, Holness in real life was clearly somewhat less clean-cut than his television persona. He once reported that his reaction to the news that Sean Connery had been cast as 007 was, 'That cunt's got my job!'

Over the subsequent decades, there have been few further Bond radio dramas, perhaps because broadcasters perceive the idea of them as pointless in light of the lush visual spectacle of Bond films.

Diamonds are Forever, the fourth Bond novel, was published on 4 April 1956.

It was serialised that month in the *Daily Express* newspaper. The *Express* was then, as now, middle-market, pitched halfway between the intellectualism of *The Times* and the populism of the *Daily Mirror*. Unlike now, it was then a top seller and the serialisation served to proffer Bond to a large captive audience who may not have previously been aware of the character. The *Express* would from that point on routinely run Bond novel serialisations, albeit condensed and sanitised for a family audience.

In the first recounted Bond mission with no involvement on the part of Russia, Bond is dispatched to the United States to disrupt a diamond-smuggling route to there from Africa. The American end of the smuggling operation is here referred to as 'American gangsters' or 'The Mob' but for some reason never 'The Mafia'. Bond has a contempt for such types, whom he considers 'Italian bums with monogrammed shirts who spend the day eating spaghetti and meat-balls and squirting scent over themselves'.

Bond is able to get into the diamond-smuggling pipeline because he can pass as intended courier Peter Franks to someone who has only a description on which to go – a situation so lacking in what would now be basic security requirements as to remind us that the world of Fleming's Bond is as close to the nineteenth century as it is to our own. Bond quickly starts unravelling a trail of diverse but intertwined criminality involving fixed horse races in Saratoga Springs and rigged blackjack games in Las Vegas. Bond is unexpectedly assisted/shadowed by Felix Leiter, now working for the famous private detective agency Pinkerton's. Leiter has a steel hook in place of his right hand, and a false left leg. Not for the first or last time, Bond has a romantic coupling with a woman whose name is simultaneously ridiculous and sublime: Tiffany Case.

On his seaborne passage home with Tiffany, Bond discovers that also aboard are Mr Wint and Mr Kidd, a pair of Mob-employed homosexual killers. After dispatching them, Bond is compelled to cover his tracks to make the deaths look like an argument that has ended in murder and suicide. This is realistic, but somewhat less intoxicating than the cavalier attitude of the cinema Bond, who has never given a stuff about the carnage and official headaches caused by his actions.

Chapter 9 marks the first time we are told that Bond likes a Martini to be 'shaken and not stirred'. We're still not quite there with the phrase 'licence to kill', though: Leiter says to Bond, 'You've still got that double O number that means you're allowed to kill?'

As so often, Fleming mixes wince-making romantic dialogue ('I have always been in step with the thought of you, but you didn't come, and I have spent my life listening to a different drummer') with descriptive prose that is exquisite ('The great six-lane highway stretched on through a forest of multi-coloured signs and frontages until it lost itself downtown in a dancing lake of heatwaves . . . A glittering gunfire of light splinters shot at Bond's eyes from the windscreens of oncoming cars and from their blaze of chrome styling . . .')

The proactive 007 of *Diamonds are Forever* is a figure less dependent than previously on coincidences and the good work of others. Despite this, as well as the acute portrayal of the glitz and greed of Vegas and the way plot strands are wrapped up ingeniously and even a little poetically, this Bond book never seems to shake itself out of a low-key state.

Fleming himself had decided that it was a last gasp. He told Raymond Chandler, 'I have absolutely nothing more up my sleeve.' His difficulty in devising plots – something which he would lament again and again – was at the time compounded by the fact that Bond seemed to have bumped up against the ceiling of his commercial potential. None of the books had become bestsellers in the UK, those issued in the States had flopped and the intermittent interest from Hollywood never seemed to translate into green-lit projects.

From Russia with Love, the fifth Bond novel, published on 8 April 1957, is the first Bond book to deviate in significant ways from the established template.

Bond does not appear at all in the first third of the book. Instead, we are introduced to Donovan Grant, a psychotic defector, Colonel

Rosa Klebb – charmless and insanely loyal head of SMERSH executions – and Corporal Tatiana Romanova, a young, beautiful and malleably loyal employee of Soviet intelligence. The last of these is chosen for the task of providing a honey trap for 'Angliski Spion' Bond, on whom SMERSH have a 'bulky file'. After Klebb briefs Tatiana, she then tries to, as it were, debrief her. The corporal flees from the sexual overtures of a woman Fleming describes as looking like 'the oldest and ugliest whore in the world'.

Bond finally makes an appearance at around the one-hundred-page mark in the form of his traditional adventure-heralding summons to the office of M. Bond is rather taken aback when informed by his boss that Tatiana has made contact with the Secret Service's station in Istanbul and has offered to bring to the West a much-coveted code cracker called the Spektor – on the condition that she be retrieved by Bond, with whom she has fallen in love from the details on him in his file.

The Service's Q Branch supplies 007 an attaché case, in the lining of which is hidden .25 ammunition, throwing-knives, fifty gold sovereigns and a cyanide pill. His sponge bag contains a tube of shaving cream that unscrews to reveal the silencer for his Beretta. This is the low-key beginning of the gadgetry that the Bond films would ultimately take into the realms of science fiction.

Upon their first meeting, the supposedly loyal Tatiana develops such a crush on Bond that she determines to defect for real. The exchanges between the pair are symptomatic of Fleming's perennial Achilles heel: being unable to portray romance as anything but gushing cliché.

At Tatiana's insistence, the two of them take the Spektor machine to the West via the Orient Express, an anachronistic decision in the jet age but clearly engineered by Fleming so as to provide lashings of luxury travel porn. Ostensible backup arrives in the form of fellow service agent Norman Nash. It is Donovan Grant, able to pass himself off as friendly via some intercepted code phrases. Later Bond is woken in the train compartment by Grant and merrily told, 'No Bulldog Drummond stuff'll get you out of this one' – an echo of a similarly postmodern taunt by Le Chiffre in *Casino Royale* that this 'is not a romantic adventure story in which the villain is finally routed'. In point of fact, Bond does pull off something Sapper's hero would likely do: insert a silver cigarette case between the pages of a book that he holds over his heart as his deadshot enemy lets rip with his gun. Bond plays possum before fatally making use of one of his concealed knives.

Prior to his death, Grant hadn't been able to resist boasting of his forthcoming meeting with Rosa Klebb, at which he expects to collect the Order of Lenin. In fact, it is Bond who makes the meeting in Room 204 of the Ritz Hotel in Paris, where, for the first time in any of the books, he says, 'My name is Bond, James Bond.' Klebb transpires to be a fiery fighter: even as she is taken into custody, she produces a poison-tipped blade from the toe of a shoe, which she propels into Bond's right calf. The book ends with 007 crashing to the floor.

The author bewilders us by having Bond reflect that he 'had never killed in cold blood' when it was explained way back in the first book that that is exactly how his double-O number was acquired. This, though, may not be sloppiness but one of the first signs of a penchant Fleming would increasingly display for revising his hero's universe in response to criticism. On this occasion, it might be the case that he was reacting to complaints of the brutality in Bond books. However, the latter cause is hardly helped by the pro-rape and wife-beating philosophising of Turkish supporting character

Darko Kerim, a vicious catfight between two gypsies and Tatiana's imploring of Bond, 'You will beat me if I eat too much?'

Curiously structured though the book may be, the switching of the spotlight in *From Russia with Love* onto things that would be unseen or background in a normal Bond book ultimately comes across as an interesting sideways view of a familiar character.

Although Bond's continued existence is in peril at the end of *From Russia with Love*, there is paradoxical evidence that Fleming was using the book as his tilt at being taken seriously as a writer. In correspondence with Raymond Chandler leading up to its writing, Fleming said he would endeavour to 'order my life so as to put more feeling into my typewriter'. In a letter to Michael Howard of Cape, he said, '... my main satisfaction ... with the book is that a Formula which was getting stale has been broken ... one simply can't go on writing the simple bang-bang, kiss-kiss type of book.'

BACKLASHES
AND BOOSTS

Regardless of his apparent satisfaction with *From Russia with Love*, as 1956 turned into 1957 Ian Fleming was pessimistic about being able to produce another Bond adventure. He told his publisher, '. . . the vein of my inventiveness is running extremely dry and I seriously doubt if I shall be able to complete a book in Jamaica this year.' However, if he had genuinely toyed with the idea of making the knife wound inflicted by Rosa Klebb fatal, Fleming clearly quickly decided against it.

When not in Jamaica, the Flemings would rent out Goldeneye and, in November 1956, it so happened that Anthony Eden – family friend as well as British Prime Minister – decided to stay there. The names of Fleming and his fictional hero were suddenly plastered across the newspapers, with a resultant spike in Bond book sales. Nine months after Fleming had penned the scene in which Bond appears to die at the end of the not-yet-published

From Russia with Love, there was suddenly a significantly enhanced financial incentive to produce more Bond adventures.

Moreover, the author had at his disposal a ready-made Bond tale. It dated from another of his unsuccessful brushes with moving pictures. In mid-1956, NBC-TV producer Henry Morgenthau III had asked him to come up with a proposal for a television drama. Fleming proffered a project with a Caribbean backdrop variously known as *Commander Jamaica* and *James Gunn, Secret Agent*. The author barely bothered to pretend the hero was not an Americanised Bond in his twenty-eight-page pilot script. The project failed to attract backers. Fleming simply recycled the story for *Dr No*, his sixth James Bond novel, published on 31 March 1958.

The book opens with a scene in which three hitmen kill John Strangways, regional officer for the Secret Service in Jamaica, by dressing up as beggars and forming the chain required by the fact of their pretending to be blind. This serves only to compound the conspicuousness they already possess by virtue of being 'Chinese-Negro'. Its absurd lack of realism is emblematic of a book that definitively takes Bond away from a common-or-garden espionage milieu into grandiose, even pulpy, terrain.

Following Bond's recovery from the poison administered him by Rosa Klebb, he is eased back into work with what M considers the cushy assignment of sending him to look into Strangways's disappearance. Strangways's last case had been an investigation into one Julius No, who owns an island between Jamaica and Cuba named Crab Key, bought for its valuable guano deposits. During Bond's briefing, M takes the opportunity to replace the Beretta the agent has always thus far favoured but whose silencer had got caught in his clothing during his tussle with Klebb. The armourer presses onto a reluctant Bond a Walther PPK 7.65mm, 'a real stopping gun'.

Doctor No (despite the book's title, the diminutive for his bogus medical designation is never used, although in the States the book was titled *Doctor No*) lives beneath the waterline of a cliff in shagpile-carpeted splendour, observing the sea life through a giant transparent wall. Of German-Chinese descent, the tall, bald, gliding No looks to the captured Bond like a 'giant venomous worm'. The bizarre appearance is completed by hooks compensating for the hands amputated as a punishment for stealing from his own Tong.

Although possessed of the usual Fleming-villain traits of psychopathy and megalomania, No is not without self-knowledge about the roots of his behaviour. 'No love, you see, Mister Bond,' he says. 'Lack of parental care . . . I became involved with the Tongs, with their illicit proceedings . . . They represented revolt against the father figure who had betrayed me.' Mr Big had previously spoken to Bond of his accidie. There would be other passages in Fleming's books wherein the villains pronounced on their own psychology. This is something that would seem to date back to Fleming's time in Kitzbühel. As well as being a novelist, Phyllis Bottome was an adherent of the work of psychotherapist Alfred Adler, whose biography she wrote. Bond's psychology, though, would never be explored by Fleming, the one way in which the author remained true to his original objective of depicting a cypher of a human being.

Not content with the fortune generated by investing his stolen loot in guano, No is now working with the Russians in jamming the telemetered instructions of American test missiles. Once again, Fleming is shoehorning in the Cold War when the villain could have worked perfectly well as unaffiliated. No's grandiose plans have been jeopardised by mere 'twitchers': bird preservationists the Audubon Society are planning to build a hotel on a corner of the island on which they own a lease.

This backstory is related by No to a sardonic Bond as a preamble to a terrible fate No has devised: a deadly endurance test in which Bond is forced to worm his way through endless narrow tunnels – horizontal and vertical – littered with obstacles such as electrified metal, extreme heat and tarantulas. Waiting in the pool beyond the exit is a giant squid whose suckered arms have the power to tear him apart. A canny Bond appropriates and defends himself with a cigarette lighter, a knife and a ventilation grille fashioned into a spear.

Having become the first-ever survivor of this bizarre assault course, Bond finds Doctor No supervising the loading of a shipment. The secret agent commandeers a crane and dispatches the villain by dumping on his head a load of his precious guano. The book culminates in a rendezvous with Honeychile Rider, an orphaned, beautiful local child-woman who has become ensnared in Bond's escapades.

For the first time, the phrase 'licence to kill' is employed. So poetic is the passage in which it is – 'The licence to kill for the Secret Service, the double-o prefix, was a great honour. It had been earned hardly. It brought Bond the only assignments he enjoyed, the dangerous ones' – that Britain's Pan Books used it (and a slight variation) as a blurb inside their sixties Bond paperbacks. It sat beneath a logo that stylishly superimposed the silhouette of a gun over the numerals '007'.

Dr No – a real page-turner – has some powerful episodes. One is a truly creepy section where a petrified Bond has to endure a giant centipede making its remorseless, multi-legged way up the entire length of his sweating body. Also pleasing are Fleming's evocative descriptions of Crab Key's stinking, sulphurous marshes and the godforsaken, windswept landscape of the *guanera*.

The *Daily Express* serialisations, the Eden visit to Goldeneye, the build-up of an audience over the course of five previous books and the graduation of the series to the wallet-friendly paperback format, had all played a part in a mushrooming of Bond's popularity. *Dr No* was the first Bond book to sell in big numbers. Combined James Bond novel paperback sales were 41,000 in 1955. They were 670,000 by 1961, a point still a year distant from the first Bond movie, which event would send sales onto another plane entirely.

Nobody, though, would know any of this from some of the reviews *Dr No* garnered. It was this book's publication that saw Fleming come under quite vicious attack.

The most quoted slating of any Bond book is probably the review of *Dr No* that appeared in the 5 April 1958 edition of *New Statesman*. It was written by Paul Johnson, a socialist journalist with a high profile. 'I have just finished what is without a doubt the nastiest book I have ever read' is a memorable opening line for any review, but what really stuck in the public mind was the heading: 'Sex, snobbery and sadism'. The latter was the subeditor's summary of Johnson's adjudgement of Fleming's signatures: 'There are three basic ingredients in *Dr No*, all unhealthy, all thoroughly English: the sadism of a school boy bully, the mechanical two-dimensional sex-longings of a frustrated adolescent, and the crude, snob-cravings of a suburban adult.' In addition, Johnson averred, 'Mr. Fleming has no literary skill, the construction of the book is chaotic, and entire incidents and situations are inserted, and then forgotten in a haphazard manner.' He conceded, though, that 'the three ingredients are manufactured and blended with deliberate, professional precision; Mr. Fleming dishes up his recipe with all the calculated accountancy of a Lyons Corner House.'

That Johnson's objection to Fleming was as much political as moral or literary was betrayed by his comments:

> . . . both its hero and its author are unquestionably members of the Establishment. Bond is an ex-Royal Navy Commander and belongs to Blades, a sort-of super-White's. Mr. Fleming was educated at Eton and Sandhurst, and is married to a prominent society hostess, the ex-wife of Lord Rothermere. He is the foreign manager of that austere and respectable newspaper, *The Sunday Times*, owned by an elderly fuddy-duddy called Lord Kemsley . . .

History shows that Johnson was on a journey that would transform him from a passionate left-winger into a virulent right-winger. Unfortunately, the issue of whether his savaging was a classic case of overcompensation is one never addressed by those who invoke the review, especially American critics who have often heard of Johnson only through this piece of writing.

However, it must be admitted that Johnson was riding a wave. A month before *Dr No*'s publication, Bernard Bergonzi complained in a nine-page article in literary monthly *The Twentieth Century* of Fleming's 'voyeurism and sado-masochism', an appraisal that seems to have opened the floodgates. *The Guardian* was shortly decrying Fleming for promoting 'the cult of luxury for its own sake'.

Such reviewers' objections almost seem bewildering now when Fleming's sex, violence and product porn pales compared with what can be seen today on television screens in peak hours, but, as can be gleaned from the Johnson review, the disdain in which Fleming was held in some quarters was less a matter of objective analysis than the perceived requisites of changing times. The Western world was entering its most left-wing phase in history, one in which Establishment men like Fleming and his creation were perceived to be part of an oppressive and outmoded paradigm. During the decade it still had to run, such sentiment would only increase in intensity, culminating in the riot-strewn year of 1968.

In an introduction to a 2009 reissue of *The Ipcress File*, the 1962 novel that was the start of his trilogy featuring an espionage agent with a working-class background, author Len Deighton wrote:

Publication of *The Ipcress File* coincided with the arrival of the first of the James Bond films. My book was given very generous reviews and more than one of my friends was moved to confide that the critics were using me as a blunt instrument to batter Ian Fleming about the head.

He is not a lone voice. Asked if *zeitgeist* leftism motivated some of Fleming's increasingly vitriolic reviews, John Pearson simply says, 'Undoubtedly. Of course.'

One can only imagine the effect of this on the psyche of Fleming, a man already in possession of a deep lack of self-worth.

Despite the spikes in 007's public profile created by the *Express* serialisations and the visit by Anthony Eden to Goldeneye, up until 1958 James Bond was not a significant cultural figure.

Although reading was more prevalent across society in the days before universal television ownership (Bond was, more than plausibly, portrayed as not possessing a set in 1957's *From Russia with Love*), the character was still invisible to the majority who restricted their reading to their daily newspaper, the odd magazine and the book they took with them on holiday. In 1958, 007's profile began to change significantly with the introduction of a James Bond comic strip in the *Daily Express*.

When the *Express* first suggested the idea, Fleming expressed 'grave doubts'. He felt that the medium of the comic strip might divest his books of a 'certain cachet', especially if he succumbed to a temptation to 'write down'. These thoughts were expressed in a letter to Wren Howard, co-founder of Cape. Fleming consulted William Plomer about whether he should agree to the *Express*'s suggestion, and then ignored his editor's emphatic advice that he shouldn't. The £1,500 fee per adaptation (over £30,000 in today's money) plus syndication royalties – as well as the knock-on effect on Bond book sales – would seem to have been inducements he felt he could not afford to spurn.

The *Express* James Bond comic strip debuted on 7 July 1958 with the first instalment of an adaptation of *Casino Royale*. It was written by Anthony Hern, who Fleming felt had done a good job in abbreviating his books for serialisation in the same paper. Its illustrator was John McLusky.

The first printed depiction of James Bond had come on the front of the 1955 UK Pan paperback edition of *Casino Royale*. The artwork of Roger Hall featured a good-looking man at a card table in a light-coloured tuxedo. Few would have found in it a discrepancy with the picture planted in their minds by Fleming's prose, aside perhaps from the man's blond hair. In the comic strip, McLusky realised well Fleming's written description of Bond's good looks, untidy comma of black hair and facial scar, even if he did make 007 look a tad older than the average reader might have imagined him. Curiously, his depiction of Bond in the first panel of the opening strip made him look a little like Ian Fleming.

As with most examples of the medium, the Bond *Express* strip comprised three panels. Ordinarily, a reading experience literally lasting seconds motivates writers and illustrators to jam as much action into each strip as possible. However, Hern & McLusky, at Fleming's suggestion, employed the stately pace of the original novel, dwelling on incidental and sensual detail in the same manner as Fleming's prose. One entire instalment was dedicated to the details of a meal, another to the changes wrought on Royale-Les-Eaux by gentrification. There was, of course, some action. The testicle-torture scene was necessarily made vague, but a preamble where Bond was ordered to strip was disturbing in itself.

Bond was now appearing every single weekday in a national paper, and would do for the next three-and-a-half years. Newspapers, of course, tend to be passed around homes and picked up by third parties in workplaces. By this process, the number of people who understood who was being spoken of when the name James Bond came up in conversation was increasing exponentially.

Only Fleming would ever have been able to reveal whether it led to his writing down.

In *Goldfinger*, the seventh Bond novel, published on 23 March 1959, M instructs Bond to investigate the suspected bullion-smuggling activities of one Auric Goldfinger, the richest man in England.

That gold bars with Goldfinger's 'Z' inscription are repeatedly found in the possession of SMERSH operatives suggests that Goldfinger is nothing less than the foreign banker of the Soviet terror organisation.

It so happens that Bond knows the man from his private life: he had exposed his card-cheating scam in the opening chapters. This is as awkward and unlikely as – and almost identical to – the coincidence of Bond being assigned to the Moonraker site the day after his contretemps with Hugo Drax over a card table. Moreover, Fleming has already tested our suspension of disbelief to breaking point by giving a character with a mania for gold the surname Goldfinger and the forename Auric ('of, relating to, or derived from gold' – Merriam-Webster). This is symptomatic of a book that is as preposterous as it is readable.

Bond selects from the car pool a battleship-grey Aston Martin DB III and sweeps down to the Royal St Marks Club at Sandwich, where Goldfinger has told him he tends to play golf. It is revealed to be the stamping ground of Bond's teens: club pro Alfred Blacking had told him he could make him a scratch player with enough practice but 'something had told Bond that there wasn't going to be a great deal of golf in his life . . .'

Goldfinger is diminutive with a large round head covered in a carroty crew cut. 'It was the short men that caused all the trouble in the world' is Bond's opinion. Bond outwits Goldfinger on the greens but their subsequent dinner doesn't lead to the job offer for which Bond is angling.

Bond goes off to investigate Goldfinger's plant in Switzerland. There he runs into Tilly Masterton, out for revenge for her sister Jill, whom Goldfinger had punished for colluding with Bond by fatally painting her gold. The two of them get discovered by

Goldfinger's bowler-hatted, cleft-palated, physically terrifying Korean manservant Oddjob.

'Mr Bond, they have a saying in Chicago: "Once is happenstance. Twice is coincidence. The third time it's enemy action."' These words to Bond from Goldfinger give the book its triptych structure. It's also an example of Fleming's ability to work into his texts memorable, poetic phrases. Strangely, though, Goldfinger doesn't kill 007 and Tilly but instead spirits them to America, where they are required to assist in what Goldfinger has termed Operation Grand Slam.

The scheme is ambitious: a plan to rob Fort Knox. With the connivance of bosses of various mafias (unlike in *Diamonds Are Forever*, that word is used), America's gold depository will be stripped of its contents. Tilly is very taken with one particular mafia boss, 'Miss Pussy Galore', leader of the lesbian organisation the Cement Mixers. Pussy seems more taken with Bond, or 'Handsome', as she addresses him.

Unknown to the mobsters, Goldfinger is planning to contaminate the water supply of the town of Fort Knox not with a sedative but deadly poison. He is also planning to rendezvous with a Russian ship, apparently neither he nor Fleming imagining that his intention to be 'the richest man in history' might be jeopardised by relocating to a land opposed to Western decadence.

The holes in the plot really begin to mount up at the point that Goldfinger and co. board what is disguised as a supply train of medical supplies and staff destined for the stricken and quarantined Fort Knox. Bond, of all people, is entrusted with the job of alerting Goldfinger by walkie-talkie of hiccups in the proceedings.

Seeing bodies littering the Fort and its surrounds, Bond initially fears the worst. However, a note he has left aboard Goldfinger's chartered plane has got through to Felix Leiter. The apparently dead soldiers spring to life when the villains are at the door of Fort Knox. This is arguably plausible, but that the townsfolk have also been playing possum on request – and have been doing so well enough to trick the eye of someone like Bond – is idiotic. That a mere Pinkerton agent like Leiter is allowed on the scene to give Bond protection seems unlikely, but somewhat less so than the fact that he is seen 'pounding up the platform'. What happened to his artificial leg?

After Oddjob has killed Tilly by breaking her neck with his steel-rimmed bowler hat, Bond ends up on a plane hijacked by Goldfinger headed for Russia. Bond uses one of the retractable daggers hidden in his shoe heels to smash a window, through which Oddjob is sucked. As the plane is depressurised Bond goes berserk 'for the first time in his life' and strangles Goldfinger to death. Bond then holds a gun on the cabin staff while he arranges a pickup crew over the radio. That Fleming spends an inordinate amount of time on this dialogue-heavy scene, but perfunctorily summarises the potentially exciting crash-landing, is not explicable, but, then, so little here is.

Fleming's fears about self-parody have come true in the shape of Goldfinger's eloquence and contained rage. ('Mr Bond, the word "pain" comes from the Latin *poena* meaning "penalty" – that which must be paid. You must now pay for the inquisitiveness . . .') Moreover, Paul Johnson's complaints about *Dr No* – chaotic construction and forgotten incidents and situations – would seem to apply far more to this book. As would Johnson's acknowledging that the sub-par ingredients are manufactured and blended with deliberate, professional precision: *Goldfinger* may not stand up to reflective scrutiny but it flows along smoothly under Fleming's masterful guidance.

Bond is shown to possess surprisingly liberal sentiments about the recent banning of heroin in the UK ('Prohibition is the trigger of crime'). Elsewhere, though, Bond is far from broadminded. He is found thinking of Koreans as 'rather lower than apes in mammalian hierarchy'. When he smiles at the end of a soliloquy from Goldfinger about how his staff sometimes occasionally accidentally kill white prostitutes whom they enjoy subjecting to 'the grossest indignities', it is not absolutely clear that this is pretend-amusement in the object of maintaining his cover. However, the danger of attributing Bond's viewpoints to the author is illustrated by 007's opinion that 'pansies of both sexes' are proliferating as 'a direct consequence of giving votes to women and "sex equality" . . . He was sorry for them, but he had no time for them.' Among Fleming's friends numbered homosexuals such as William Plomer and Noël Coward. Moreover, *Reflections in a Golden Eye*, which on occasion Fleming had no problem citing as the source for the name of his Jamaican house, was a notably gay-themed work.

The eyebrow-raising statement herein that Bond has been in the double-O section for only six years – he was clearly a veteran of the section in *Casino Royale* six books ago – reveals that Fleming is beginning to regret having, in *Moonraker*, pinned down Bond's age to thirty-seven. Fleming was starting to encounter the classic dilemma afflicting writers of action series. Most such writers learned to get around it by never specifying their hero's age and simply ignoring the fact that no one individual could possibly have so many adventures in a lifetime, yet alone that part of a lifetime where a protagonist's bodily abilities are the match of those of his adversaries. Fleming's solution was to keep altering the facts and shifting the goalposts.

In May 1959, a new James Bond tale was printed in a most unlikely outlet. It was *Cosmopolitan* that played host to 'Quantum of Solace'.

The women's magazine provided no particular fanfare for what was the first published 007 short story. Although its front cover was, as ever, emblazoned with details of its contents, 'Quantum of Solace' wasn't listed among them, while the story's standfirst ('Marriage can survive every disaster but one . . .') drew no attention to the identity of its protagonist. Nonetheless, the outlet was appropriate. 'Quantum of Solace' is a uniquely female-friendly Bond tale, wherein the agent takes a back seat to a recounted soap opera. The story would be reprinted in Britain in *Modern Woman* that November.

The next Bond appearances were also short stories. 'James Bond and the Murder Before Breakfast' was serialised in the *Daily Express* in September 1959. 'The Hildebrand Rarity' was published in March 1960 in *Playboy*.

The latter periodical certainly seemed more consistent with the Bond brand than *Cosmopolitan*. Hugh Hefner had started the magazine in 1953, the year that Fleming had launched Bond on the world. The publication's mixture of liberal politics, adventurous prose and nude women made it the bible of those who felt they were throwing off the shackles of the Victorian morality then still widespread – and to which M had admitted in *From Russia with Love* – for a libertarian and hedonist ethos. It was a suitable outlet for a character now synonymous with sexual promiscuity and high living.

Playboy was also a suitable outlet for writing of the quality of

Fleming's. Although easy to mock as the epitome of one-handed reading, the magazine was on a higher plane than *Stag*, which serialised *Dr No* and *The Spy Who Loved Me*. *Playboy* published high-calibre wordsmiths such as Jack Kerouac, John Steinbeck and Arthur C. Clarke, while its massive celebrity interviews often transpired to be definitive explorations of their subjects' psyches.

'*Playboy* continued to publish short stories and excerpts from his novels in the early sixties, and went on to do pictorials from the movies,' explains Raymond Benson. He asserts, '*Playboy* was a pretty big deal. I say that *Playboy* and John F. Kennedy were the main instrumental things to bring Bond into the public consciousness in America.'

In mid-1958, Fleming was approached by CBS about a Bond television series.

Fleming wrote treatments – detailed plot synopses – for thirteen episodes of this putative thirty-two-episode series. Judging by a memo he provided to CBS, it appears that by this point the network had accepted that 007 should not be an American. Fleming was actually imploring them not to go too far the other way with 'stage Englishness', which he defined as, 'monocles, moustaches, bowler hats, bobbies . . . blatant English slang . . . public-school ties and accents . . .' The series was never made, apparently because Fleming offended the relevant producer by discussing a different project with a counterpart at the network.

Another television project that failed to materialise stemmed from a 1959 $10,000 bid from production company Hubbell Robinson to make a ninety-minute TV movie of *From Russia with Love* to be sponsored by Ford and to star James Mason as Bond.

While live-action Bond floundered, literary Bond continued, if with its own problems. In a letter to Plomer after the completion of *Goldfinger*, Fleming asserted that it was 'the last full-length folio on Bond. Though I may be able to think up some episodes for him in the future, I shall never be able to give him 70,000 words again.' Plomer must have been weary of this sort of doom-mongering from the author, but this time at least Fleming didn't seem to be being unduly pessimistic. The follow-up to *Goldfinger* was *For Your Eyes Only*, published on 11 April 1960. The UK publisher called the contents 'Five Secret Occasions in the Life of James Bond', the US publisher 'Exploits', but, either way, they were short stories. Moreover, three of the five were previously published.

Not known by the public at the time was an additional reason for viewing the project as ersatz: four of the stories recycled plots Fleming had devised for the aborted CBS television series. This is not to mention that two of the stories – 'Quantum of Solace' and 'The Hildebrand Rarity' – are experimental, suggesting that Fleming was casting around for ways to perpetuate his character.

Fleming's bewilderment about what to do with Bond – mixed perhaps with a determination to innovate as a stung reaction to the critical backlash he had endured – kicked in at precisely the halfway mark of the fourteen Bond books (which count includes the posthumously published *Octopussy and The Living Daylights*). *For Your Eyes Only* was succeeded by *Thunderball*, effectively a novelisation of an unmade film for whose script Fleming was only partly responsible. That itself was succeeded by *The Spy Who Loved Me*, in which Bond is a mere bit-player. Repetition, laziness and whimsy often marred the books after that, despite their qualities. Ironically, this apparently uncertain groping for inspiration started just prior to the Bond films making the character vastly more famous. What is generally considered the worst Bond book, *The Spy Who Loved Me*, appeared in the same year as the film that inaugurated 007's explosion into fame, *Dr. No*.

For Your Eyes Only's opening story is 'From A View To A Kill', a retitled 'Murder Before Breakfast'. Bond is instructed to investigate the murder of a Royal Corps of Signals dispatch rider in France. Bond mounts a patient surveillance operation on the remains of a nearby gypsy caravan site that had aroused the interest of sniffer dogs. An artificial, moving flower stem gives away the presence of a Soviet spy unit's underground bunker. Bond decides to do a dummy dispatch run the next morning, much to the consternation of fellow agent Mary Ann Russell. He takes exception to her characterising the Secret Service as 'a lot of children playing at Red Indians', a criticism he had accepted from Le Chiffre back in *Casino Royale*, and responds, 'Now, be a good girl and do as you're told.'

Sure enough, retracing the murdered driver's route lures from the hidey-hole a would-be assassin, who – unaware of Bond's prior knowledge and .45 Colt – meets a brutal end. Bond, hoping that no more fatalities will be necessary, makes his way to the bunker in the company of some station agents. He meets unexpected resistance and is convinced he is about to die, but the man poised to shoot him collapses in a heap. The person whose deft shot has saved Bond's life is the young woman he had patronised earlier. (Bond repays Mary Ann the favour by, it's implied, pleasuring her in the adjacent forest.)

This twist in the tale is, of course, the sort of thing often found in short-form fiction, but, despite this, the story overall reads like a mini-Bond novel. As in other stories here, we are even made privy to details that are so character-defining that they seem almost too important to be sprinkled into such a vehicle – for instance, that Bond lost his virginity in Paris at the age of sixteen. (The fact that he lost his notebook – i.e. wallet – on the same evening has been interpreted by some as meaning that the person to whom he lost his virginity was a prostitute.) Yet we are left with something of a 'So what?' feeling, something that applies with all the stories in the volume, despite flashes of good writing.

The title story opens with the gunning down of an old white couple who refuse to sell their Jamaican property to three interlopers. It turns out that the couple, named Havelock, were very good friends of M, who stamps 'For Your Eyes Only' on the file he passes to Bond in acknowledgement of the extracurricular and vigilante nature of his task.

Bond flies to the Canadian lair of the villain, Herr von Hammerstein, an ex-Gestapo man buying up land in the Caribbean as a security against the possible rise to power in Cuba of leftist rebel Fidel Castro. There, 007 runs into Judy Havelock, a young woman armed with bow and arrows, intent on vengeance for the murder of her parents. The two team up to deadly effect in a well-written long-distance showdown.

Even in such a short piece of prose, there are stylistic errors and plot inconsistencies. Additionally, when Bond's plans are jeopardised by his encountering Judy, it strikes one as not only too similar to the Tilly Masterton situation in *Goldfinger* but too soon after it, with the fact that she happens to be beautiful (does Bond ever encounter unattractive or old women?) ratcheting up the predictability level to pretty near crushing. Oh, and he also threatens to spank her.

The fourth story, 'Risico', was serialised (as 'The Double Take') in the *Daily Express* simultaneously with the book's publication. In it, 007 is dispatched to Rome to deal with the growing menace of the opium export business. The opium is supplied free of charge by Russia because the country views the social problems caused by the drug as a useful weapon in the Cold War. Bond's running away from the heavies of local contact Colombo when he mistakenly perceives menace is a nicely prosaic touch among the heroics.

The third and fifth stories not only feature little or no espionage, but could easily not be Bond tales at all.

'Quantum of Solace' is a real curiosity, starting with an opening that finds Bond at the aftermath of a dinner party, a territory instantly recognisable as alien for a man whose recreational backdrops are roads, restaurants, gentlemen's clubs and bedrooms. Sure enough, Bond is discomforted by being seated on a softly cushioned sofa with the Governor of Nassau, a scenario he finds inappropriately 'feminine'. Bond is in the area because he has been ordered to stop arms reaching the Cuban supporters of Castro.

The ice begins to break after a half-joking remark by Bond that if he ever got married it would be to an air hostess. The Governor proceeds to tell Bond the story of a man who had achieved that then-newish fantasy, a civil servant he gives the pseudonym Philip Masters. Once the air hostess married Masters, she behaved in a lazy, cruel and faithless way that brought out a not-necessarily beneficial inner steel in her husband. The latter refused to grant a 'quantum of solace' to the wife he spurned and discarded. This is a term of the Governor's coinage, meaning a residue of humanity in a wounded spouse. The woman was left destitute but fell into luck by marrying a Canadian millionaire. A twist in the tale is provided by the Governor's dropping the bombshell that the woman is one half of the couple with whom Bond and the Governor have just dined, a woman Bond found dull. This all leaves Bond thinking that 'Fate plays a more authentic game than any Secret Service conspiracy devised by Governments'.

The story is an interesting failure. Fleming would have been better advised to depict the drama rather than have it relayed: lines like, 'Philip Masters gazed out of the window, seeing her in the sea of white clouds below' do not convince as having come out of a human mouth.

Even here, we learn important things about 007. Very unexpectedly, Bond's attitude towards the Cuban situation is that, 'If anything, his sympathies were with the rebels'. One wonders whether this is a response by Fleming to the recent attacks on him by left-wing critics. It's not the last time in the series that Bond's attitudes suggest an authorial tweaking in the cause of such appeasement, and Fleming even took it into the interview sphere, telling *Playboy* of Bond, 'I should think what politics he has are just a little bit left of centre.'

Closer 'The Hildebrand Rarity' is another experimental story that does not need to include Bond for whatever power it possesses. It finds 007 awaiting his ship home from the Seychelles after having completed a report on whether the location is susceptible to Communist infiltration. A local friend persuades Bond to accompany him on an errand aboard *The Wavekrest*, a yacht owned by Milton Krest. The latter is an American millionaire who, to help justify the tax-exempt status of his foundation, is seeking a specimen of a fish called the Hildebrand Rarity.

Krest disciplines his young and cowed wife Liz with 'The Corrector', the amputated tail of a stingray. His method of killing the Hildebrand Rarity is a toxin that will make many other fish collateral damage. Despite his own blood-drenched profession, Bond takes such an exception to Krest that he tries to sabotage the mission. It doesn't work and Krest throws a party to celebrate the capture of his valuable specimen, at which the American drunkenly offends Bond's friend Barbey and frightens his own wife. Later that night, both Bond and Krest sleep on deck, where Krest's snoring is abruptly terminated. Bond finds him with the Hildebrand Rarity fatally stuffed into his mouth. Mindful of the prospect of the scandal and embarrassment of a murder trial in which a secret agent might be a suspect, Bond throws the body overboard. On the trip home, he studies Liz and Barbey closely to try to work out who is responsible for the bizarre slaying, but neither gives anything away and the story ends on an inconclusive note.

In a story centred on water, Fleming is inevitably on strong ground. Moreover, the way the author depicts Bond, detective-like, testing the reactions of Barbey and Liz to Krest's death, is impressive for its economy. ('. . . Liz Krest had a short but credible fit of hysterics.')

It should be noted that, at the time, *For Your Eyes Only* was not necessarily perceived as the start of a downward gradient. Some reviewers previously hostile to Fleming's full-length Bond prose felt that these miniature Bond adventures removed excesses from the author's outlandish plots, while others were impressed by the exploration of new pastures.

In hindsight, 'Quantum of Solace' and 'The Hildebrand Rarity' are very interesting for what they say about the workings of Flemings's mind. Via such only nominally Bond writing, Fleming seems to have been surreptitiously producing 'worthy' work without breaking the cover granted by genre fiction and thus leaving himself open to the ridicule of his wife's set. He was also, it would seem, trying to break out of what James Bond had become for him: a gilded cage.

By the turn of the sixties, a flurry of activity indicated that James Bond's repeated failure to graduate to any further live-action representation was nearing an end. Multiple parties were now involved in a veritable race to bring Bond to the big screen.

Fleming himself was involved in one of those film projects. It was the only one not based on an existing Bond novel. Explains Raymond Benson, 'Nineteen fifty-eight, Ivar Bryce was working with Kevin McClory as a producer. Kevin had this movie called *The Boy and the Bridge* that Bryce produced and McClory wrote and directed. They thought that was going to be Ian's ticket to get Bond on the silver screen.' *The Boy and the Bridge* won several film-festival awards. In May 1959, a group gathered at the Essex home of Ivar Bryce. He was a lifelong friend of Fleming: they attended Eton together and both worked in intelligence during the war. The rest of the party comprised Fleming, McClory and Ernest Cuneo, a lawyer friend of both Fleming and Bryce. Benson: 'They were throwing around ideas for a Bond movie. McClory didn't want to adapt an existing book. He wanted to do an original screenplay and he wanted to make it in the Bahamas 'cause he lived there and did underwater stuff and he thought that would be very visual.'

Duns: 'They'd decided that none of the books were going to work, we'll do a new story from scratch. So the idea as far as McClory saw it was we're going to use all this new technology and this is all going to be brilliant, and this is going to be the first James Bond film – hopefully of a series.'

Benson: 'It was Ernest Cuneo who came up with this two-page outline of a plot that weekend and he sold it to Ivar Bryce for a dollar, relinquishing any rights to it 'cause he didn't care. Bryce was acting as producer. Fleming took the first stab at writing a screenplay. It was terrible. It was called *James Bond of the Secret Service*. Then McClory gave him notes and Fleming wrote another treatment. He retitled it *Longitude 78 West*. Then McClory hired another writer named Jack Whittingham to come in and rewrite it, 'cause Fleming really wasn't a screenwriter. There were a couple of drafts of the script that Whittingham wrote. He was a professional screenwriter. Somewhere along the way the title got changed to *Thunderball*.'

In his Fleming biography, John Pearson dated to 1958 Fleming's stated preference for an actor to play Bond: David Niven. That McClory demurred is understandable. Niven was a debonair and usually mustachioed man who didn't give the impression of being able to look after himself in a fight. He was also already pushing fifty. Perhaps Fleming was blinded by sentimentality: the two were friends. (Possibly as recompense for not pushing Niven's case hard enough, Niven got an adoring mention from the character Kissy Suzuki in the Bond book *You Only Live Twice*.)

By August 1959 a letter Fleming wrote to Bryce showed a new preference: 'Richard Burton would be by far the best James Bond!' Fleming was on more solid ground here. Burton had been criticised in 1959 for looking too old for the part of Jimmy Porter in the film version of John Osborne's angry-young-man stage play *Look Back in Anger*. He was, though, pretty much ideal for the part of 007: thirty-four and possessed of a brawny physique, smouldering good looks and a voice of booming authority.

Meanwhile, in July 1960 the Ratoff-produced, 20th Century-Fox-funded *Casino Royale* once again flickered into life. The *Los Angeles Times* reported that Ratoff would be the director and

Peter Finch the lead actor. Although this wasn't the first time the announcement of a Ratoff-helmed Bond flick had been made, it was still news to McClory. Duns: 'Kevin McClory had been told that he had the right to make the first Bond film . . . He says, "What the fuck is going on? Who is this Ratoff guy?" Basically, the problem is that Fleming had sold off different books.'

Gregory Ratoff died in December 1960 with the filming of *Casino Royale* still not yet begun. However, if McClory thought that was the end – or even the extent – of his unexpected competition troubles, he was mistaken. In June 1961 it was reported that the production partnership of Albert 'Cubby' Broccoli and Harry Saltzman was set to bring 007 to the big screen. Saltzman enthused in the press, 'Actors are falling over themselves to play Bond: Cary Grant, David Niven, Trevor Howard, James Mason, all are interested but I want to use an unknown.' Further media stories made clearer the picture about their rights: Saltzman and Broccoli had bought seven of the books.

This in turn reactivated the *Casino Royale* project that had seemed to die with Gregory Ratoff. The right to adapt the first Bond novel to the big screen was one of several film properties sold by Ratoff's widow to ease her financial difficulties. The buyer was agent Charles K. Feldman. It so happened that Feldman had once been an employer of Cubby Broccoli, who started his film career as a talent agent for Feldman's company Famous Artists. (Broccoli would later claim that he had tried to buy the *Casino Royale* rights from Mrs Ratoff but was rebuffed.) 'Feldman did it as a favour to the widow,' says Duns. 'He wasn't particularly thinking about anything to do with James Bond. Then suddenly he realises, "Christ, Broccoli – the guy who used to work for me – has bought seven of these damn things and it's all over the press."'

Feldman decided to go full steam ahead with his own Bond project. The seriousness of his intent is illustrated by the fact that he engaged the ultra-expensive services of legendary screenwriter Ben Hecht. Dubbed the 'Shakespeare of Hollywood', Hecht had been responsible for the scripts of *It's a Wonderful World*, *Spellbound*, *Notorious* and several other cinema classics. However, his renown in the industry was far greater than among that part of the public who paid attention during the credits: as often as not, he polished scripts without credit.

When in 2011 Duns tracked down several drafts of Hecht's *Casino Royale* – which had lain undisturbed in the Newberry Library in Chicago since 1979, and no doubt had been similarly neglected before being deposited there – he found them, one or two outlandish drafts aside, to be 'a masterclass in thriller-writing'.

Hecht seems to have been fifty years ahead of his time: the tone of his *Casino Royale* script is comparable to the one filmed with Daniel Craig. Duns says, 'Hecht was trying to do in sixty-three, sixty-four what they did in [2006], which is to film a near-unfilmable novella, really, in which not an awful lot happens and most of it's a card game, and a torture scene which is a little unacceptable for cinema audiences, and to try and make it into an exciting thriller . . . It's grim but it's totally brilliant. It's possible that Hecht's version would have flopped. It's very dark. It's got the ending from the novel, with her dying and a heartbroken Bond having proposed marriage. It's got some very dark stuff about paedophilia in it.' However, Duns also says, 'It's a very Hitchcockian film. It's got chases on water skis. It's got an incredible torture scene. It's got all of the stuff there for the best Bond film ever made.'

Broccoli and Saltzman, though, beat Feldman to the punch by releasing *Dr. No*. Duns says of Hecht's Bond scripts, 'It looks like the first stuff that he was doing was late 1963. It's informed by [the film] *Dr. No* and, while he's writing it, it's informed by [the film] *From Russia with Love*.' Apart from a single scene in a draft around halfway through the process where he makes Bond an American who has inherited the 007 number, Hecht's Bond is British. Or perhaps that should more accurately be Scottish. Duns: 'The character of James Bond is a very, very subtle and clever melding of Ian Fleming's character and Sean Connery.'

Unfortunately, at this point death entered the story again: Hecht succumbed to a heart attack in April 1964 without having completed a planned next draft of *Casino Royale*.

The spikes in interest in James Bond caused by newspaper serialisations, the prime-ministerial visit to Goldeneye and the *Express* strip were as nothing compared with some positive publicity generated in March 1961. It was in that month that Fleming's writing was granted an unexpected endorsement from the most powerful man in the world.

Ian Fleming had met John Fitzgerald Kennedy in March 1960 through the aegis of his friend Marion 'Oatsie' Leiter, wife of Tommy Leiter, a couple after whom Fleming had named Bond's CIA chum. At the relevant dinner party at the home of the then Senator Kennedy, Fleming proceeded to amuse his host with his semi-facetious proposals to undermine the recently installed Castro regime in Cuba. A year to the month after their meeting, Kennedy – now ensconced in his position as young, handsome, hatless President for a new liberal era – was the subject of a feature in *Life* magazine. The puff piece by Hugh Sidey was titled 'The President's Voracious Reading Habits' and boasted that Kennedy had a reading speed almost five times the national average. It also contained a list of the President's ten favourite books. They were mostly ostentatiously erudite works, but in ninth position sat *From Russia with Love*.

'That was bullshit,' says John Pearson. 'Kennedy didn't read for pleasure ever. He did get a rather fancy list of books up, which included Lord David Cecil's *The Young Melbourne*, a most unlikely book for Kennedy to have [read], and several others. It was Sidey who actually slipped in *From Russia with Love*.'

In a more deferential age, the motivation for, and authenticity of, the article's contents wasn't the subject of much discussion, but the consensus that has grown in the years since is that the article was a calculated attempt to provide specific dimensions to the President's image. Contrary to what Pearson suggests, Kennedy certainly read and enjoyed the Bond books, having been introduced to them either (sources differ) by his wife Jacqueline with *From Russia with Love* itself or by Oatsie Leiter with *Casino Royale*. However, it can be reasonably assumed that the book's inclusion on the list was for a reason other than admiration. It's in the nature of such politician puff pieces that they attempt to suggest the subject shares some of the tastes of the average – and much less well-educated – man. Kennedy's being a Bond-lover made him one of the guys.

Of course, it hardly mattered that the endorsement was a bogus, or at least exaggerated, one. It had an electrifying effect on the standing in the world – general and literary – of both Ian Fleming and James Bond. The visit of the British Prime Minister to Fleming's house hadn't been attended by any public endorsement of his works, yet it prompted people to go into bookshops to buy them. The explicit approval conferred by the American President was exponentially more beneficial, not only in terms of the simple fact of spotlighting the books but in the implication that they proffered an accurate depiction of the behaviour of the Soviet intelligence organisations with which Kennedy had to grapple daily. Capitalising on this, Fleming's American paperback publisher, Signet, launched a major advertising campaign. By the end of the year, Fleming was the biggest-selling thriller writer in the USA.

It may even be the case that Bond finally made it to the medium of cinema after so many failed previous attempts precisely because Kennedy was a fan. 'JFK' was a friend of Arthur Krim, chairman of United Artists studios, and had spoken to him of his liking for the Bond books.

Fleming was in the habit of rewarding other writers for their friendship and support by portraying Bond reading their books (in *Goldfinger*, Raymond Chandler had become the latest to be paid that compliment). He would reciprocate Kennedy's endorsement via complimentary references to him and his writing in future Bond stories. There was really no way, though, of returning the favour of one of the greatest boons that could possibly be conferred on any author.

However, Fleming received the good tidings about the Kennedy endorsement on the same day as he received some worrying news: he was facing legal action over his next Bond novel, due to be published imminently. This action would cause him considerable stress and embarrassment, and arguably severely reduce the number of Bond books he would write by the simple fact of shortening his life.

By 1960, Fleming's film project was, as far as he could see, floundering.

Benson: 'McClory and Bryce had been trying to sell this idea to studios and had no luck, so the project just died. It just fell apart. So Fleming went off and wrote his next novel and he used the plot that was in these screenplays.' The result was *Thunderball*, Fleming's ninth Bond book, published on 27 March 1961.

'. . . these jobs with people like SMERSH that I used to get tangled up in.' With that past-tense reference by 007 to Smert Shpionam, *Thunderball* delineates, rather quietly, a new Bond era. The organisation whose evil way back in *Casino Royale* provided Bond a life-mission is herein wound up via Fleming claiming that it was abolished by Soviet premier Nikita Khrushchev in 1958.

The Special Executive for Counterintelligence, Terrorism, Revenge, and Extortion (the American comma before the 'and' is, peculiarly, Fleming's) is a private syndicate unaffiliated to any government or ideology. That Fleming decided to make SPECTRE Bond's new nemesis was a bad misjudgement. Author Robert Sellers unearthed a memo in which Fleming told his movie-script collaborators, 'It might be very unwise to point directly at Russia as the enemy . . . the film will take about two years to produce, and peace might conceivably break out in the meantime . . .' Occurrences in the Soviet Union such as the reforms of Khrushchev had convinced Fleming that the Cold War was nearing an end. However, Bond's thoughts in this book – such as, 'With the Cold War easing off, it was not like the old days' – were the types of things that would within two years seem a bitter joke as the world was shocked by such events as the Cuban Missile Crisis and the construction of the Berlin Wall. The Cold War would remain very much 'on' and the defining focus of global relations for a further quarter of a century. Fleming would later recognise his mistake and begin bringing the KGB (under that name) into the Bond texts.

Significantly, the brand names thrown in by Fleming at the start of *Thunderball* are Phensic (a type of aspirin) and Enos (a liquid stomach settler). M has been disturbed by Bond's latest medical. Accordingly, M – a recent convert to health regimes – has booked 007 into a Brighton health farm called Shrublands. We have never seen Bond so emasculated as in his horrified reaction: he speaks in a 'strangled' voice and tries to protest. ('But, sir, I mean, I'm perfectly all right.') Once outside, Bond vents his spleen at Moneypenny in what is actually the series' first long exchange between the pair.

Bond's taxi to Shrublands is driven by a cocksure young man with a duck-tail hairstyle. This leads to a silent soliloquy by Bond that is anti-Beveridge and anti-rock'n'roll: 'This youth, thought Bond, makes about twenty pounds a week, despises his parents, and would like to be Tommy Steele . . . He was born into the buyers' market of the Welfare State and into the age of atomic bombs and space flight. For him life is easy and meaningless.' Yet, in the conversation Bond then initiates, the youth reveals that he has been industrious enough to have already saved up half of the money he needs for a new car, leading Bond to decide that he has misjudged him and to tip him handsomely. We, once again, wonder whether the author is trying to placate the politically minded Bond-haters. However, Fleming could never reinvent 007 as working-class and, when later summoned by red telephone, Bond races to Regent's Park in his new Mark II Continental Bentley, which has cost him £4,500 – in today's money in the area of eighty-five grand.

At Shrublands, the contretemps into which Bond gets with one Count Lippe, who bears a Tong tattoo, features extraordinarily pulpy text. Bond, for instance, vocally impersonates no fewer than two of the facility's staff, one of them at length. It seems to betray *Thunderball*'s origins as a project intended for a coarser and generally more stylised medium.

Bond – euphoric over raised energy levels and enhanced wellbeing – is carefully masticating his food, consuming yoghurt and restricting his smoking to low-tar cigarettes. Housekeeper May is disgusted by the 'pap' that 'Mister James' is eating. She thinks such sustenance will be insufficient when he is dispatched on another of the dangerous assignments she is not supposed to know about. The Scots brogue in which Fleming renders May's admonition ('I'm knowing more about yer life than mebbe ye were wishing I did') is both delightful and a lot more convincing than the taxi driver's Estuary English.

Once in the office of M – who is back to his harrumphing, unhealthy self – Bond is handed a blackmail letter that the Prime Minister has received from SPECTRE. The organisation reveals it is in possession of a missing British aircraft carrying two atomic weapons. It demands for the bombs' return £100,000,000 in gold bullion, upon pain of detonation. In stating, 'This, Mr. Prime Minister, is a single and final communication,' SPECTRE are displaying a faith in the efficacy of the Royal Mail uncommon even for the late fifties. It also strikes one as odd that the villains don't just request the traditional and far more readily transportable banknotes with non-consecutive serial numbers. The real credibility problem, though, lies in the fact that it will transpire that Count Lippe is an employee of SPECTRE. It is truly remarkable how often Bond happens to run into villains in his off-duty life just before he is assigned to deal with them via his work.

SPECTRE is headed by Ernst Stavro Blofeld, a Pole concerned

only with the accumulation of money, whatever the means. His lack of interest in sex, cigarettes and alcohol is something common enough in Bond villains to make one suspect Fleming considers an abstentious state as much a shorthand for evil as ugliness. Despite being twenty stone and having eyes with no discernible irises, Blofeld is not the often-deformed figure of film adaptation but a man with a crew cut and ageless face. Nor does he stroke a cat. (He also has a birthdate – 28 May 1908 – that Fleming's family would have found familiar.)

The official response to the crisis is styled 'Operation Thunderball'. M sends Bond to the Bermuda/Bahamas area to investigate a suspicious radar reading. Before he departs, a failed assassination attempt on him by Lippe makes Bond realise that life is short and he has May cook him up a gloriously unhealthy send-off meal. Once overseas, Bond inveigles his way into the circle of Emilio Largo, SPECTRE's man on the ground. The denouement is a mass underwater fight between Largo's frogmen and some Royal Navy men Bond has recruited who are equipped with nothing more hi-tech than knives attached to broom handles. Bond's life is saved by the intervention of the book's romantic interest, Domino, armed with a harpoon gun. Thus ends what is by a considerable margin the weakest Bond book so far.

Bond's health-farm encounter with Lippe is just the start of the unlikely coincidences and improbabilities. In Nassau, Bond by simple happenstance hooks up with Domino, who is not just the kept woman of Largo but – unknown to Largo – the long-lost sister of one Giuseppe Petacchi, an Italian pilot who was subcontracted by SPECTRE to hijack the missile-carrying plane before being murdered. That it was reportedly Jack Whittingham's idea to make the book's Bond girl related to the hijack pilot raises another possibility about the reason for the book's preponderance of shortcomings, namely the 'too many cooks' principle. Fleming also seems to be straining to make the necessary wordage. Among several examples of tedious digression is Domino's imagined backstory of the sailor with 'Hero' on his cap band featured on packets of Player's cigarettes.

Meanwhile, Fleming's penchant for real-life brand names is taken to an absurd degree when Bond notices that the sweat boxes at Shrublands are manufactured by the Medikalischer Maschinenbau GmbH, 44 Franziskanerstrasse, Ulm, Bavaria. One can only hope he is taking the piss.

Kevin McClory had been provided an advance copy of *Thunderball* in the hope that it would quell the noises he was making about litigation. It had the opposite effect. McClory and Jack Whittingham tried to secure an injunction preventing *Thunderball*'s publication. They failed on the grounds that the book had already shipped to bookshops and reviewers, but the presiding judge made the point that this ruling was without prejudice to the validity of the plaintiffs' claims. McClory and Whittingham immediately launched a civil action in pursuit of rights and recompense.

'McClory sued for plagiarism,' explains Benson. 'He sued both Fleming and Bryce.' Bryce was on the receiving end of a writ because of what McClory claimed was his involvement as a 'false partner' in Xanadu, a production company set up by the two to make the first Bond picture.

One strand of McClory's claims was that the organisation SPECTRE was not a Fleming invention but had been devised by committee. This was potentially important because, by the time the court case was heard in November 1963, Fleming had used the organisation again in his novel *On Her Majesty's Secret Service*. Even more importantly, Eon – the Broccoli–Saltzman production company that McClory clearly felt had usurped his rightful role as the captain of 007's cinematic voyages – had also used SPECTRE, if in a more background role.

The original meaning of the SPECTRE acronym was actually less cartoonish than the final one: the Special Executive for Terrorism, Revolution and Espionage. What was more important, though, is who devised the organisation. 'We don't know,' says Benson. 'Bryce told me that McClory did. Ernest Cuneo told me that McClory did. However, there is evidence that Fleming was the one who invented it. It just sounds like his kind of work. Maybe McClory said, "Let's create a criminal organisation that works for hire" and Fleming came up with the name SPECTRE. In Cuneo's first outline, the Mafia was the bad guys. Then it became the Russians and finally SPECTRE.'

The name in various ways did speckle Fleming's previous writing: the ghost town Spectreville in *Diamonds are Forever* and the Spektor code cracker in *From Russia with Love*. Benson: 'But who created it really didn't matter. It was who owned it.'

The month after McClory's failed injunction, Fleming suffered a heart attack. It wasn't, of course, a consequence of McClory's action. Although that may have contributed to it, Fleming's prodigious intake of cigarettes, fatty food and alcohol and his lack of exercise and overwork were the chief culprits. Although Fleming did make a serious attempt to reform his ways afterwards – even resorting to a hypnotist to try to give up smoking – pretty soon he abandoned any efforts to prolong his life. Fleming could not even be dissuaded from this long, slow act of suicide by the news in August 1961 that the deal had been made between Eon and United Artists to produce a Bond motion picture, the breakthrough of which he had been dreaming for years.

THE
CELLULOID
AGENT

In 1959, *The Sunday Times* was sold to Roy Thomson. The new owner seems not to have perceived Ian Fleming as an *ex facie* member of the newspaper aristocracy and to have therefore questioned his cushy arrangements. Fleming subsequently left the staff of the paper to set up as a freelancer. However, Fleming was now a big and prestigious name. As such, he continued to have close links to *The Sunday Times*. He received a retainer of £1,000 a year, attended its Tuesday morning conferences and in 1962 was given the important role of setting up *The Sunday Times Colour Section* (later *The Sunday Times Colour Magazine*).

This innovation was a matter of no little controversy, its implications ranging from whether British newspapers were being dragged downmarket by a garish, foreign gimmick to whether newspapers giving them away might destroy the market for paid magazines. Fleming helped make the 4 February 1962 inaugural edition of the 'supplement' an even bigger deal than it already was by gifting it a new Bond short story, 'The Living Daylights'. Although he was no doubt properly remunerated, it is nonetheless remarkable that that story was no throwaway. (The story appeared in US title *Argosy* the following June.)

Bond is sent to Berlin to enable agent number 272, based in Russia since the war, to cross Checkpoint Charlie. To prevent 272 being picked off by the East, 007 keeps a Sniperscope trained in an apartment overlooking the crossing point. Inconveniently, it is not known on which night 272 will make his dash for freedom. For three days Bond and the rather uptight Captain Paul Sender have to bear each other's company as they await the appearance of their colleague.

During the third day, Sender rebukes Bond for pouring a stiff whisky. Bond replies, 'I've got to commit a murder tonight. Not you. Me . . . I'd be quite happy for you to get me sacked from the double-O section.' At five minutes past six, Sender – acting as Bond's eyes at the crossing point in lieu of Bond's ability to take his attention from the suspected sniper's nest in a building opposite – spots the figure of 272 making his way across the wasteland towards the West. Noticing something moving in a darkened window, Bond realises 272 has been spotted. Bond is amazed to see that the would-be assassin opposite is a golden haired, beautiful female. He hastily alters his aim and his bullet merely disables his target. Bond has to interrupt Sender's celebrations about the fact that 272 has made it over the Wall to tell him to get down: a searchlight sweeps over their window and bullets start howling into the room.

When everything has quietened down, Sender confronts Bond with the fact that he had seen him adjust his aim, pointing out,

'KGB have got plenty of women agents – and women gunners.' Bond knows that the girl is in worse trouble than he is: she has possibly lost her left hand and – having had the living daylights scared out of her – had her nerve broken.

Bond's humanity-dictated unprofessionalism probably provided the interesting tension in the story for readers unfamiliar with 007 fiction. However, the regular Bond reader would have been *au fait* with the fact that bucking orders and succumbing to emotion – for reasons of whim as often as humanity – is so common with 007 as to make him something approaching a loose cannon.

Fleming impresses with his knowledge of rifle handling and espionage routine in a story whose gloominess, location and circumstances make it a quintessential Cold War tale.

Despite Ian Fleming's stated determination to 'write the spy story to end all spy stories', the word 'spy' does not occur much in his Bond books.

Although the terms 'spy' and 'secret agent' have become conflated in the public mind, spying more suggests inveigling oneself into a long-term position in enemy territory in order to procure intelligence, something that Bond did not do. Fleming tends to employ the term 'secret agent'. Bond himself – as a function of being an employee of an organisation that at the time did not officially exist – explains his role to members of the public by saying he is 'a kind of policeman', 'from Scotland Yard' or 'from the Ministry of Defence'.

He is, though, sometimes referred to as a spy by third parties. In *Casino Royale*, the assassin of Le Chiffre brands him with an abbreviation of 'Shpion', Russian for 'spy'. In *From Russia with*

Love, the Soviets discussing Bond refer to him as both secret agent and spy. Bond is also referred to as a spy in the title of the tenth Bond book.

Published on 16 April 1962, *The Spy Who Loved Me* is a unique James Bond novel. In place of the broadly objective, third-person narration of all the books thus far, we are presented with a first-person account that gives us a rounded view of Bond's arrival into another individual's life. This is unusual enough, but an even more unexpected departure is that the narrator is a woman.

The Spy Who Loved Me originally appeared credited to 'Ian Fleming with Vivienne Michel', the latter being the book's narrator. In the American edition, Fleming included a whimsical note stating that he had found Michel's manuscript on his desk. Fleming would soon distance himself from the work in a somewhat less playful way. The author was so bitterly disappointed by the reception given to *The Spy Who Loved Me* that he quickly became ashamed of it. Nothing better demonstrates the way that Fleming increasingly came to resemble a weathervane in his reaction to criticism of his work than what he did next. Although he could hardly recall the circulated editions, he did the nearest thing by refusing in his lifetime to allow a paperback edition to be published and by banning any film version.

Those coming to the novel after having learned this will be surprised at how good it is. The two-thirds of it neither involving nor requiring Bond's presence – and especially the parts about the narrator's youth and sexual liaisons – form a highly respectable literary novel. The departure from the series template works enormously well in that we feel and cheer for this protagonist, her narration creating an intense empathy that the cold tone of normal Bond books could never engender. That the book actually declines in quality with Bond's arrival is a matter of regret for the 007 fan but a separate issue.

Vivienne 'Viv' Michel is a French-Canadian in her early twenties who is house-sitting Dreamy Pines, a remote New York State motel that is closing up as the tourist season comes to an end. Due to hand over the keys the next day to the owner, one Mr Sanguinetti, she is driven by her isolation to reminisce about her life. This part of the book is titled 'Me'. In it, Viv takes us through the backstory that has led her here. Viv's prose is, in literary first-person tradition, often implausibly eloquent. However, her Quebec childhood, student life and coming-of-age are rendered very convincingly. Particularly powerful is a deflowering scene in a private cinema box: breathless date Derek arrives back from a chemist with a 'thing' but the two are humiliatingly discovered.

Her next lover dispenses with her when Viv – now an up-and-coming journalist – falls pregnant and has to be bought an abortion in Switzerland, where it is legal. A devastated Viv sets off aboard a Vespa on a solo journey across America.

Bizarrely, 'Me' feels like nothing so much as a precursor to the prose depictions of Swinging London and 'promiscuous' culture that the availability of the contraceptive pill was soon to make fashionable. Its distaff perspective is astoundingly convincing. Viv in no way comes across as a dummy manipulated by a patriarchal author-ventriloquist. We have never had any reason to believe that a male who had never wanted for anything materially could understand a young woman living on a budget, nor had we been given any reason to believe that such an apparent advocate of sexually predatory behaviour would have insight into how badly this person might feel treated by the men she has known intimately.

'Me' is, remarkably, far more sexually explicit than any previous Bond book. We are not prepared for lines like, '. . . as he told me, it was essential to a happy marriage that the climax should be reached simultaneously by the partners', nor the jaw-droppingly candid recounting of being discovered in the cinema ('I imagined what the manager must have seen when Derek got up from me. Ugh! I shivered with disgust').

In Part 2 of the book – 'Them' – an unsavoury pair of characters nicknamed Sluggsy and Horror turn up unexpectedly at the motel on the night before the handover. Viv is just about to be raped when the door buzzer sounds – the transition from 'Them' to 'Him'.

Forced to open the door to allay suspicion, Viv is confronted by the sight of a man whose hat, belted raincoat and cruel good looks make her think, God, it's another of them! It's the series' first third-party sight of Bond that seems organic, not contrived. Bond's car has a puncture and he has been attracted by the lit 'Vacancy' sign. Viv warms to Bond when he smiles, and then further when she sees in his eyes his quick apprehension that something is wrong.

Bond contrives to get inside, where he explains to Viv, 'We've got to sit these two hoodlums out. Wait until they make a move . . .' In order to help pass the time, Bond explains to Viv how he came to be in this neck of the woods. Cue an amazingly implausible piece of indiscretion and boastfulness in which Bond spills the details of a just-completed case. Also implausible is the absence of colloquialism in Bond's recounted story.

Eventually, it transpires that the gangster pair have been employed by Sanguinetti to burn down the motel for the insurance money. That Viv was to have been portrayed as the cause of the blaze necessitated her death. Bond ensures that Sluggsy and Horror fail to dispatch either Viv or him, but the action depicted is disjointed. Viv's mounting adoration for Bond, meanwhile, is a lurch back to the cliché of femininity Fleming has spent much of the book avoiding. In the action's aftermath, a policeman named Captain Stoner delivers Viv a lecture about Bond types. 'Keep away from *all* these men,' he sternly tells her. 'They are not for you, whether they're called James Bond or Sluggsy Morant.' Fleming's tacking-on of this cautionary note is absurd: Stoner has never met Bond, who has saved Viv's life. It all makes for a disappointing conclusion to a text that had started at a high level of quality.

Nonetheless, *The Spy Who Loved Me* is more than merely a worthwhile experiment. While one would not wish all Bond books to be like it, one is glad that this lateral view of 007 exists.

Harry Saltzman was an odd choice for Ian Fleming to entrust with the character who represented his greatest professional achievement in life.

It was Saltzman to whom, in December 1960, Fleming sold an option regarding motion pictures for all of his existing and future Bond books except *Casino Royale*. Born in Quebec in 1915, Saltzman was most well known for kitchen-sink dramas and Angry Young Man vehicles: *Look Back in Anger, Saturday Night and Sunday Morning* and *The Entertainer*. These films were both very good and innovative in providing a window on the world of the proletariat that had hitherto been largely denied British society. Their tableaux, however, were the antithesis of Bond's rarefied environs. Saltzman's daughter Hilary has suggested that Saltzman may have gained the rights to Fleming's character because of his classified work for the Psychological Warfare Division of the US Office of War Information during World War II. In October 2012,

Hilary told David Kamp of *Vanity Fair*, '. . . they had a similar background during the war, which was in confidential missions, they had a mutual understanding. Even though they couldn't publicise it, I really think Ian felt that this series was safe in my father's hands.' Some suspect that the two men even met during the war.

However, Saltzman's live-action option on Bond might well have – like those of almost everyone before him – come to nothing. With only around a month of his option remaining, there remained no apparent prospect of studio funding. It was then that Albert R. Broccoli entered the picture.

Broccoli – known to one and all as 'Cubby' – was born in New York in 1909. He was also a producer with a good track record, if with slightly less 'worthy' fare. Among his nineteen pictures as either producer or executive producer were *The Red Beret*, *Cockleshell Heroes* and *Safari*, although *The Trials of Oscar Wilde* (1960) was an early cinematic tilt at compassion for homosexuals. Broccoli had actually spotted the celluloid potential of Bond books before. He had tried to interest Irving Allen – his partner in the production company Warwick Films – in licensing them. According to the (admittedly often unreliable) word of Broccoli, Allen's scepticism about the Bond property alienated Fleming and his literary agent, Robert Fenn. David V. Picker of United Artists heard a slightly different story: that Fleming's putative CBS Bond TV series and Fleming's dislike of movies alienated Allen. The latter story has one convincing element: Fleming was never much of a moviegoer; his stepdaughter Fionn's memory is of his going off of an evening to the Portland Club to play bridge, not off to the local Odeon.

Whichever story was true, it was ultimately all for the good, according to Richard Maibaum, who would become a long-term Bond scriptwriter. Speaking in Pat McGilligan's *Backstory* (1986), he said, '. . . with the censorship of pictures that existed then, you couldn't even have the minimal sex and violence that we eventually put into the pictures. They just wouldn't have been the same.'

One or two years after this (his dates varied), Broccoli had a meeting with novelist and screenwriter Wolf Mankowitz, whom he sometimes employed. Broccoli mentioned that he'd long wanted to make a James Bond film and lamented that someone else now had the options on the properties. Mankowitz revealed that he knew that person. Mankowitz further revealed that Saltzman had been unable to put a deal together. The writer offered to arrange a meeting between the pair.

The meeting occurred the very next morning. By the end of it, Broccoli and Saltzman had agreed to enter into a partnership. Broccoli always maintained that he never wanted a partnership but that it was his only way to ensure the Bond property came his way: with Saltzman's option expiring within three weeks, Broccoli was worried the rights would be snapped up by someone else. This reluctance is in some ways understandable, for the two men made for an odd couple. Norman Wanstall, soundman on five Broccoli–Saltzman Bond films, says, 'I always found Harry a little bit scary really. He was a very strong, silent character and I would have always called him "Mr Saltzman", whereas Broccoli was always a father figure. I would have been very relaxed with Broccoli.'

'Harry was a peculiar man,' says Monty Norman, who wrote music for Broccoli–Saltzman films. 'A friend of mine did a film with him and he was having trouble getting paid, and Harry said something like, "But I've just bought a Cadillac – I can't do it!" Like you're supposed to sympathise. He was a difficult man. Whereas Cubby . . . was basically a really nice guy.'

The mismatched pair had meetings about James Bond with United Artists and Columbia Pictures. Some sources cite the UA meeting as taking place on 20 June 1961 but Broccoli has stated 21 June, a date one might assume to be reliable from being embedded in his brain: it was his wedding anniversary. Picker, then United Artists' head of production, recalls of the planned meeting, 'Bud Ornstein, who was our man in London, told me about it. I was absolutely thrilled because I had been trying to see if we could get those rights and had been told by Fleming's agent that he wasn't prepared to sell.'

Both Broccoli and Picker are in agreement that the meeting ended on a handshake production agreement. Memories differ on specifics. Broccoli recalled a profit division of 60 per cent to Broccoli–Saltzman, 40 per cent to the studio. Picker recalls a 50–50 deal. Not in dispute is that Broccoli and Saltzman more than once got their margins raised over the succeeding years. Picker: 'When they came to us and the projects were obviously turning out to be successful, we had no trouble whatsoever in renegotiating the deal.' However, he also points out that this was essentially largesse on the part of UA: 'Under no circumstances could they have ever taken [the Bond films] elsewhere simply because we refused to renegotiate a deal that we had in place. We had the right to option all the projects.'

Although of course Broccoli and Saltzman were at the time very pleased to have made the deal, it would come to be seen by the pair as a poisoned chalice. When UA was taken over in 1967 by Transamerica Corporation, it set the pattern for what would happen over the following decades, when the studio was incrementally reduced to little more than a logo by predators who at the same time brought their own financial crises to the table.

Broccoli and Saltzman set up a production company called Eon, short for a phrase that had the smack of a Bond title: Everything or Nothing. Danjaq – a portmanteau of the first syllables of the men's respective wives' first names – was the company set up to control the copyright of Eon's films

Eon decided to make *Thunderball* the first 007 motion picture and commissioned Richard Maibaum to provide the screenplay. It has been contended that Maibaum was handed a Jack Whittingham *Thunderball* script to rework. This appears to be true: although his script was generally faithful to Fleming's book, Maibaum's inclusion of a plastic-surgery element emanates from a Whittingham script, not Fleming's treatment or prose. This shortly became moot when it was decided to make the first Bond film *Dr. No*. The switch was executed, according to both Broccoli and Maibaum, because of the legal case Kevin McClory instituted with regard to *Thunderball*. Not so moot is the suggestion that Whittingham – though now permanently out of the 007 picture – had a profound effect on the moulding of the cinema Bond by dint of his script's interpretation of the character – less intense, more charming and humorous – being adopted by Maibaum, and thence naturally by every succeeding screenwriter. Germane to the ongoing *Thunderball* court case is that Maibaum's reworking a Whittingham script would suggest that Eon knew full well that Fleming had sold elsewhere the film rights to *Thunderball*.

Broccoli and Saltzman decided to reward Wolf Mankowitz for being the broker to their partnership by appointing him as co-screenwriter with Maibaum on *Dr. No*. Things did not get off to a flying start. Maibaum recalled in Broccoli's autobiography *When the Snow Melts*, '. . . we decided that Fleming's *Dr. No* was the most ludicrous character in the world. He was just Fu Manchu with two steel hooks. It was 1961, and we felt that audiences wouldn't stand for that kind of stuff anymore.' Their solution to this absurdity, however, seems even more ludicrous. Their forty-page treatment gave the name 'Dr No' not to the human villain but a marmoset monkey sitting on his shoulder. After a dressing-down from the producers, the writing pair set to work again, with the instruction to stick more closely to the literary antecedent.

Bond's creator attended several script meetings, but Fleming had no contractual approval over the scripts and did not try to interfere. Broccoli – who was glad of his pleasingly louche presence – recalled that Fleming instead offered notes about espionage protocol and weaponry. He also provided a memo that sounds similar to, or the same as, the one he gave to CBS regarding their proposed Bond TV show, containing as it did warnings against cartoon Englishness. It also stressed the need to make the audiences like Bond.

The final screenwriting credit for *Dr. No* was shared by Richard Maibaum, Johanna Harwood and Berkely Mather. Maibaum was irritated that Harwood got a formal credit when he felt her role had been merely to anglicise the dialogue. Harwood – a long-term scriptwriting employee of Saltzman – has insisted that she actually wrote a first draft before anyone else set to work. In any case, it was swings and roundabouts: Mankowitz does not appear in the credits because he was initially disgusted with his and Maibaum's script and, by the time he had changed his mind, the titles had been completed and he didn't want to pay to have them redone. Broccoli also

claimed that director Terence Young and his own wife Dana –
an established screenwriter – threw in ideas.

That tangled tale had an upshot that might not on the surface
be the expected one: Maibaum went on to be a fixture in Bond
scriptwriting credits, writing or co-writing thirteen of the first
sixteen official 007 movies. Although the collaborative nature of
filmmaking means it is always difficult to pinpoint and evaluate
individual contributions, Maibaum must go down as one of the
people principally responsible for the personality of the cinema
Bond. Maibaum clearly felt so. He said, '. . . my work on the
first four films set the pattern and had something to do with the
character of Bond – his humour, his *savoir faire*. I know I insisted
on the elegance of the villains – especially after I saw how great
Joseph Wiseman was in *Dr. No*.' Yet, of course, Jack Whittingham
might suggest that, in the process described above, Maibaum was
merely picking up the thread Whittingham had started to sew in
his *Thunderball* scripts.

In any case, a lot of people could claim the father-of-cinema-
Bond title. Many of them had worked together previously.
Maibaum's retention would seem to be related to the fact that for
Dr. No and its successors Broccoli imported wholesale the staff
of Warwick Films. Not only had Maibaum worked for this outfit,
but so had Terence Young, editor Peter Hunt, set designer Ken
Adam, cinematographer Ted Moore, stuntman/stunt coordinator
Bob Simmons and sound technician Norman Wanstall.

'It was always said that we had a family atmosphere,' says
Wanstall of the crew on Bond films. 'I think it was because it was
very unusual for there to be a series, where a film finished and soon
after that another one was made and then another one was made.'
Eon's Bond productions were a family affair in another sense.

Anecdotes abound of behaviour by Saltzman and (especially) Broccoli that was more the method of indulgent parents keen to keep those around them happy than of hard-ass movie producers with an eye on the bottom line. This veritable Bond family crafted the 007 movie signatures over a sufficiently long period as to make them immutable.

Adam created the sort of elaborate, towering sets – especially for villains' lairs – that are comparatively unremarkable today but were awe-inspiring when he pioneered them.

Hunt's editing spurned the stateliness then common in cinema for something approaching frenetic and almost illogical: he would abandon pans in what would normally be the middle and start a cut with action that contrasted with what was seen in the previous frame. Wanstall says of Hunt's work on *Dr. No*, 'When he first saw the rushes and he began to see how the film was being directed, he said to me, "We don't want people stopping and thinking about this and that and 'Why didn't he do that?' Let's keep the film moving" . . . The other films followed in the same way.' Interestingly, this approach was something that had been in Fleming's mind at the time of his 1959 script for *Thunderball*. He advised his collaborators 'not to allow the audience time to worry about probabilities'.

Wanstall had his own part to play in the unconscious building-up of franchise hallmarks. Operating in the days before large sound libraries and computer-generated effects, he had to seek out or improvise wild and weird sonics to provide accompaniment to sights never before seen on screen. Those often futuristic sounds were ratcheted up to exaggerated levels by directors, making Bond films even more exclamatory than their action already dictated.

Then there was Bob Simmons. When a budding young actor,

Simmons had been mates with both Sean Connery and Roger Moore. When fate put him into the stunt game and Connery and Moore successively into the Bond role, he ended up doubling for them, tussling with them and choreographing their fights. His contribution went further than many might assume. It is he, not Connery, in the 'gun barrel' sequence at the beginning of the first three Bond films. Moreover, it was a confab with Simmons, Sean Connery and Ken Adam that led to the iconic moment in *Goldfinger* when Oddjob is electrocuted while reaching for his bowler hat. Simmons noted in his autobiography, 'There were no clues in the screenplay as to how Oddjob . . . was going to be beaten in a fight with Sean Connery . . . I choreographed the entire sequence . . . '

With the studio and producers behind the picture being North American, it could easily have been the case that Eon followed in the footsteps of CBS and Gregory Ratoff before them by making 007 a nephew of Uncle Sam. However, Broccoli and Saltzman concluded that only a Briton should play James Bond. Picker was in agreement. 'Why would anybody possibly think that's a good idea?' Picker laughs in response to the possibility of an American Bond.

Cary Grant – handsome, English, big box-office, a close friend of Broccoli, an acquaintance of Fleming and a Bond fan – was a logical choice for the part of Bond. Although soon to turn fifty-eight, he looked twenty years younger. However, he turned down Eon's overture. Money may have been a part – *Dr. No*'s entire budget was adjacent to his normal fee – but the consensus seems to be that his unwillingness to commit to more than one picture was no use to producers trying to create a franchise. Patrick McGoohan, already familiar as a British espionage figure from the TV series *Danger Man* (a.k.a. *Secret Agent*), turned down

Bond for moral reasons. James Fox had similar misgivings. The suave Richard Johnson told *Cinema Retro* in 2008, 'I turned the job down . . . I was under contract to MGM anyway, so that gave me a reasonable excuse to say no, because they told me I'd have to be under exclusive contract to them for seven years.'

The reasons for Grant's and Johnson's reluctance might be why a belief began to develop that an unknown was needed for the role. Picker explains, 'Whoever played that first role had to be signed up to do all the subsequent movies if it turned out they were successful. The only way you can do that is if you hire somebody who is prepared to give you the options you want. Most major "stars" are not going to do that. An unknown actor is going to be delighted to do that because he wants the opportunity.' Additionally, Broccoli said he felt a newcomer would ensure that the audience would not be distracted by familiarity.

Broccoli couldn't stop thinking about an actor to whom he had been introduced a year previously. Sean Connery, born in Edinburgh in 1930, was dark-haired, handsome, six-foot-two and powerfully built. That he had a rough-hewn quality not quite in keeping with Fleming's suave template was no longer an issue. Now lost in the folds of history is the fact that when the Eon partners decided to cast Connery it was as what Broccoli called a 'subliminal spoof'. He is backed up by others, if in a roundabout way. In 1983, Richard Maibaum told Lee Goldberg of *Starlog*, 'Sean was *nothing* like Fleming's concept of James Bond . . . the very fact that Sean was a rough, tough, Scottish soccer player made him unlike the kind of English actors that Americans don't like . . . The fact that we attributed to him such a high-style epicure was part of the joke . . . It was a slight takeoff, not belaboured or done consciously. But it came off as if it *was* planned and was a great, great plus.' Richard Johnson offered, 'Sean . . . was completely wrong for the part. But in getting the wrong man they got the right man, because it turned the thing on its head and he made it funny.'

Perhaps because he had been pushing for Johnson, Terence Young adjudged Connery's casting a 'disaster', although his opinion carried at least a little weight insofar as he had directed Connery in *Action of the Tiger* (1957). Fleming also demurred.

When Connery's name was raised, United Artists sent Eon a telegram which simply read, 'NO – KEEP TRYING.' Eon squared up to the studio and were triumphant. This, at least, is according to Broccoli, whose autobiography is littered with things ranging from the questionable to the demonstrably incorrect that have the common factor of placing Broccoli in a better light than all the fools around him. Picker simply says, 'The picture was cast out of London. Sean was submitted to us as their choice. We looked at him and we said, "Well, he's the best one of the people you suggested and if you want to go with him, we approve him." And that was the end of the conversation.'

Connery resisted Eon's original demands that he agree to two Bond movies a year. This worked out well for everyone. An annual (eventually biannual) Bond film was a special event in a way that a semiannual 007 picture would not be.

Young agreed to make the best of what he considered a bad fist. Picker says he opted for Young as director over Eon's other suggestion, Guy Hamilton, because he felt he could do a Henry Higgins-style mentoring job on Connery. Although he was in his mid-forties with a receding hairline, it seems to be universally agreed that the suave, handsome, upper-class Young was, to use Picker's phrase, 'a walking James Bond all by himself'. Young duly took Connery under his wing, introducing him to tailors, maître d's and other fixtures of society unfamiliar to the son of a lorry driver and charwoman.

Asked if he knows what Fleming thought about the casting of Sean Connery as his creation, John Pearson says, 'Er . . . I think he enjoyed his work. [Chuckles.] I don't want to talk about it really.' Connery later avowed that Fleming had described him to a third party as an 'overdeveloped stuntman'. In fairness, Fleming's doubts about the casting must have seemed legitimate at the time. It would have been a shock for Fleming, for instance, that his quintessential Englishman was now audibly a Scot. Monty Norman – who, as the man tasked with scoring *Dr. No*, watched it being filmed – recalls Connery's accent as being an issue with the author: 'Ian Fleming wasn't that keen on the idea. Terence Young also had reservations at the very beginning.' However, he also says, 'Both of them were really won over very quickly.'

Monty Norman – a singer turned composer – was offered the *Dr. No* gig because he had written the score and lyrics of *Belle, or The Ballad of Dr Crippen*, a stage musical of which Broccoli had been a backer. At the time of *Dr. No*, Norman happened to be very busy. He recalls, 'I was just about to stall and say, "Give me a little while to think about it" when Harry Saltzman said, "We're going to do all the locations in Jamaica. Why don't you come over with us and write some of the Caribbean music and get the atmosphere of the place, and bring your wife, all expenses paid?"'

The film has the same opening as the book. Norman recalls, 'When you first see those three blind beggars walking along in single file, I could have done a really dramatic thing, but I thought, "No, as we're in Jamaica, as it's all light, I'll do a calypso-type song."'

And I did "The Kingston Calypso".' This jolly piece incorporates a section that gives new words to the children's nursery rhyme 'Three Blind Mice'. 'I suppose I was taking a bit of a risk because one would expect something a bit more serious, but, funnily enough, that set up for all time to come the sort of thing that you get out of a Bond film, which is that you don't take it a hundred per cent seriously.'

Once back in England, Norman turned his attention to a piece of music designed to serve as a theme for the film's hero. He says he received no specific instructions from Eon on this. 'Somebody – I can't remember who now – wanted to use "Underneath the Mango Tree" 'cause they liked it so much. Of course it would have been silly to do that even if it was a big, big hit because they weren't all going to be set in the Caribbean.' He goes on, 'I'd tried one or two pieces while I was in Jamaica, and one was pretty good – in fact, in the end Count Basie did a recording of it – but I didn't feel it had all the qualities of James Bond.

'I suddenly remembered another musical that I was doing in London a year or two before.' *A House for Mr Biswas* had been abandoned because of the difficulties of assembling an exclusively Trinidad-Indian cast, but, 'I put a few melodies in my bottom drawer. I kept thinking about this melody of a song called "Bad Sign, Good Sign". It went, [singing] "I was born with this unlucky sneeze / And what is worse I came into the world the wrong way round." And I thought, "What would happen if I split the notes and tried to get rid of the Asian quality?" Immediately, I realised that this was right and had all the qualities of James Bond. So I worked on that, completed it and that became the song.'

Norman wrote down the piece of music ('It was a bit more

than notation') but didn't make an audio version: 'Things were happening too fast for that. I think we were in a studio within three or four weeks.' Said studio was Pinewood. 'I brought in John Barry to orchestrate,' Norman says.

Barry was an arranger and producer responsible for hits by Adam Faith, the theme to TV's *Juke Box Jury* and the score for the movie *Beat Girl*. As leader and trumpeter of the pop-jazz ensembles the John Barry Seven and the John Barry Orchestra, he had also achieved several British chart hits of his own. Norman: 'He did a wonderful job. The definitive orchestration, actually. One of the reasons that we wanted somebody like John Barry was to get a kind of pop quality of the day.'

Part of that contemporaneous pop quality was a surf-music characteristic to the guitar lick that now played what had been – in a slower variation – the vocal melody of 'Bad Sign, Good Sign'. Such a move was fairly audacious for a film score in the early sixties. 'At that time, the guitar was used in the odd rock-type film or whatever, but not generally,' Norman notes.

This makes it all the more surprising that 'The James Bond Theme' is not just exhilarating, catchy and evocative but also timeless. The *dang-der-dang-DANG-dang-dang* guitar figures that kick in after the opening parping brass should really now sound like a period piece in the way of old rockabilly records, yet 'The James Bond Theme' still somehow feels modern. The enduring vitality may also be something to do with the fact that those figures are perfectly suited to the subject, seeming to resonate with intrigue and danger. In any event, the guitar is only part of the theme's brilliance. It bristles with stylish, explosive brass riffs, especially in its wild central section. A deflated note concludes proceedings in an unexpectedly, but delectably, sardonic manner.

There has subsequently been much debate about the overall provenance of 'The James Bond Theme'. Some have insinuated that the true composer was Barry, who went on to score eleven Bond films and wrote the music to some of 007's most famous theme tunes. Barry supported those insinuations when asked about it in 1997 by *Mojo* magazine. He replied, 'If I didn't do it, why the hell did they not continue to employ Mr. Norman for the following 14 Bond movies? Name another two scores that Mr. Norman has composed.' When a *Sunday Times* story followed up the claim, it led to a libel action by Norman, heard in 2001.

Although not a defendant, Barry gave evidence in the libel case on behalf of *The Sunday Times*. He stated that he had been brought in by Broccoli and Saltzman because the score Norman had provided for *Dr. No* was inadequate. Norman, it was claimed, understood perfectly that, while he, Norman, would receive the credit, Barry had *carte blanche* to do as he liked with the theme. 'Go ahead, I'm not proud,' Norman is reported to have responded. Barry stated that he used the bare minimum of what Norman had written in rearranging his title theme. Barry felt that, apart from the melody played on the guitar riff, just about everything in the final theme – which includes riffs and countermelodies just as famous as the guitar riff – was his. Norman won the libel trial.

Asked if he felt John Barry added anything to his theme in terms of riffs or countermelodies, Norman says, 'I wouldn't say countermelodies.' When Barry claimed that 'The James Bond Theme' was essentially his creation, did he think it was a lapse of memory or an outright mistruth? 'I certainly couldn't answer that, but what I would say is that there were certainly people around him, not necessarily friends, who were pushing that kind of Chinese-whisper thing. To this day – he's dead now so there's no way of knowing anyway – I don't know whether he truly thought he wrote it. But I doubt it. It's very difficult to say. Music is so ephemeral. You're never quite sure. But one thing I am quite sure of is that I wrote it.'

Because 'The James Bond Theme' became a staple of Bond films, people might think they know its every note, but in fact the arrangement is different each time. Norman: 'Obviously, over the last fifty years, there've been a lot of very top orchestrators and composers working on the films and they've all bought something to it in their way and in their time. I wouldn't say I think every one of them's great, but certainly quite a few are. Each man has his own way of doing it. And I'm very thrilled to hear what they do with it.'

A version of 'The James Bond Theme' was issued on disc by the John Barry Seven and Orchestra to coincide with *Dr. No*'s release. It gave the public a chance to hear the theme in full that the movie – despite sprinkling parts of it throughout its running length – did not. Barry's version went to No. 13 in the British charts in late 1962, thus increasing Bond's profile. However, a *Dr. No* soundtrack album did not appear until mid-1963, only a few months before the release of the second Bond film. Moreover, it included some material not even heard in the film while omitting the by-now famous melodramatic tarantula-scene music.

As to why Broccoli and Saltzman never again asked him to contribute to a Bond soundtrack, Norman says, 'They'd asked me to do their next film, which was a Bob Hope comedy called *Call Me Bwana*. When I'd finished it, I still hadn't got a contract, so I said to Harry, "Isn't it time we talked money?" He looked at me

and said, "Monty, if you want to talk money, we can't do business."
I got my lawyer to get me a contract and that was it. I can't be sure
if that was the reason that they didn't use me, but it could well
have been.'

Be that as it may, Norman is associated with James Bond for all
time. How does he feel about a single piece of work from half a
century ago serving almost to define him? 'Well, you can't argue
with something as iconic as that,' he reasons. 'If people want to
remember me just for that, that's fine.'

Dr. No opens with a design like moving, separating spotlights to
the background of space-age sound effects. The final spotlight
becomes a gun barrel through which we are provided a view of
a be-hatted Bond walking across the screen in virtual silhouette.
He spins to shoot at the unseen holder of the gun. The screen
freezes as a wash of blood-alluding red materialises, and, when it
unfreezes, the barrel is wobbling, by which point the blaring brass
riffs of 'The James Bond Theme' have kicked in. Said theme is
used in syncopation with patterns of multi-coloured circles into
which the gun barrel/spotlight has morphed. As the credits
unfold – flashing at us – the theme's sharp, circular guitar work
starts up.

The gun-barrel sequence was designed by Maurice Binder. It was
at the time not just a lapel-grabber but achingly modern. Instantly
iconic, it, or a variation, has been used in all official Bond films
since. So stirring was the combination of imagery and theme that
people shunted aside their feelings that it didn't really make sense.
Surely, the view should be through a scope rather than a barrel.
And, surely, the blood wouldn't drip down a barrel opening. The
really observant would have detected something wrong – lack of

height and barrel chest – about the Bond figure strolling screen-right to screen-left. It wasn't until the fourth movie, *Thunderball*, that the Bob Simmons clip was replaced by footage of Connery. Since then, each successive Bond actor has shot his own gun-barrel sequence and for both audience and actor the 007 experience is not considered complete without one.

Binder also supplied *Dr. No*'s opening credits, which feature colourful, dancing silhouettes. Although Robert Brownjohn would design the opening credits for the next two Bond pictures, Binder would make the job his own for a quarter-century from *Thunderball* (1965) on. Binder's trademark would be gyrating female outlines that had the thrilling whiff of being naked.

Our first sight of Bond is in a gambling club called Le Cercle. That we hear him and see his back and hands for a protracted length before we are allowed a view of his face was a mocking homage by Terence Young to a similarly extended build-up to the unveiling of Paul Muni in *Juarez* (1939). When 007 is finally shown, it is to the accompaniment of the instantly classic line, 'Bond, James Bond'. Although it had appeared in the books, here the line is actually a quasi-sarcastic echoing of the way fellow *chemin de fer* player Sylvia Trench (Eunice Gay) introduces herself to him surname first. However, that the producers knew it would be iconic is suggested by its heralding the use of 'The James Bond Theme'. The phrase would become a fixture of the film series, although surprisingly not so much in Connery's tenure, being unused in *From Russia with Love*, *Thunderball* and *You Only Live Twice*. Another example of what would become a series trademark is the fact that Bond is dressed in a tuxedo.

Sean Connery does not look like Hoagy Carmichael and his still-audible Scottish brogue was not the normal soundtrack to plush London gentlemen's clubs of the era. However, the public – including that section of it familiar with the Bond books – accepted Connery as 007 because his appearance did not constitute a juxtaposition with the material. He may have been from a dirt-poor background and self-educated, but his poise and presence ensure he glides through establishment backdrops as if he were to the manor born. The rough edges of his Glaswegian accent are already gone and his voice on its way to being generically British. A physique powerful enough to have seen him compete in a Mr Universe contest ensures that he looks as if he is used to hand-to-hand combat. Facially, he needed not so much to look like Hoagy Carmichael – even if a thespian could be found with that lookalike quality, it would have constituted a distracting novelty – but like someone intense, suffused with extraordinary experience and irresistible to women. Connery scores on all counts. He's handsome, but also weather-beaten, the beginnings of a permanent grimace etching their way into his face. His unusually dark looks lend him a brooding mien.

Future Bond movie signatures are piling up thick and fast as 007 enters through an upholstered door the antechamber office of Moneypenny (who is unexpectedly North American owing to the casting of Canadian Lois Maxwell) and tosses his trilby across the room to land perfectly on a hat stand. Courtesy of Fleming's bare-headed friend John F. Kennedy, hats were already becoming granddad apparel. However, the hat-tossing became a long-running motif completely abandoned only in the late eighties with the Timothy Dalton Bond. Moneypenny's swooning flirtatiousness and Bond's not unkind brush-offs – never an element of the books – begin their long history here. The movies' spotlight on M's 'girl' has rather written Loelia Ponsonby out of Bond lore. Secretary in the books to the three double-O agents, 'Lil' was someone to whom Bond felt very affectionate.

Bond's maverick qualities are illustrated by his attempt to sneak his old Beretta out of M's office after being instructed to switch over to a Walther PPK. Bernard Lee is crustily perfect as M as he fills in Bond on his Jamaican mission. Although at this stage the adaptations of the Bond books were broadly faithful, the multiple differences between the page and screen *Dr. No* start with the fact that 007's mission is not quite the one described in the source book. While loss of communication with the murdered Strangways arouses suspicions at 'Universal Exports' (as the films plurally rendered the Secret Service's cover name), the Service is already on to attempts to disrupt space launches from Cape Canaveral, which itself is distinct from disrupting missile launches.

Other changes include the substitution of a tarantula for a giant centipede, the villain having steel claws instead of hooks, the inclusion of Felix Leiter (Jack Lord), the creation of a minion of No's named Dent (Anthony Dawson), Bond's cold-blooded murder of Dent and the fact of Bond's passage through narrow, hazardous tunnels being simply an escape attempt rather than a forced participation in a sadistic obstacle course.

Additionally, the producers create a new climax where Bond causes an overload of the nuclear reactor that powers the radio beams utilised for bringing down American rockets. It admittedly feels a little pat and generic – particularly the way Bond smuggles himself onto the control-room floor by knocking out a technician and donning his handily anonymous safety uniform – but is undeniably more cinematic than would have been the book's intrinsically slow-motion water-based combat with lugubrious sea life. While dumping a load of birdshit on the villain would probably have been a plus point – certainly, later Bond films would revel in such quasi-comic dispatchings – a good replacement is proffered: Dr No is consigned to a watery grave because his steel claws can't grip the frame over the cooling vat of the nuclear reactor.

Another change from the novel was made for impenetrable reasons. 'With your disregard for human life, you must be working for the East,' Bond taunts Dr No at dinner. No responds, 'I'm a member of SPECTRE . . . The Americans are fools. I offered my services. They refused. So did the East. Now they can both pay for their mistake.' While the background presence of SPECTRE may lie in the fact that the first Bond movie script on which Eon worked was an adaptation of *Thunderball*, the book where said organisation made its entrée, it doesn't explain why the Bond series consistently declined to pit the British Secret Service against SMERSH, the KGB or any other instrument – fictional or real – of the Eastern Bloc. Broccoli later tried to sell the explanation, 'We decided to steer 007 and the scripts clear of politics . . . None of the protagonists would be the stereotyped Iron Curtain or "inscrutable Oriental" villain. First, it's old-fashioned; second, it's calculated to induce pointless controversy . . .' The Cold War was certainly not old-fashioned – it would continue throughout almost the whole of the rest of Broccoli's life – and since when have filmmakers considered controversy a minus? That said, there doesn't seem any more comprehensible a reason for the decision. It might be assumed that the removal of Cold War politics was felt necessary so as to not jeopardise a lucrative inroad into foreign markets, but, as Bond films were banned in the USSR throughout the Cold War, one wonders what the territories in question might be. Even had such a motivation existed in the beginning, it seems logical that it would have been abandoned as soon as it became clear that the

Soviet censors were going to remain unyielding. Another possible explanation – that it was a mealy-mouthed rationale from Western left-wingers with a blind spot for Soviet human-rights abuses – hardly seems likely. Broccoli cited American right-winger George H.W. Bush as 'a President I greatly admired'.

Another change is more understandable but one that fundamentally altered the character of Bond. Anxious both that the public would not warm to a vista of unrelenting violence and that censors might cut the film to ribbons, Terence Young decided to sprinkle Bond's dialogue with quips. When Bond delivers to Government House the dead body of a No henchman who has swallowed cyanide rather than talk, Bond tells a doorman, 'Sergeant, make sure he doesn't get away.' When assassins chase Bond in a hearse and end up going over a cliff, an unperturbed Bond notes to a witness, 'I think they were on their way to a funeral.' From here on in, villains dispatched by the movie Bond would be given similar sardonic eulogies. This didn't have the effect of making 007 a comedy character, but provided stylish leavening.

Although Bond books would have seemed cinematic to readers before the movie series started, the transference to screen provided a dimension to James Bond that even the quality of Fleming's writing could not. The lush terrains of Jamaica on display in *Dr. No* were virtually landscapes from other planets for a low-waged British populace who took their holidays in UK coastal resorts such as Blackpool and Bournemouth. Then there is the physical manifestation of the character of Honey Ryder (as the film's credits render her). Her fractured English meant that her dialogue had to be re-voiced by Nikki van der Zyl, but, physically, Ursula Andress was perfect. Her parading around naked as she does in the book was, of course, out of the question, but the white bikini in which she emerges from the surf during her entrée was shockingly revealing for 1962, when one-piece swimsuits were the norm. Only Dr No's metallic dragon – much smaller than in the book, where its wheels were twice the height of a man – fails to bring something more to the party visually.

Some things, though, were clearly destined for transference unchanged. 'Medium-dry vodka martini, mixed like you said, sir, and not stirred,' says a waiter to Bond, thus bringing to the common man a fastidiousness about alcohol then unknown to him. The first specific use of 'shaken, not stirred' (Fleming's 'and' would never feature) comes when Dr No offers Bond a drink. Bond himself would first use the phrase in *Goldfinger*. The phrase would become another famous signature of the films.

Some fans cleave to the idea of the early Bond films possessing a gritty realism that was gradually sacrificed for gadgetry and gimmicks, but watching *Dr. No* gives the lie to that. Among its absurdities are the fact that Sylvia Trench is able to sneak her way into an intelligence officer's home; the fact that Bond lets go a female photographer clearly in league with evil forces; and the fact that Bond and Honey are decontaminated of the radiation permeating Crab Key by a perfunctory scrubbing at their clothes and a shower.

The biggest offence against plausibility, however, is the film's most famous scene: Bond's shooting of Dent when he has him cornered in Miss Taro's house. Angered by his reaching for his gun, Bond pumps two bullets into a helpless Dent to the accompaniment of the line, 'That's a Smith & Wesson and you've had your six.' The scene was sensational for the time: heroes did not kill in movies unless their lives were in direct danger. It was also illogical. Just as he is killed, Dent is literally on the point of yielding up to 007 the identity of the person who ordered Bond's assassination. It makes sense only as a tilt for headlines or a heady act of defiance of the censors.

Dr No makes his first appearance (apart from a scene that conceals his face) around twenty minutes before the end. While Joseph Wiseman may not be on screen long, he is magnetically menacing when he is. His calm and cultured manner is a world removed from the 'Wiseguy, huh?' baddies that then proliferated in cinema.

Upon Bond's sabotaging of the nuclear reactor, Dr No's minions scramble to evacuate Crab Key, throughout which alarms resound. Bond finds Honey and makes his escape with her before the island blows sky-high. The movie ends with Bond and Honey canoodling in the boat he has forcibly commandeered. It's Bond's third conquest of the movie after Trench and Miss Taro, a seduction rate not even Fleming depicted him attaining: in only two of Fleming's novels did Bond seduce more than one woman.

Dr. No's lushness is particularly impressive considering the production's financial limitations. The budget allowed by United Artists was so inadequate for mounting such an extravagant story that anecdotes abound of pathetic begging-bowl tactics and ingenious improvisation during the shoot. David V. Picker – who claims to have got the budget raised from an initial $1.1 million to $1.35 million – bristles at talk of such stories. 'It was enough to do what we wanted to do for the first picture,' he says. 'That's chitchat.' *Dr. No*'s soundman has different recollections. Says Norman Wanstall, 'It was quite aggravating when, every time I tried to ask for a theatre or recording session for something, I was always told, "Well, do you really need it? You're costing us a fortune, Norm." How Ken Adam ever built those sets for that money I will never, ever understand.' Wanstall even suspects the limited money available was an unofficial reason for casting an unknown as Bond. Miraculously, the threadbare reality behind the glossy illusion is really visible only in the patently false shelf of book spines disguising the radio equipment in Strangway's office. The back projection on roads and water may be shoddy but was not unusual for movies of the period, regardless of budget.

'Nobody – and I really, really mean nobody – knew whether or not that film would be a success,' insists Wanstall. 'I always remember when we had that sneak preview in a cinema in Ealing, as people were filing out the look on Saltzman's face was sheer terror. I'd never seen Saltzman look like that before – he was always so laid back.'

He continues, 'Everybody knew that we had a fantastic star in Sean. It didn't take long to realise, "My God, we've scored here." We knew that Ursula was going to cause a sensation because she was terribly glamorous. We knew the locations were going to be very, very effective. And the sets were out of this world. And we had a scene like the tarantula which was going to knock people out. So we knew there was quality and something different in this film. But we knew we had eventually to introduce Dr No . . . He was a pretty bizarre character, this guy who was living in this extraordinary environment, underground with fish in a massive aquarium. He had metal hands. His whole setup was so extraordinary. It was a question of whether or not people would think he was laughable . . . We thought, "God, if people don't accept him, then the film will be a flop." But somehow everybody just accepted it.'

An audience reaction Wanstall describes as 'very, very favourable' fanned out from humble little Ealing across the world. Following its British premiere on 5 October 1962, the 105-minute film was an instant success in Europe, quickly recouping its costs.

According to Broccoli, United Artists, despite their original enthusiasm, were unsure of *Dr. No*'s prospects in the world's single most important movie market and therefore bypassed US metropolises, showing it at drive-in theatres in backwaters. Monty Norman also remembers a lack of fervour from the Americans. He says, 'After I'd spent four weeks in Jamaica, Harry Saltzman asked me to go and see the suits, the people involved in Bond on the New York side. I went there and I could see that there wasn't that much enthusiasm.' Yet Picker says of Broccoli's claim, 'That's total bullshit. We opened it on Broadway in two theatres. We didn't open in the sticks anywhere.' While at the time *The Hollywood Reporter* stated that the film was to premiere in the Midwest and Southwest, it adjudged its 450-theatre engagement 'massive'. Either way, both audiences and the likes of *Variety* and *Time* were enthusiastic in their reception. In fact, the latter's review was printed in October 1962, fully seven months before the US premiere.

Altogether, *Dr. No* took back more than twenty times its budget. This was not a figure bulked up by television residuals: United Artists refused to sanction any TV broadcasts of Bond films for a decade. (Eon had the option of making a Bond TV series after having completed three feature films but never exercised it.)

Ian Fleming's remuneration for his largely passive role in the making of the Eon Bond films was impressive: an advance for each film of $100,000 – around $800,000 in today's coinage – all of which went into trust for Caspar. The addition of 5 per cent of the producers' profits was, of course, a more abstract remuneration, and theoretically meaningless: if the Bond films made no money, neither would Fleming. History shows, however, that Eon's Bond contrived to become among the most profitable series in motion-picture history. This is not to mention the knock-on effect on sales of Fleming's Bond novels.

In public, Fleming's opinions on the cinema Bond seemed backhanded compliments. Of *Dr. No*, he said, 'Those who've read the book are likely to be disappointed, but those who haven't will find it a wonderful movie.' Of Connery, he offered, 'Not quite the idea I had of Bond, but he would be if I wrote the books over again.' Yet there is a suspicion that he did warm to Connery's portrayal of his creation. He privately wrote to his lover Blanche Blackwell in October 1961 that Connery was 'a real charmer . . . a god actor with the right looks and physique.' In his books he began making Bond incrementally more Scottish.

Richard Maibaum said to Pat McGilligan, 'In my opinion, [the Bond films] started this whole larger-than-life approach to action-adventure pictures . . . and then everybody else climbed on the bandwagon . . . You know, Hitchcock once told me, "If I have thirteen bumps in a picture, I think I've got a picture." A bump is something like someone says, "I'm looking for a man who has a short index finger," and a totally unexpected guy says, "You mean like this?" That's in *The 39 Steps*. After *Dr. No*, Cubby, Harry and myself decided that we weren't going to be satisfied with thirteen bumps in a Bond story, we wanted thirty-nine.'

Such a contrived, incident-packed approach, of course, was rather at odds with Fleming's slowly unfolding Bond books. As the poet Philip Larkin noted in *The Spectator* in 1966, 'No sooner were we told that the Bond novels represented a vulgarisation and brutalisation of Western values than the Bond films came along to vulgarise and brutalise – and in a way sterilise – the Bond novels.'

Within two years, the revolutionary approach seen in *Dr. No* had, with the follow-up Bond films, settled into a loveable formula. Within five years, the plethora of pastiches, spoofs and imitations had made that formula a cliché. Yet it did at the time genuinely define a new paradigm. *Dr. No* felt topical because of the Cuban Missile Crisis that happened to occur in its month of release, but that was not the only impression of aching modernity it conveyed. Its sensuality and brazenness about non-marital sex was extraordinary in a film world across which lay the shadow of the Hays Code and the British Board of Film Censors (now known as the British Board of Film Classification). Moviegoers were used to big and exotic productions, but such big and exotic productions were usually American and, as such, were laced with all-American, cornball high-mindedness rather than British scepticism and sardonicism. While British leading men before Connery were manly, they were also overly polite, even effete. Connery introduced an unapologeticness and swagger to UK male acting. And, if Bond's being an establishment rebel was a contradiction in terms, it was not a dichotomy over which the audience were inclined to agonise. Not for nothing did the Vatican condemn *Dr. No* as 'a dangerous mixture of violence, vulgarity, sadism and sex'.

Fame often ripples out in an unexpected fashion. As James Bond films began to change the world, Connery himself had his own smaller effect. The given name Sean – hitherto an arcane, Irish variant of John – suddenly became popular, and specifically in Connery's spelling rather than the more phonetic 'Shaun'.

Although the *Daily Express* had recognised 007's potential before the movie industry, the explosion of interest in James Bond created by *Dr. No* was something on which the newspaper was unable to capitalise.

The Bond strip had disappeared from its pages in February of the year of the movie's release. An adaptation of *Thunderball* abruptly ended after the hijack section. A cursory, even insulting, final entry was mostly composed of text summarising the remainder of the story. 'Bond finds them and the world is saved,' it helpfully informed the readers regarding the missing bombs.

The reason for the strip being thus wrenched from the paper was the fury of the paper's owner, Lord Beaverbrook, over the appearance of 'The Living Daylights' in *The Sunday Times Colour Section*. Beaverbrook considered it a breach of his newspaper's exclusive UK right to publish Bond prose in non-volume form, although this arrangement doesn't seem to have been formalised in contract and, even if it had, would seem to have been called into question by the fact that the *Express* had declined to serialise *The Spy Who Loved Me*.

Press barons of the era were liable to make such peremptory gestures. This one was costly to both Beaverbrook and Fleming. Beaverbrook lost out on the publicity bonanza attached to the newly famous Bond, while Fleming lost out on both revenue from further comic-strip adaptations and further book serialisations, which also ceased. Some grovelling from Fleming – still not financially secure – ensured the two men's rapprochement and the resumption of both serialisations (March 1963) and comic strip (June 1964).

Beaverbrook died three weeks before the Bond comic strip returned to the *Express*. Fleming was dead within two months of that return. The Bond comic strip, though, ran for many years. Its final *Daily Express* instalment was in 1977, whereupon it moved over to the Sunday edition of the paper, plus a daily strip in the *Daily Star*, a new part of the stable. It completely ceased appearing only in 1984.

The success of the Bond comic strip is a stark contrast to the failure of 007 to thrive in a closely related medium, the comic (or comic book in American parlance).

The release of the *Dr. No* movie saw the appearance of the first Bond comic. *Classics Illustrated* from New York's Gilberton Company, Inc., was a self-conscious cut above the average comic, ostentatiously bringing literature to the kids, as demonstrated by its cover strapline, 'Featuring stories by the world's greatest authors'. Ian Fleming may or may not have fitted that description, but the decision to run an adaptation of *Dr. No* was certainly incongruous for a publication devoted to disseminating adaptations of the works of such people as Lewis Carroll, Robert Louis Stevenson and Mark Twain. Moreover, the comic was not, in fact, an adaptation of one of Fleming's books but its film incarnation, albeit rendered, unlike both (UK) book and film, as '*Doctor No*'.

The comic had the usual *Classics Illustrated* classy and undemonstrative painted cover. However, the artwork by Norman J. Nodel in the thirty-two-page adaptation inside was rudimentary and, in places, almost childlike. The rumour that Nodel had no access to the actual film and was working from a script and publicity stills seems borne out by inconsistencies (the room in which Dent is upbraided by Dr No lacks the film's famous huge roof grille) and what might be termed over-consistencies (i.e. the familiar and frozen nature of some of the tableaux).

The sex and violence of the film is understandably toned down for a young readership. Bond beds no one, and his sadism is transformed into traditional comics' Queensberry-rules stuff (he merely wounds Dent). Other changes had less benign purposes. There are no black characters in this Caribbean adventure, with Bond's local aide Quarrel made as Caucasian as Bond.

While Gilberton managed to get the publication distributed in the UK as usual, the lack of the typical 'classic' content caused problems in their home country, where the purchasers of *Classics Illustrated* were as much schools and libraries as retail outlets. Accordingly, it was not issued Stateside under the *Classics Illustrated* banner but, instead, was sublicensed to DC. A new cover, drawn by Bob Brown and more in keeping with the house style of the publishers of *Superman*, *Batman* and *Wonder Woman*, was wrapped around the *Classics Illustrated* work. The newly upholstered publication was released as an edition of DC's *Showcase* title.

DC published at precisely the wrong time. Although, courtesy of their president, a lot of adult Americans knew who James Bond was, few children did. Releasing the comic in January 1963, four months before *Dr. No*'s Stateside premiere, was, therefore, pretty close to pointless. Sales were inevitably poor.

Even had the publication date been synchronised with *Dr. No*'s US release, such was the low quality of the comic that it's to be doubted that it would have led to a public demand for a regular Bond title from DC. That option was there, though. Blogger Mark Evanier has written of the DC sublicence:

The contract . . . included an option clause that would allow DC to do a regular series for a modest fee . . . George Kashdan, who was the editor at DC involved in the *Doctor No* one-shot, told me that DC Management felt it was in the business of promoting Superman and Batman, not properties owned by others ... Kashdan did not know why they made an exception for the *Doctor No* adaptation but theorized that it was cheap (the material was already drawn and the Bond people didn't want a lot for the rights) and maybe that someone was doing a favour for someone else.

Yet, while it's understandable that DC didn't exercise their option for a regular Bond title at this point, it's inexplicable that over the following years – as Bond became a phenomenon whose name was known to every man, woman and child in America – they didn't revisit the property. It's perfectly plausible that a mid-sixties James Bond title would have become the biggest-selling comic on the planet. Instead, again according to Evanier by way of Kashdan, there was no further discussion of a James Bond title at the company until early 1972, when its business division mentioned to publisher Carmine Infantino that their ten-year option on the character was nearing its end. A surprised Infantino then entered into discussions about a DC Bond title, and even got to the stage of considering artists such as Jack Kirby and Alex Toth for illustration duties. However, he ultimately decided against the project. One of the considerations was the fact that, at that point in history, a question mark was felt to hang over the Bond film franchise.

The story is symptomatic of 007 in this medium. For a character with an all-conquering track record in prose, film, music and merchandise, James Bond has been the subject of an amazingly small number of comics. In the decade after DC's US option expired, no other publisher showed any inclination to produce a Bond title. This was a juncture where it might be assumed that Gold Key – who specialised in comics based on licensed properties, most notably *Star Trek* and Tarzan but also manqué Bond *The Man from U.N.C.L.E.* – would axiomatically be interested. Meanwhile, although Bond's home country had a tradition of weekly titles such as *TV Comic* and the renowned *TV 21* that were oriented around licensed live-action properties, no publisher appears to have ever enquired about 007 being given the same treatment.

YOU ONLY
LIVE ONCE

Ian Fleming told Jonathan Cape that *The Spy Who Loved Me* 'wrote rather easily', an unusually – possibly uniquely – upbeat comment to his publishers about his Bond writing. However, that didn't stop him suggesting to Plomer that he should use the book to kill off his character 'appropriately & gracefully'. Plomer demurred and/or Fleming changed his mind and *On Her Majesty's Secret Service* – published on 1 April 1963 – became the first of Fleming's Bond books released after 007's fame had been massively expanded by the *Dr. No* movie.

In it, Bond gets involved with a beautiful but unhappy young woman who is formally known as La Comtesse Teresa di Vicenzo but who prefers to go by 'Tracy'. Her father turns out to be Marc-Ange Draco, head of the Union Corse, which runs nearly all organised crime in France. To Bond's surprise, Draco has, courtesy of his high connections, heard of him: 'You are a member, an important member, of Her Majesty's Secret Service.' Although the story is that Fleming took the book's title from a nineteenth-century sailing-adventure novel, it would also seem to be a play on the legend 'On Her Majesty's Service', which at that point in history (and for quite a while thereafter) adorned the brown envelopes in which arrived letters from British governmental departments.

Loelia Ponsonby has married and left the Service. She has been replaced by a woman with the extremely Bondian name Mary Goodnight, who, we are told, is a 'honey'. In our first exposure to her, Goodnight tells Bond he is to report to the College of Arms, who have a new lead on the elusive Ernst Stavro Blofeld.

In a chapter that verges on comedy, Bond is granted an audience with the Pursuivant, Griffon Or. Under the impression that Bond is here to research his family background, he pumps him with questions, something that grants the long-term Fleming reader new information: Bond's father was from the Highlands, near Glencoe, and his mother was Swiss. The speculation that providing Bond a Scottish hinterland was Fleming's way of conferring approval on the casting of Sean Connery as his hero would certainly fit timeframe-wise: this book was written in January and February 1962 at the very time *Dr. No* was being filmed in locations near Fleming's Jamaican home. (He almost wandered into shot during one beach scene.) Moreover, the author's determination to attribute a Scots grounding to his creation became more and more pronounced. However, the proof is not conclusive. It could just as easily have been another example of weathervane Fleming bending with the wind; plus, there is the fact of the Caledonian background of Fleming's own parents.

Fleming has clearly engaged the services of a real-life Griffon Or, as he has the character run through genuine Bonds who might have been ancestors of his fictional one, including the baronet who gave his name to London's famous Bond Street and whose family motto was 'The World is Not Enough'.

Or's colleague, Sable Basilisk, informs Bond that the College has been approached by a firm of Zürich solicitors whose client, Blofeld, wishes to have it confirmed that he is the rightful heir to the title Monsieur le Comte Balthazar de Bleuville. 'He wants to become a new, respectable personality,' theorises Basilisk, a man seasoned in such vanities.

In Switzerland, Bond – posing as geologist Sir Hilary Bray – finds himself in the company of a group of ten women who have in common a British farming background and a lack of intellectual sophistication. They are resident at the mountain resort of Blofeld (who has had extensive plastic surgery to disguise his identity) and his 'personal secretary', Irma Bunt, because they are receiving treatment from him for various allergies. The girls seem to make Bond as sweaty and gauche as a teenager, although his nocturnal fun with one Ruby yields the information that her allergy cure is effected via deep hypnosis each midnight. One of the resort's guests, incidentally, happens to be the actress Ursula Andress, recently made famous by a film Fleming doesn't quite stoop to naming.

Bond has to make his escape when his identity is in danger of discovery. The night-time ski chase that ensues provides some of the few examples here of the fine writing usually so common in Fleming's prose: 'The three-quarter moon burned down with an almost dazzling fire and the snow crystals scintillated back at it like a carpet of diamond dust'; 'The first vertical drop had a spine-chilling bliss to it.'

Reaching a railway track, Bond is gruesomely drenched in blood when one of his pursuers is diced by a train's snow fan.

Knowing that the Swiss police will also now be after him, Bond tries to recover from the chase, '. . . the breath sobbing in his throat'. Although it is refreshing to see the vulnerable side of 007, his state of exhaustion, dread and despair as he wanders through a busy local town seems inordinate. He has been through worse than this. It's as though Fleming had transferred to him the fatigue – mental and physical – of a man in his mid-fifties recovering from a heart attack.

With some relief, Bond comes across a familiar and friendly face in the crowds of seasonal celebrants: Tracy, directed to the vicinity by her father. As Bond had been searching for Blofeld's Swiss lair for months, the odds of their being in the area at the same time are slim. Tracy's reward for providing with her car a *deus ex machina* is a marriage proposal from Bond the following morning. The snap decision is made at least a little credible by Bond thinking, 'I'm fed up with all these untidy, casual affairs that leave me with a bad conscience.'

Back in Britain, the Service works out that Blofeld is scheming with the Russians to launch a biological attack on Britain's agricultural and livestock resources, something that would render the country bankrupt within months. With his soon-to-be father-in-law's help, Bond launches an assault on Blofeld's mountain lair. (M seems utterly unconcerned about an agent fraternising with, and even about to be related to, a gangster.) Bond loses Blofeld in a bobsleigh chase.

With – Blofeld excepted – the case tidied up, Bond and Tracy travel to Munich for their New Year's Day nuptials. The 'playing Red Indians' dismissal of Bond's job crops up for the third time in the series as Bond contemplates that life '. . . would now be fuller, have more meaning, for having someone to share it with'.

Driving off on honeymoon, Tracy notices a car behind them on the autobahn and asks her husband if she should try to 'lose' it. 'No,' says Bond. 'Let him go. We have all the time in the world.'

The overtaking car delivers tragedy ('The wind-screen of the Lancia disappeared as if hit by a monster fist'). As a gun-wielding Blofeld sails by, the Bonds' car goes off the road. An autobahn patrolman finds a shattered Bond cradling a dead Tracy. Bond assures the man that everything is all right because they have all the time in the world.

As ever, some of the new things learned about Bond during the course of the book contradict previously established facts, but this time inconsistencies seem more due to things other than carelessness. Bond's claim to Marc-Ange that he has no 'inherited money' raises the question of what was the yearly, tax-free private income of £1,000 mentioned in *Moonraker* and how he was ever able to afford a £4,500 Bentley. Once again, Fleming seems to be moving the goalposts to make his character less of an easy target for the Left. However, when Bond abandons with relief his nobleman's prop of *The Times* for the more populist *Daily Express* (contradicting what we were told in *From Russia with Love* that *The Times* is his paper of choice) it strikes one as not so much a tilt at belatedly making Bond a man of the people but part of the campaign of grovelling Fleming undertook to get the Bond serialisations and comic strip reinstated by Beaverbrook.

Although there is not a return to the explicitness that the distaff perspective of *The Spy Who Loved Me* seemed to give Fleming the confidence to deploy, there is some rare and bawdy humour from Bond. When told by Griffon Or that the Sir Thomas Bond coat of arms had three golden balls, Bond quips, 'That is certainly a valuable bonus . . .' Although it's more ribald than anything in the *Dr. No* film, perhaps significantly one can easily imagine it emerging from Connery's mouth.

Despite the shocking and moving ending, Fleming has – bizarrely, in the wake of the explosion of the fame of his character in the previous year – proffered probably the least interesting, most hackneyed and least well-written Bond book of all. The blizzard of brand names feels like self-parody. Repeatedly, Fleming ends sentences with exclamation marks, a hack's tactic to convey tension. Time and again we come across sentences that, though they aren't technically terrible, seem for Fleming either lazy or low-rent: 'He guessed that he might have to get away from this place. But quick!'; 'He listened, his ears pricked like an animal's'; 'Bond was gaining, gaining.'

Yet the poor quality turned out not to matter a whit. The six months in which the world had had the chance to see Connery bringing Bond to life had an astounding effect on the success of the character's literary incarnation. *On Her Majesty's Secret Service* received 42,000 advance orders, more than any previous 007 adventure by almost one quarter. It immediately secured a reprint of 15,000 and, by the end of April, had sold more than 60,000 copies. This was as nothing compared with the 1965 paperback. *On Her Majesty's Secret Service* made history twice over: no previous UK paperback had had a million-copy print run, let alone this book's 1.5 million.

Norman Wanstall recalls the filming of *From Russia with Love*, the second James Bond motion picture, as being a very different affair from that of *Dr. No*. 'I remember looking at the scene for a gypsy encampment,' he says. 'It was meant to be in Turkey but in fact it was shot on the backlot of Pinewood. I walked into the production office and I said, "I want ten Turkish men, ten Turkish women and as many Russians as you could get." And the production manager just looked at the calendar, he said, "Would Thursday be all right?" I thought, "Jesus Christ! Now we're making movies." From then on, whatever I asked for on the Bond films, I got.'

From Russia with Love saw the debut of what would be another Bond movie institution: the pre-title sequence, a mini-drama that precedes everything except the gun-barrel section. Sometimes it was a disconnected aperitif; other times, as in *From Russia with Love*, it took the form of a prologue. During this pre-title sequence, we see 007 apparently executed by this movie's chief villain Red Grant (Donovan Grant from the book, played by Robert Shaw) via a garrotte hidden in a wristwatch. However, this turns out to be a SPECTRE training exercise: a face mask is peeled from the corpse to reveal another man entirely.

The theme song is the first to give a Bond film its title rather than the other way around: it's playing on Bond's radio when he is called into HQ. Although John Barry – co-composer of most of the Bond themes people remember – was formally on board to score the picture, the song was not written by him. Lionel Bart fails to bring to his pedestrian, slushy creation any of the sprightliness and colour that marked his compositions for the likes of *Oliver!*. Nonetheless, Matt Monro's rendering was the first Bond theme to become a pop hit, reaching No. 20 in the UK. Far better was Barry's noble, stately, brass-dominated '007', whose perennial presence in Bond films over the next decade-and-a-half made it a sort of alternative 'James Bond Theme'.

From Russia with Love – a book in which Bond is meagrely represented – is a peculiar choice to film so early in the series. Perhaps the decision had something to do with Kennedy's endorsement having made the novel famous. It's also a peculiar choice for a series whose production team had decided to sidestep the Cold War. However, Richard Maibaum (credited with the screenplay) and Johanna Harwood ('adaptation') get around this by making completely innocent the Russian to whom the title alludes: Tatiana is forced into a mission to tempt Bond with the cryptographic machine (here called a Lektor, to avoid Spektor/ SPECTRE confusion) upon pain of death. Her superior, Rosa Klebb (the superbly villainous Lotte Lenya), is only nominally working for the Soviets, having – as *her* superior puts it – 'come over from the Russians' to SPECTRE. Said superior is depicted merely as a pair of arms stroking a white cat and referred to as 'Number One'.

For the only time in the series, we see Bond as the driver of a Bentley. This one has a telephone, highly unusual for motor cars in 1963. 'I've just been reviewing an old case,' he tells Moneypenny over the line, a reference to Sylvia Trench, with whom he has just been canoodling on a moored boat. After this encore, the very first 'Bond girl' never reappeared, but variants of Bond's dialogue here – 'I'll be there in an hour. [Glance at girl.] Er, make that an hour-and-a-half' – did become another 007 film motif.

In *Dr. No*, the armourer who brought Bond his new gun was played by Peter Burton. Here the equivalent character is the equipment officer of Q Branch and played by Desmond Llewelyn. By the next movie – and ever after – he would be gadget provider 'Q'. In this film, Q provides Bond a more complex version of the briefcase that Bond is issued in the book, the contents augmented by a collapsible rifle and a teargas canister that explodes if the case is opened incorrectly.

The comic-book-like pre-title sequence is actually at odds

with the rest of the film. Notwithstanding the presence of the stylisation and gimmickry that would always be hallmarks of the movie world's version of Bond, there is something realistic and pleasantly small-scale about *From Russia with Love*. It manages to possess a leisurely, procedural quality and often feels as cramped as the compartments on the Orient Express, on which almost thirty minutes of the movie are set, an unthinkable stasis for a modern Bond picture.

The sensuality is even more pronounced than in *Dr. No*. Bond's conquest tally this time is four – including an implied threesome with the gypsy girls. Grant's masseuse, completely unnecessarily, strips to her underwear and there is even some fleeting nudity when Tatiana is seen from a gauzy distance slipping into bed.

Fleming had instituted in the books the Bond tradition of an action coda. It makes its first movie appearance here in the form of the showdown with Klebb. The closing credits inaugurate another Bond movie tradition when we are provided the teaser, 'The End. Not quite the End. James Bond will return in the next Ian Fleming thriller "Goldfinger".'

From Russia with Love premiered on 10 October 1963. Terence Young considered it the finest Bond film of all time, while Sean Connery feels it was the best he himself appeared in. It's certainly a connoisseur's Bond picture, one that subscribers to Bond magazines and visitors to 007 fansites disproportionately cite as their favourite.

Nineteen sixty-three saw the appearance of two further Bond short stories: 'Agent 007 in New York', printed in the *New York Herald Tribune* in October, and 'The Property of a Lady', commissioned from Fleming by the famous London auction house Sotheby's and printed in their *Ivory Hammer* annual in November, later reprinted in *Playboy*. The New York story was reprinted (as '007 in New York', the title it has kept in subsequent appearances) in the American edition of Fleming's travelogue book *Thrilling Cities* (1964), specifically to head off US outrage over Fleming's unflattering assessment in said tome of the Big Apple.

Barely more than half a dozen pages long in book form, '007 in New York' sees Bond travelling to America's East Coast to warn an ex-service employee that her live-in lover is a KGB man. As Bond morosely contemplates the decline into homogeneity of a city he knows well, it hardly constitutes an antidote to Fleming's *Thrilling Cities* assessment of the same place. Nor does the ending. A perfunctory twist in the tale revolves around the fact that Bond's rendezvous almost ends in catastrophe because the planned location – the reptile house at Central Park Zoo – does not exist, proving that, contrary to his earlier musing, 'New York had *not* got everything'. A lengthy footnote detailing Bond's recipe for scrambled eggs doesn't exactly dispel the air of insubstantiality.

In 'The Property of a Lady', Maria Freudenstein, a Communications Department member of the Secret Service, has been sent a Fabergé egg. It is suspected to be a reward for services rendered as a double agent. Freudenstein has put the item up for auction at Sotheby's, its catalogue billing 'The Property of a Lady'.

Knowing that the Russians will use an 'underbidder', someone in the auction room raising the bidding artificially to get the best price possible for their woman, Bond has a brainwave. The underbidder will be the KGB's British Resident Director; as tradition and expedience dictates he will be the only person who knows of the double agent's payment method. The Service can finally identify the Resident Director and get him declared *persona non grata*.

Although there is no violent action whatsoever, the narrative is compelling. Fleming, as usual, keenly observes and eloquently annotates the customs of a different world, in this case auction houses. Almost nowhere does 'The Property of a Lady' show signs of being the gimmick it really is. Fleming, though, considered it so slight that he refused to accept payment for it.

The *Thunderball* court battle began on 20 November 1963 at the Chancery Division of the High Court. Despite the case having been fought all the way for three years, it was all over by 2 December.

Kevin McClory came away with £50,000 damages. This is close to a million in today's coinage, possibly enough to bankrupt Fleming. Luckily for the author, his costs and damages were paid by his co-respondent Ivar Bryce, a very wealthy man through marriage to A&P heiress Josephine Hartford. McClory also won all film rights to the story. Although Fleming was allowed to keep book rights and the ability to use SPECTRE in his novels, it was decreed that the title pages of all future editions of *Thunderball* carry the line, 'Based on a script treatment by Kevin McClory, Jack Whittingham and Ian Fleming', the sequence of names court-mandated. This line was the sort of attribution normally to be found in film novelisations and, accordingly, was a matter of no little confusion to people reading *Thunderball* for the first time. Another upshot of the judgment was that Eon had to license from McClory the right to use SPECTRE in further Bond films.

Some people point to the fact of Fleming's frail health – there is talk of his having suffered two heart attacks during the hearings – as a reason for his settling. However, the author seems to have come under strong pressure from his lawyers to concede the case. There is evidence that Fleming and Bryce deliberately undermined and obstructed McClory in his attempts to make a Bond picture, and even that he committed perjury.

In Fleming's defence, a reason for his disenchantment with McClory may have been the fact that the Irishman repeatedly failed to provide Ivar Bryce accounts relating to the Bryce-funded *The Boy and the Bridge*, which didn't bode well for the interrelated Bond finances. Moreover, by failing to formally set up a company to make the film, McClory was in breach of the agreement entered into with him to produce a Bond movie.

Furthermore, as with his previous recycling of ideas from *Commander Jamaica/James Gunn, Secret Agent* and the aborted CBS Bond TV series, Fleming may have considered what he was doing just a harmless exploitation of a property that was apparently going nowhere. Moreover, *Moonraker* had started life as an idea for a film script, even if one not previously pledged to third parties. The fact that *Thunderball* concerned a character who was indubitably his own must have been a powerful plank in his reasoning, as must the fact that his own first screenplay included the same story arc and some of the major elements of the subsequent committee-devised plots and Whittingham screenplays.

What may have ultimately made Fleming do what he did, though, was the fact that he was bereft of ideas. Before starting the *Thunderball* novel, Fleming told Plomer he was 'terribly stuck with James Bond. What was easy at 40 is very difficult at 50.' Part of the problem was his wife and child. 'They knock the ruthlessness out of one.' He added, 'I shall definitely kill off Bond with my next book – better a poor bang than a rich whimper!' Something not mentioned by Fleming is that his diminishing libido may have played a part in his increasing distance from Bond and his voracious interests. In 1962, he had written in a notebook, 'Suddenly you reach the age when it crosses your mind to say no to pleasure. For an instant you think that you have been virtuous. Then you realise the desire was not there. It was dead, and you are sad because sensuality is leaving you.'

Jack Whittingham acted as principal witness for McClory despite health problems. Giving evidence wasn't the first act by Whittingham on McClory's behalf that could partly be construed as one of generosity. In November 1959, Whittingham agreed to write the *Thunderball* screenplay for £1,000 less than his normal fee – a difference of approximately £20,000 today – on the understanding that he would be the screenwriter of choice if James Bond became a series of movies. One of the few things with which McClory did not emerge from the court case was the cinematic Bond rights he thought he had been granted by Fleming, so Whittingham's assuming the role of regular Bond screenwriter was not in his gift. However, when McClory did bring *Thunderball* to the screen two years later by going into partnership with Eon, he did not bring Whittingham aboard.

This wasn't the only *Thunderball*-related disappointment for Whittingham. A week after the 1963 court case had been wrapped up, Whittingham issued a writ against Ian Fleming for libel, malicious falsehood and damage to professional reputation. As he would be relying on the same evidence that resulted in McClory's triumph, it would seem he had a good case. Fleming's August 1964 death, however, caused its abandonment, leaving Whittingham with considerable legal costs, ones with which the newly rich McClory did not help.

Whittingham, who died in 1972, might well have agreed with the assessment of Jeremy Vaughn, a friend of McClory, who told author Robert Sellers, 'He's been very cruel to a number of people over the years who thought they were his friends.'

The tragedy about the *Thunderball* court case is that so much bitterness, tarnishing of reputation and depletion of health revolved around such a substandard novel.

At the start of the next Bond novel, *You Only Live Twice*, published on 26 March 1964, 007 is anything but the swaggering character portrayed by Connery.

Rather, he is a wreck, broken by the death of Tracy in *On Her Majesty's Secret Service*. He takes solace in prostitutes. (Contrary to his superstud aura, this is not too unusual: as well as the arguable case of his losing his virginity to a hooker, in *Dr. No* he admits to Honeychile that he has paid for sex, while he contemplates visiting a brothel in 'The Living Daylights'.) Adjudging him on the edge of becoming a security risk, M decides to send Bond on a job to make him forget his personal troubles. He tells Bond that he is taking him out of the double-O section and giving him acting promotion to the Diplomatic Service. He will be leaving for Japan, where his job will be to persuade Tiger Tanaka, head of the Japanese Secret Service, to yield up the secrets of his country's code-cracking machine and break the Service's dependence on a CIA increasingly uncooperative in the wake of British intelligence scandals. Bond is given a new number: 7777.

In Japan, Tanaka offers Bond a *quid pro quo*. He talks of a man who entered his country six months previously whom he considers a 'fiend in human form' but whom geopolitical sensitivities prevent the Japanese authorities dealing with. The man is the splendidly named Doctor Guntram Shatterhand, who lives in a castle on a southern island where he has built around himself a death trap. His grounds are filled with poisonous plants and deadly snakes, scorpions, spiders and fish. Moreover, the highly volcanic grounds contain many geysers and fumaroles, which, like the flora and fauna, are a magnet for suicide-seekers in a country with deep-seated notions of shame.

Bond agrees to Tanaka's proposal that he 'enter this Castle of Death and slay the Dragon within', but before he does he must first be acclimatised to Japanese conduct and culture so as not to attract attention. Cue a travelogue, much of it interesting.

When Tanaka suggests Bond try his hand at *haiku* poetry, the agent is game. His effort reads:

You only live twice
Once when you are born
And once when you look death in the face

Although translating it into Japanese reveals it does not have the form's requisite number of syllables, Tanaka is delighted at this 'most honourable attempt'.

When Bond is shown a photograph of Shatterhand, he is staggered: it is Blofeld. Naturally, his wife Emmy is Irma Bunt. This turn of events is ridiculous, pointless and disappointing, and not simply because of the pulpy improbability of Bond's and Blofeld's paths crossing with such frequency (or, as Fleming would rather have us believe, 'the long, strong gut of fate had lassoed him to them'). It rather spoils what had seemed an intriguing villainous addition to the series.

Bond uses the island of Kuro as a base while he awaits a manageable tide that will allow him to scale the towering seaward wall of Shatterhand's castle. Here he meets the beautiful and sensuous Kissy Suzuki.

Secreted in the grounds, it doesn't take Bond long to bear witness to suicides, one via an immersion into piranha-infested waters, the other by the stepping into of a bubbling fumarole. Bond awakes to screams: from his hiding-place he observes the horrifying sight of the guards' morning tidying process whereby they laughingly slaughter those nocturnal callers who have changed their mind or lost their nerve.

Bond inevitably gets captured and is subjected by the villain to a speech that even Fleming states to be 'expository'. It's also not for the first time that a villain in the series admits to 'accidie'; Blofeld's denunciation of 007 as a 'blunt instrument', however, is the inaugural appearance for the term mentioned in so many Fleming letters and interviews.

This denouement feels a little limp: Bond merely throttles Shatterhand when Fleming should surely have engineered a fate for the villain suffused with grisly poetic justice via one of the perils with which he had packed the grounds of his lair. However, Bond adroitly demolishes the castle, twisting closed a wheel that acts as a vent for a geyser before making a Douglas Fairbanks-like escape via a canvas banner. Unfortunately, because 007 is rendered unconscious by a bullet grazing his head, we don't coherently experience the consequence of diverting the geyser: it's initially unclear whether the crumbling of the castle walls is a hallucination.

That said, Bond's delirium is poetic stuff, and the final line of the chapter – 'Bond let go with hands and feet and plummeted down towards peace, towards the rippling feathers of some childhood dream of softness and escape from pain' – would actually have made a good ending to the novel, and indeed to the series as a whole.

Instead we are presented with two further and rather peculiar chapters. The first is a *Times* obituary for 'Commander James Bond, CMG, RNVR', which includes that newspaper's masthead. (Not the string-pulling it might seem, as at that point there was no connection between *The Times* and *The Sunday Times*.) The reason for the eulogy is the fact that Bond is 'missing, believed killed, while on an official mission to Japan'. It is presumably because Fleming is so bored with his creation that he then proceeds to get transcendentally silly with him. The obit – written by M – states that the publicity accorded Bond's adventures, particularly overseas, had the 'inevitable result that a series of popular books came to be written about him by a personal friend and former colleague of James Bond'. Although it may be endearing that it is stated that only the poor quality and caricatured nature of these books has prevented Fleming being prosecuted under the Official Secrets Act, this whimsical conceit raises all sorts of problems, even leaving aside the innate awkwardness of the breaking of the fourth wall. Why, for instance, did the wide broadcasting of Bond's adventures never cause problems to a man whose trade is secrecy? And why was the existence of the Fleming Bond books never mentioned in, er, any of the Fleming Bond books? And, furthermore, is *You Only Live Twice* one of these aforesaid 'caricatures' or is it – as the supposed myth-debunking of the obituary it contains implies – on a higher plane of authenticity?

The final chapter shows Kissy – who had rescued Bond from the sea after his escape – shamelessly exploiting Bond's loss of memory, telling him they are lovers. Although Bond proceeds to spend his days quite happily with her, he is haunted by strange dreams full of white faces and big cities. The chapter takes an even more bizarre turn when Kissy, frustrated by Bond's lack of sexual interest in her, travels to a Fukuoka sex shop to purchase an aphrodisiac partly comprising toad sweat. The potion and some *Kama Sutra*-like pornography work well enough for Kissy to wind up pregnant. However, before she can tell him the news, Bond discovers the word 'Vladivostok' on one of the newspaper squares in the toilet. The story ends with Bond determined to travel to this place to resolve the vague feelings and memories its name has stirred up.

Fleming uses the conceit of the *Times* obituary to unleash a veritable torrent of biographical information that dwarfs the dribs and drabs he has doled out in this area over the previous decade. Bond's parents were Andrew Bond of Glencoe and Monique Delacroix, from the Swiss Canton de Vaud. Because his father was a foreign rep for Vickers, James Bond's early schooling took place entirely abroad and gave him a first-class command of French and German. Both his parents were killed in a climbing accident in France when he was eleven, after which he was raised by his aunt Charmian in Kent. He attended Eton, for which his father had put him down at birth, but was transferred to his father's old school Fettes because of 'some alleged trouble with one of the boys' maids'. He left school at seventeen and, by claiming he was two years older, wangled a place in what would become the Ministry of Defence.

The obituary's statement that it was 1941 when Bond was seventeen and that he was married to Teresa in 1962 is less authorial fudging of Bond's vintage than grand resetting of the clock. Other alterations of established history seem to have a different motive. It being the case that Fettes is the Scottish equivalent of Eton but far less associated with public-school privilege, Fleming's decision to make this a Bond *alma mater* could be posited as the bisecting of his recent determination to make his creation both less posh and more Caledonian. There is also a purpose, if a more personal one, to the name Fleming chose for Bond's mother: Monique was the name of the girl to whom Fleming was engaged before his mother forced him to break it off.

Despite the perplexing concluding chapters, some nonsensicalities and some tedious padding, *You Only Live Twice* is not only a return to form but one of the best Bond books – sparklingly written, exotic, informative and ingenious. The considerable research that has gone into it is communicated unshowily. The smooth flow is assisted by the fact that, unusually, there are few instances where the narrative breaks out of Bond's point of view. Again, there seems a little more humour than usual, particularly Bond's harrumphing responses to Japanese culture and his banter with Tanaka, and again this seems a response to the quippy Bond movies.

There is another quality wholly unexpected of a Bond book, usually such a cold proposition: its protagonist is likeable.

Following Ian Fleming's 1961 heart attack, a friend suggested to him that he pass the recuperation longueurs by writing down the self-composed bedtime story he had taken to reciting to eight-year-old Caspar. The result was *Chitty-Chitty-Bang-Bang: The Magical Car*, which although quite good didn't appear until three years later, by which time Fleming was dead.

There are some sad ironies surrounding *Chitty-Chitty-Bang-Bang*. The evident love for Fleming's son that provided its impetus was, it would seem, not reflected in the pastoral care that Caspar received. The fact that Caspar committed suicide in 1975 doesn't suggest a product of a well-balanced childhood. Even more tragic and symbolic is the fact that Ian Fleming's death was a horrific twelfth-birthday present for Caspar.

Fleming suffered a heart attack on 11 August 1964 when staying at a hotel in Canterbury. He died in hospital the next day. He was just fifty-six. Fleming had lived for real Bond's existence of smoking, drinking and lovelessness, and it had killed him. Had the bypass procedure been common at the time, Fleming might have gone on to properly enjoy the fruits of his labours. However, enjoyment wasn't the wont of a 'Death-Wish Charlie', although his perennial disinclination to allow his feelings of lack of self-worth to be manifested in inconsiderateness is revealed in his comment to the ambulance staff who responded to the emergency call: 'I am sorry to trouble you chaps.'

John Pearson says Fleming was 'going downhill towards the end. He used to say he was running out of puff. Life was going very sour for him. He had medical problems. Bond had a very complicated role within what was already a very unusual life.'

Fleming's death meant he missed out on a financial bonanza. Says Pearson, 'He'd never have dreamt of the success, otherwise he'd never have sold the franchise to his friend Jock Campbell, who was the head of Booker McConnell.' Pearson is referring to the fact that, in the first quarter of 1964, Booker Brothers acquired 51 per cent of Glidrose for £100,000. The impetus for this was Fleming's desire for a tax-free capital sum. (*The New York Times* estimated that 'income tax takes about $2.73 of every $2.80 he earns.') However, the low figure raised eyebrows: an auction might have generated far more. Moreover, in a sickening twist of fate, the £100,000 was lost in death duties upon Fleming's passing. 'It was a sad story, really, because everyone made money out of it except poor old Ian,' says Pearson. 'He died before the Bond boom really started.'

As Fleming passed, his creation assumed the mantle of immortality. August 1964 was the very month that saw the start of the process of the mythologisation of the Bond literary canon.

O.F. Snelling, a writer and expert on rare books, got to know Fleming through Sotheby's, where he worked in the Rare Book Department. He assisted Fleming with some research for his Bond stories and got Fleming's blessing for his *007 James Bond: A Report*. That Fleming died just days after the appearance of what was the first book-length study of the Bond phenomenon caused the work to seem almost a tribute to the deceased man. It eventually sold, by Snelling's estimation, a million copies around the world.

By the following year, there was a deluge of books about Bond. Some were lightweight, such as *Ian Fleming's Incredible Creation*, split into two parts: 'My Friend Ian Fleming' by Paul Anthony, and 'The World of James Bond' by Jacquelyn Fried. Some were heavyweight, such as Kingsley Amis's *The James Bond Dossier*, similar to Snelling's sober study. Others were playful, such as the one Amis published under the pseudonym 'Lt Col. William "Bill" Tanner,' *The Book of Bond, or, Every Man His Own 007*, a slender volume that provided tongue-in-cheek instruction on how to live like the secret agent. Some books were rather specialist. In *James Bond: Modern-day Dragonslayer*, Ann S. Boyd wrote from a Christian point of view, and her Bible-quote-littered text turned cartwheels to impose a religiosity on Bond that Fleming never intended.

The most stern-browed Bond publication was *Il Caso Bond*, an Italian collection of seven essays, co-edited by Oreste Del Buono and a young Umberto Eco. Eco's own contribution to the collection was an essay titled 'The Narrative Structures in Fleming', in which he compared Fleming's novels to matches played by the Harlem Globetrotters exhibition basketball team: 'We know with absolute confidence that the Globetrotters will win: the pleasure lies in watching the trained virtuosity with which they defer the final moment, with what ingenious deviations they reconfirm the foregone conclusion, with what trickeries they make rings round their opponents.'

That constricted but definite pleasure was now gone for ever.

WORLD DOMINATION

D ue to a dispute about money, Terence Young was replaced on *Goldfinger* by Guy Hamilton.

The film's screenplay was credited to Paul Dehn and Richard Maibaum. Maibaum told Pat McGilligan, 'On *Goldfinger*, I did a first draft. Saltzman didn't like it, and he brought in Paul Dehn, a good writer, to revise. Then Sean Connery didn't like the revisions, and I came back to do the final screenplay.' An uncredited contribution is reported to have been made by Wolf Mankowitz. This sort of screenwriter merry-go-round and shadow assistance is common in Movieland, and certainly common in the history of the Bond franchise. Not every example will be listed herein in the interests of skirting tedium.

When writing the *Goldfinger* novel, Fleming clearly conducted a considerable amount of research: the book features a visual aid in the form of a map of Fort Knox and its surrounds. It was all for naught. Several critics observed that stealing the gold from

Fort Knox posed practical problems that weren't all related to the heavy security. Or, as Maibaum and/or Dehn had Bond note to Goldfinger, 'Sixty men would take twelve days to load it onto two hundred trucks.' Accordingly, Goldfinger's plan was changed by the writer(s) to one that involved irradiating the Fort Knox gold where it sat, thus increasing by tenfold the value of the villain's existing stocks while the government of China – who supplied him the necessary atomic device – would secure their objective of economic chaos in the West. (Unlike their disinclination to condemn the USSR, Eon had no qualms about criticism of what was then still called 'Red China', possibly because Chairman Mao's horrific policies had made him a successor to the previous Red bogeyman, Joseph Stalin.) The finale thus becomes a desperate race by Bond to overcome Goldfinger's henchmen and disarm the device.

This is indicative. While largely adhering to its structure, the screenplay of *Goldfinger* over and over again improves on the parent novel. Examples of changes for the better include the fact that Bond first encounters Goldfinger by design, not chance; a horrified Bond comes upon the gold-painted corpse of Jill Masterson (as she is named here) rather than the murder being verbally relayed to him; Bond's genitals are threatened by an industrial laser rather than a circular saw; we actually get to go inside Fort Knox instead of stopping in the grounds; the specs of the Aston Martin are profoundly sexier. An added bonus is the merciful absence of the suffocatingly ubiquitous SPECTRE, the only example of such in Connery's seven-picture tenure.

Which is not to say that the picture is without flaws. The most notable of several is when Goldfinger tells an assembly of hoods the full details of Operation Grand Slam. As Goldfinger kills them all with deadly gas immediately afterwards, it's clear that the only point of the peroration is to enable the temporarily escaped Bond to bear witness to it. An illogicality that can't be explained even by the need for exposition is Oddjob crushing plan-refusenik Mr Solo in his car without first extracting from the boot his boss's gold.

Goldfinger contains the first proper Bond pre-title sequence in the sense of one that feels like a miniature movie: in a brisk four minutes, Bond penetrates and blows up an enemy installation, keeps a rendezvous with a beautiful woman and then – just when we think the action is over – has to electrocute to death a would-be assassin ('Shocking'). This would be an exhilaratingly stylised start on its own, but we are then swept up into John Barry, Anthony Newley and Leslie Bricusse's sumptuous title theme, rendered lustily by Shirley Bassey. It was the first Bond theme as we know the term today: glossy, anthemic and slightly preposterous ('Such a cold finger!').

Another, more bizarre Bond tradition is begun with the fact that Jack Lord does not reprise his role as Felix Leiter. The CIA man is instead played by Cec Linder. Although there may have been legitimate reasons for not getting back Lord – he is reputed to have made disproportionate demands regarding billing and money – it is rather silly that, in his nine appearances in official films, Bond's CIA pal has been played by seven different actors, with David Hedison and Jeffrey Wright the only returnees.

A more agreeable tradition is inaugurated with the first proper Q scene. First, Bond walks through the testing section of Q's department, a furious and comical hive of activity where Q's minions calmly withstand explosions and gunfire in the certainty of the protection afforded by their device prototypes. Then comes an exchange between Q and Bond that emphasises that Bond is no hero to the gadgets man, who is harrumphingly resentful of having to demonstrate to 007 equipment he knows the agent will only go and destroy. Q's main gadget in this picture is the Aston Martin DB5, which comes with a rear bullet shield, a revolving licence plate, an oil dispenser, retractable wheel-spikes, machine guns and a passenger-side ejector seat. In the book, the car's add-ons were restricted to hidden compartments, changeable lights and reinforced bumpers, and Bond used none of them.

That the movie's budget constituted those of the first two Bonds combined is evident in Scene 1's luxurious, seamless panning shot. It sweeps across the exterior of Goldfinger's grand Miami hotel to its swimming pool, telescopes in on a man diving from a high board, follows him under the water, shifts to Felix Leiter observing the swimmer through an observation panel and then follows Leiter as he goes in search of Bond.

The budget is also evident in Ken Adam's designs, which exceed even his usual flights of fancy. At Broccoli's prompting, Adam spurned the prosaic nature of what is known about Fort Knox's interior to create a cathedral of gold protected by huge steel, cone-design doors. Similarly, the bomb is the size of a chest freezer, chockfull of mysterious wires, buttons, dials and blinking lights.

Some scenery, of course, needs no budget. Connery looks the veritable million dollars, especially when wearing Savile Row suits. This despite the fact that *Goldfinger* was the first film where Connery's hair – which had been thinning since he was a very young man – was artificially augmented. (Paint was applied in *From Russia with Love*.) It's curious how much of an open secret this was. In his private life and in some contemporaneous film roles, Connery didn't bother with toupees, but there was little commentary by the media on his follicle depletion.

Much of the frisson surrounding the film resulted from the name of the character played by Honor Blackman. Christening someone Pussy Galore in print is one thing, but the transference to film and the fact that the character is far more prominent than in the book meant that the name was now being enunciated on peak-time television and radio broadcasts. In 1964, it was a how-do-they-get-away-with-it? scenario.

Although Blackman's casting meant a change of nationality for Pussy, it can't be denied that the actress is as beautiful as she had been as action-girl Cathy Gale in television show *The Avengers* — only in full colour. She's also the first Bond girl of any description not to be re-voiced, Nikki van der Zyl having stood in for Andress, Eunice Gay — twice — and this film's Shirley Eaton. The last of these is arguably even more transcendently easy on the eye than Blackman: her hair of spun gold and eyes of cobalt blue would have made her brief appearance memorable even without her character Jill Masterson's iconic gold paint job.

Goldfinger is played by German actor Gert Fröbe. Rotund and red-headed, he is visually perfect. However, sonically he fell down and had to be re-voiced. Recalls Wanstall, 'It was a huge shock. Apparently, he came over here giving the impression he could speak English, but all he did was to learn his lines parrot-fashion so that he would be ready for shooting. I remember they tested a lot of actors. They all attempted to do a few lines. I synchronised them all up and then we ran them one after the other.' Michael Collins was the man chosen to put words into Goldfinger's mouth. 'I think it was a masterclass,' says Wanstall of his work. 'You will never, ever, ever, ever witness a better re-voicing example than that. You cannot tell. He captured not only the sync, but the weight of the man, the cynicism of the man and the danger of the man.

And the accent. Everything is perfect. I wish I'd been responsible for it. I was on sound effects. The dialogue man did that.'

Wanstall, however, has plenty he can claim credit for in *Goldfinger*, not least the power of the laser-beam scene. Accordingly, come 5 April 1965, Wanstall became the first Bond crew member to be presented with an Academy Award.

Goldfinger is a hugely stylish and swaggering film, from that glib-and-proud-of-it pre-title sequence, to the way Bond works his way into Goldfinger's hotel room by deftly manipulating a chambermaid, to Bond humiliating his boss by displaying superior expertise about brandy, to the stylish way Bond slides across the floor of Fort Knox to electrocute Oddjob with a severed electricity cable as the villain is reaching for his metal-lined hat, to the fact that the atomic bomb is disabled when its three-digit countdown display is on '007', to the way proceedings conclude with Bond pulling a parachute over himself and Pussy to evade a rescue so they can enjoy another tryst, the bawdy horn line of the theme music blasting out once more as he does . . .

Despite the film's vaunting tone, it's in no way devoid of humanity, even nobility. Bond is shaken by the murder of Jill and grimly aware of his culpability in it. Moreover, in Fort Knox, Bond doesn't even think about taking the opportunity he has to run and instead selflessly toils to defuse the bomb in the face of lack of resources, knowhow and time.

That *Goldfinger* was destined to be a phenomenon seemed to be assumed from the get-go. John Barry's soundtrack album charted before the film was released. At the film's world premiere in Leicester Square, London, on 17 September 1964, the print was delivered in golden canisters by four gold-clad 'dolly-birds'. The film broke the UK box-office records set by *From Russia with Love*.

Over in the States, it was accorded the privilege of being UA's major Christmas release. UA put over a thousand prints of the movie into circulation across the globe, enabling the maximum number of cinema screenings and a critical mass of publicity. *Goldfinger* made it to what was then called *The Guinness Book of Records* as the fastest-grossing movie in history.

Dr. No was rereleased at the same time and also did well. Such rereleases would, over the following decade, be an important part of the Bond revenue stream in the absence of television royalties.

During his second scene with Jill Masterson, Bond quips that drinking Dom Perignon '53 above a temperature of 38 degrees Fahrenheit is 'as bad as listening to the Beatles without earmuffs'. The putdown might have accurately reflected the prejudices of a man of Bond's breeding, but it's rather ironic in the cultural context of the time. The mania surrounding Bond from this point on tied into a feeling of which Beatlemania was the other major element. It's an arrestingly appropriate fact that the first Bond movie and the first Beatles record – 'Love Me Do' – were released on the same day.

Despite their North American producers and funding, and despite their UK crew being chiefly determined by the Eady Plan – the tax-deduction scheme by which the British government encouraged filmmaking in its country – the Bond films were quintessentially British. The other quintessentially British phenomenon of the era was the 'Fab Four'. Just as their irreverence, proletarianism and provincialism made the Beatles seem harbingers of a new classless age, the strutting, sexed-up values of James Bond seemed to epitomise the taste in the air for libertarianism, while his gadgets chimed with the impression of a gleaming, trailblazing era. A grey, class-ridden, war-weakened, empire-deprived country was suddenly beginning to believe that it had more to its credit than an illustrious history. Out of the blue, the world considered British culture ahead of the curve, a feeling culminating in April 1966 with *Time* magazine anointing England's capital 'swinging'.

In short, over the course of the next few years, it was primarily the Beatles and James Bond who made people once more proud to be British.

The decision to pitch the James Bond films at a younger demographic than had Fleming his Bond novels was one of the most commercially astute moves Eon ever made. That they had no greater a rating restriction than 'A' in the UK and – once classification started there in 1968 – 'PG' in the US meant that Bond films were consumed by children as much as they were by adults. This in turn paved the way for merchandise, the bulk of which is usually aimed at kids.

The 'Bond Market' began in a modest way. The merchandise accompanying the film *Dr. No* extended no further than the comic adaptation, the belatedly issued soundtrack album, the John Barry single of 'The James Bond Theme' that wasn't even an official version and a reprint of the original novel with stills from the film on the cover, which Fleming complained to Pan Books was using 'my books for advertising . . . films'. A similarly scanty merchandising story pertained to *From Russia with Love*.

The explanation for this would seem to be that there was almost nothing in it for Danjaq. In a letter dated April 1962, Fleming stipulated to Danjaq that, although they were free to make licensing deals, they could receive no money for them. Moreover, such deals were to be limited to five products within one year of *Dr. No*'s release and must not include toiletries.

Left: Ian Fleming, James Bond's convoluted creator.

© *Daily Mail/REX/Shutterstock*

Right: Hoagy Carmichael, the famous songwriter whom Fleming used as the visual basis for 007.

© *REX/Shutterstock*

Below: Ornithologist James Bond, whose name was appropriated by Fleming for his hero.

© *Jerry Freilich*

Right: David Niven was Fleming's first choice to play James Bond, but only got to appear in the role in derided unofficial picture *Casino Royale* (1967).

The licence to kill for the Secret Service, the double-O prefix, was a great honour. It had been earned hardly. It brought James Bond the only assignments he enjoyed—the dangerous ones

Above: This iconic blurb, familiar from sixties Bond paperbacks published by Pan Books, was lifted from the pages of sixth 007 novel *Dr No*.

Above: Fleming with the two movie producers who would ramp up the fame of his hero to levels he could never have imagined: Harry Saltzman (*left*) and Cubby Broccoli.

© *Harry Myers/REX/Shutterstock*

Below: Fleming with Sean Connery. The author's opinion of the first man to play his creation in the cinemas was – at least initially – not entirely favourable.

© *Sipa Press/REX/Shutterstock*

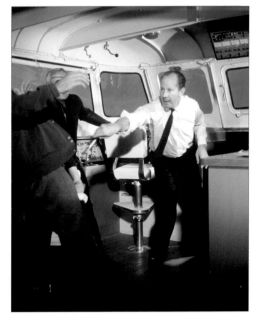

Top: Monty Norman, composer of the immortal 'James Bond Theme', with a rapt Vanessa Redgrave.

© *Daily Mail/REX/Shutterstock*

Bottom left: A 1961 publicity shot of Lois Maxwell, soon to become the first filmic Miss Moneypenny.

© *Everett/REX/Shutterstock*

Bottom right: Terence Young directs Connery and Adolfo Celi (Emilio Largo) in *Thunderball*. Many felt that Young was something of a Bond figure himself.

© *REX/Shutterstock*

Above: Corgi's Aston Martin DB5. This most iconic of all items of Bond merchandise was the biggest-selling toy of all time.

© *Ken Mckay/REX/Shutterstock*

Below: Kevin McClory attends the premiere of *Thunderball*. He would be a thorn in the side of the Bond movie producers.

© *Harry Myers/REX/Shutterstock*

Above: George Lazenby gets to grips with Diana Rigg in *On Her Majesty's Secret Service*. Lazenby's only Bond film is for many fans the best 007 picture of all.

© *PA Archive/PA Images*

Left: Sean Connery in classic Bond costume and pose. Many still regard him as the definitive 007.

© *United Archives/DPA/Press Association Images*

Above: Third official movie Bond Roger Moore (*right*) prepares to do battle with Scaramanga, the Man with the Golden Gun (Christopher Lee).

© *Anonymous/AP/Press Association Images*

Left: Timothy Dalton preparing to become the fourth movie Bond in the company of Maryam D'Abo.

© *Nils Jorgensen/REX/Shutterstock*

Below: Pierce Brosnan with Michelle Yeoh in *Tomorrow Never Dies*, the second of his quartet of Bond films.

© *dpa-Film UIP/DPA/*
Press Association Images

Left: Daniel Craig with his M, Judi Dench. They were promoting *Skyfall*, which was soon to become the most successful Bond film of all time.

© *Joel Ryan/AP/Press Association Images*

Left: Martin Campbell, the director who twice 'rebooted' the cinema Bond.

© Mirco Toniolo/REX/Shutterstock

Right: John Barry – co-composer of most of the best-known 007 movie themes – is congratulated by Bond producer Barbara Broccoli on his 2006 'Inspiration Award' from *GQ* magazine.

© Richard Young/REX/Shutterstock

Above: Craig was a much darker Bond, but that didn't prevent him also being beefcake.

© Topham/Topham Picturepoint/Press Association Images

Meanwhile, according to Broccoli, UA chief executive Arthur Krim had insisted from the get-go that the studio own all Bond-movie music rights. Merchandise, then, was useful only to draw attention to the Bond films.

The aftermath of the release of *Goldfinger* was very different. It saw shop shelves groaning with Bond jigsaws, board games, action figures, guns, walkie-talkies, bubblegum cards, attaché cases and clothing, even if much of this product did not appear until several months after the movie had been put on release. Although shortly before Fleming died Glidrose had signed an agreement with Eon to share the Bond marketing rights, one suspects that, following Fleming's death, a more hard-headed attitude was adopted by the owners of the literary Bond. Booker McConnell were in the business of making money and were not motivated by the sentimentality that would have partly informed the decisions of Glidrose when run only by the Fleming family.

From this juncture on, synchronisation became standard. No Eon Bond film would ever again reach the cinemas without the simultaneous presence on shelves of tie-in consumer goods of every description and utility. Replica guns, miniature cars and secret-agent paraphernalia in general were expected because logical, but Eon had learned the same lesson as owners of merchandising rights to other cultural phenomena such as Tarzan and the Beatles: a brand name or likeness could be plastered on any conceivable artefact and, whether germane or not, result in a mutually beneficial outcome for licensor and licensee. Thus it was that James Bond's name, the 007 logo and the likeness of the current Bond actor have ended up on everything from toy racetracks to pencil cases to magic sets to deodorant to underwear.

Hand in hand with the tidal wave of merchandise came a sharper sense of promotion. Bond films were heralded by official television documentaries, publicity jaunts and a blizzard of publicity stills. The publicists eventually honed this process to such a state of ubiquity that, whenever Bond was in the theatres, his face and name routinely appeared as much on cereal packets, crisp bags and lottery tickets as they did magazine covers.

The ultimate Bond merchandising sensation was the miniature Aston Martin DB5, manufactured by UK toy company Playcraft in their Corgi range. Although prompted by the car's appearance in *Goldfinger*, this die-cast model didn't actually appear until October 1965, only a couple of months before the release of the next Bond movie, *Thunderball* (although it did, handily, also feature in that). Although no bigger than a human palm (1:46 scale), it had several features of the vehicle seen in the film, including machine guns, bumper rams, bullet shield and – most gratifyingly – ejector seat with resident villain. These features were activated by ingenious methods, such as pressing the exhaust pipe. The car was not the silver of the film but gold, a decision made because the silver paint originally tested made the toy look as though it had in fact been denied a paint job. The kids didn't care. 'James Bond's Aston Martin D.B. 5' – Corgi model 261 – was, despite its hefty price tag (9s 11d in the UK), the retail sensation of Christmas 1965.

By February 1968, the toy had sold nearly 4 million models, during which time it had been slightly increased in size to 1:43 scale. Corgi continued the upgrades, exchanging the 261 for the 270, the paintwork of which was authentic silver birch. The gadgets were now augmented by revolving number plates and pullout tyre slashers and the product came in a 'blister pack' – as opposed to the previous rectangular box with a painted image – that enabled the prospective purchaser to instantly see what he was getting.

Some of the retoolings since then have been more to do with cost-cutting than improvement. Corgi's ownership has changed hands. Production has switched from the UK to China. There have been many other Bond-related toy vehicles, some arguably snazzier, such as the Lotus Esprit from *The Spy Who Loved Me*. Yet, throughout it all, Corgi's DB5 has remained in continuous production.

During this period, the status of the real-life DB5 has changed more than once. Formerly fashionable, it became dated. The passage of time then gave it the aura of 'classic', something that means Eon have been able to sit behind its steering wheel latter-day Bonds Pierce Brosnan and Daniel Craig without sacrificing Bond's stylishness.

Corgi's Aston Martin DB5 seems unassailable in its position as iconic 007 toy and the most famous piece of Bond merchandise of all time.

'For this is, alas, the last Bond and, again alas, I mean it, for I really have run out of both puff + zest, and I would not like to short-weight my faithful readers . . .' Ian Fleming had no way of knowing when he wrote those words to his publisher to accompany the delivery of *The Man with the Golden Gun*, his latest Bond manuscript, that this time fate would call his bluff on his assertion of a lack of a future for prose Bond.

The title may be an allusion to Nelson Algren's 1949 novel about a lowlife card dealer, *The Man with the Golden Arm*. There was an even closer involvement in Fleming's book by another author. Although he had diligently tapped away at a new Bond tale during his final months, Fleming's declining health had reduced him to a mere hour-and-a-half's typing per day. He told William Plomer that he wasn't happy with the resultant manuscript and suggested that he – for the first time – take it back to Jamaica for additional work the next time he went. He reasoned that he should 'go out with a bang instead of a whimper'. Plomer disagreed with his proposal for reworking, although may have been motivated less by quality than the fact that Bond books were now an annual fiscal bonanza for Cape not to be postponed lightly. *You Only Live Twice* – published in the same month as Fleming completed *Golden Gun* – had advance orders that were a 50 per cent increase on even *On Her Majesty's Secret Service*.

Yet Cape did eventually decide that *The Man with the Golden Gun* needed work. Perhaps their change of mind was motivated by the fact that the book had been transformed by tragedy from latest instalment to swansong. The man they engaged to take on the task was Kingsley Amis. Amis had no thriller-writing experiences, but he was both a renowned literary novelist and a Bond expert. His *The James Bond Dossier* was due for publication by Cape, and in fact was delayed in order that Amis be able to incorporate an evaluation of *The Man with the Golden Gun*. Raymond Benson says of Amis, 'Despite any kind of rumours you may have heard, he did not rewrite or write most of *The Man with the Golden Gun*. That's a myth. The manuscript was completed but it needed a lot of polishing and fixing up, and he did that. He didn't add any plot elements or anything like that. He just made it acceptable to publish.' Benson cites his sources for this as Fleming's agent Peter Janson-Smith and Amis himself. *The Man with the Golden Gun* was published on 1 April 1965.

A year after Bond's death was announced in the press, he turns up at the Service's new address in Kensington – where they now use the cover name 'Transworld Consortium'. Bond denounces M as a warmonger and unsuccessfully tries to kill him with a jet of cyanide. He is a brainwashed double agent.

That cute *Times* obituary now begins to undermine credibility at every turn as M decrees that, if Bond can be rendered fit for duty again, he should be sent off on a new mission as a means of expiation for the day's events. Even if we are to accept that Bond had previously operated in a situation of low-level fame incongruous for a secret agent, how are we now to believe that his job has not been made untenable by the explosion in his celebrity engendered by that obituary's confirmation of his existence?

It should also be noted that M comes ridiculously quickly to his decision that 007 should be required to complete a new mission – barely after the door has been closed on the overpowered Bond. The book is strewn with such nonsenses.

Bond's task is to dispose of one Francisco Scaramanga. A Latin American freelance assassin mainly under KGB control through Havana, he has killed and maimed several operatives of the Secret Service, the CIA and other friendly agencies with his trademark gold-plated, long-barrelled Colt .45. As usual, the villain has a bodily deformity: a third nipple. Not as usual, he is hot-headed and not very articulate.

Bond catches up with Scaramanga in Jamaica. When the undercover 007 tells the gunman his line of employment is insurance investigation, Scaramanga offers him some security work at an imminent conference of stockholders of a holiday-resort development. A convincing reason for this overture is never really provided. Perhaps the wrinkle would have been ironed out by the further work made impossible by Fleming's death and the author would have realised that Scaramanga's homosexuality provided the logical motive.

Bond uncovers murder, the disturbing precedent of the Mafia consorting with the KGB and a scheme to increase the world price of sugar to aid Castro's regime. A hunting trip on a private train culminates in Bond chasing Scaramanga through marshland and taking a bullet before fatally putting Scaramanga out of business.

Bond is offered a knighthood. M is inexplicably in favour, despite its being established in both *Moonraker* and *Goldfinger* that working secret agents can't accept honours. Bond, though, is contemptuous, stating that he is a 'Scottish peasant', a yet further downgrading of the social class Fleming had once been proud to make unambiguously upper-middle. Despite this authorial muddle-headedness, Fleming then evocatively writes of Service reunions where ex-agents 'talked about dusty triumphs and tragedies which, since they would never be recorded in the history books, must be told again that night'.

An unexpected motif of the book is dreams, with Bond experiencing several – including a daytime reverie – all of which possess a persuasive flavour of fractured reality. In fact, in this book, Bond gets off with someone – Mary Goodnight – only via this method. One wonders whether the dream aspect is the major contribution to the book by Amis, who suggested in his *James Bond Dossier*, 'What about a few dreams? – known as the handy off-the-peg method of injecting significance into any form of fiction.'

Reviews of *The Man with the Golden Gun* tended to focus not on whether it was a good read but on whether it constituted a fitting valedictory. It is indeed the latter because, like so much of Fleming's oeuvre, the fact that it is full of flaws doesn't prevent it being an assured, stately page-turner.

That having been said, the thought also occurs that Fleming, had he lived, would have been wise to make good on his insistence to Plomer that he would not write any more Bonds. Not only had Fleming painted himself into a corner with the *Times* obituary, but his weariness is becoming ever more evident. We are used to his continuity errors, but the lapses of concentration seem to be accumulating: he speaks of Honeychile 'Wilder' and Maria 'Freudenstadt' and states that Bond and Leiter have never shaken hands in their lives when we saw them do exactly that when they met in *Live and Let Die*. Moreover, the franchise is moving towards antiquatedness. Goodnight's furious blushes when Bond describes a building as a 'whorehouse' are part of a portrayal of women as a simpering breed that is disappearing into history.

That the bomb in *Goldfinger* ended its countdown on '007' was cute, but it was an afterthought: those at the premiere saw it stop at '003'. This was not the only alteration to the original print of *Goldfinger*.

The credits had initially ended with the information that the movie in which Bond would return was *On Her Majesty's Secret Service*. Maibaum had already begun a treatment on that adaptation. However, with Kevin McClory now in possession of the right to make a James Bond movie of his own, Broccoli and Saltzman decided that joining forces with him was a less objectionable vista than the prospect of a rival picture. Accordingly, future prints declared 'James Bond will return in *Thunderball*'.

McClory had originally intended to make his own Bond film independently of Eon. Laurence Harvey and Richard Burton were talked of as playing Bond. However, McClory had second thoughts and announced, '. . . deep down I knew I wanted Sean.'

Thunderball underlined that Connery certainly had a special something. Because Eon were now shooting in Panavision, a new gun-barrel sequence was required. The difference between a stuntman and an actor immediately becomes apparent: Connery strolls, swivels and shoots with the utmost panache.

The theme tune – Barry's music decorated by Don Black's lyric, which is sung by Tom Jones – is, like that of *Goldfinger*, both rousing and risible.

Terence Young returned as director. Richard Maibaum shared the screenplay credit with John Hopkins, although the project's tangled history is illustrated by the addendum, 'Based on an original screenplay by Jack Whittingham', which has its own addendum: 'Based on the original story by Kevin McClory, Jack Whittingham and Ian Fleming'. McClory is credited as producer, Broccoli–Saltzman as executive producers.

Those members of the public who did not take interest in such behind-the-scenes stuff perceived *Thunderball* as simply the latest Bond flick. The latest Bond flick was by now a momentous thing. When McClory had launched his suit, nobody knew for sure that James Bond movies would be money-spinners. By the time *Thunderball* premiered on 9 December 1965 in Tokyo (the series' first non-British entrée), 007 pictures were cinema 'events' more than a decade before *Jaws* supposedly inaugurated the concept. In fact, anticipation of its arrival and fond regard for its predecessors enabled *Thunderball* to achieve a success out of all proportion to its quality.

There is something 'off' about *Thunderball*. It's a little over the top and a little conceited. When Maibaum had first started work on a *Thunderball* screenplay four years previously, there was no self-consciousness about the process. Now he admitted, 'I realise how much we have been influenced by audience reaction.' The alternate pandering and laziness is evident in many places. An otherwise good pre-title sequence that sees Bond make an escape via a jetpack ends limply with his departing Aston Martin spraying the camera with water. Bond inanely rattles off to a romantic partner the line, 'See you later, alligator,' as if he were a bequiffed leading man in a teenage-oriented rock'n'roll movie. He endangers himself by smugly delaying his departure from an enemy's room for the sake of stealing a grape. The dialogue is pat and knowing: 'That gun looks more fitting for a woman'; 'You know much about guns, Mr Bond?'; 'No, I know a little about women.' The narrative injects idiotic coincidences into Fleming source material already burdened with implausibilities, one example being the fact that, direct from an underwater skirmish with Largo's men, Bond hitches a lift on land from a woman who turns out to be a SPECTRE agent. This overall glibness has the result of our never feeling that Bond is in danger.

Meanwhile, 007's customary cocksure attitude towards the fairer sex is beginning to cross a line. When asked for something to put on by a woman he catches in the bath, he proffers a pair of shoes and then settles back to watch; he virtually blackmails into sex a Shrublands employee fearful of losing her job.

There are other fundamental problems. However well shot and choreographed are the frogmen fights, they can't ultimately overcome the obstacle of being fundamentally slow. That the man who agrees to hijack the nuclear weapons has undergone plastic surgery to make him the real pilot's exact double would be a science-fiction concept even today. Additionally, a certain sense of *déjà vu* is beginning to creep in. When we see Bond smuggle himself into the heart of the enemy's operations by donning an antagonist's identity-veiling apparel, we are instantly reminded of the climactic scene in *Dr. No*.

However debased, Bond was still impressive on one level. John Stears won an Oscar for his visual effects. Stears, incidentally, was the man responsible for bringing to life the Aston Martin DB5 in this and the previous movie.

Thunderball so vexed British censors that it was almost given an 'X' certificate, which would have barred admission to it for anyone under sixteen. This was an unthinkable scenario considering the series' vast youth demographic. The British Board of Film Censorship wanted thirty changes made to a film they stated to be characterised by 'sex, sadism and violence'. Eon's powers of persuasion seem to have been considerable. The film was so unscathed that it still ran to 125 minutes (the longest yet), the BBFC settling for changes only to the scene in which Bond is stroking a woman's back with a mink glove. That *Thunderball* was granted the usual UK 'A' certificate – accessible to children, although some local councils insisted on an accompanying adult – paved the way to its enjoying the status of highest-grossing Bond film. This achievement was not that remarkable at a time when the franchise was three years old. What is remarkable is that it held on to that status for nearly half a century.

With vast success comes imitation.

One of the first significant riders on the coattails of Fleming was Donald Hamilton, whose character Matt Helm debuted in 1960 in the blood-and-revenge-strewn *Death of a Citizen*. Helm went on to appear in twenty-six other novels up to 1993. He did not merely have a licence to kill but was specifically employed as a government assassin, albeit one who usually killed only Communist agents or terrorists.

Bond-style fiction ballooned in print with the success of the

Bond films, and from that point often tended to conflate the literary and cinematic 007s.

Nick Carter was a character originating in nineteenth-century pulp magazines. In the wake of the first two cinema Bonds, he was resurrected, updated and recalibrated, metamorphosing from a police detective to a secret agent with the blunt rank of 'Killmaster'. The pulp traditions were maintained, however: of the more than 250 Nick Carter Killmaster novels that appeared over a quarter-century from *Run, Spy, Run* (1964), none carried an author credit.

Adam Diment's secret agent Philip McAlpine made his debut in 1967 in *The Dolly Dolly Spy*. Naturally, the hero was sexually promiscuous, but it was the promiscuity of a new generation, one that went hand in hand with long hair, Swinging London 'gear', hipster speak and joints. The hero worked for British intelligence only on threat of drug-related prosecution. This counterculture James Bond was in large part just a version of his creator. Diment was, astoundingly a mere twenty-three years old when his first McAlpine novel appeared. For a brief period, Diment had the aura of a pop star, gracing magazine spreads dressed in regency coats and candy-stripe trousers, sometimes in the company of mini-skirted admirers.

Even Richard Llewellyn, best known for Welsh-mining-village novel *How Green Was My Valley*, got in on the Bond act. Between 1969 and 1974, he penned three books about Edmund Trothe. The trilogy proved that the profession of secret agent did not prohibit a rather pompous and staid personality: Trothe objects to his children listening to the product of pop stars he considers 'callow importunates' and is discomforted by his daughter's boyfriend being black.

There were also what could be termed 'anti-Bonds'. *The Ipcress File* (1962) and its sequels saw Len Deighton create a new secret agent paradigm: unlike Bulldog Drummond, Richard Hannay or James Bond, its nameless hero was not only from the lower orders but had severe misgivings about upper-class values. John le Carré's depictions of the inhabitants of the 'Circus' – the British intelligence services – in books such as *Call for the Dead* (1961) and *The Spy Who Came in from the Cold* (1963) posited a mundane, paranoid and grey world devoid of Bond-style sex and glamour.

Although he financially benefited from the way Fleming's success broadened the espionage market, John le Carré disliked Bond. In a 1966 BBC interview, he told Malcolm Muggeridge, 'I'm not sure that Bond is a spy . . . he's more some kind of international gangster with, as it is said, a licence to kill . . . He's a man entirely out of the political context. It's of no interest to Bond who, for instance, is president of the United States or of the Union of Soviet Republics.' This lack of accuracy about Bond – whose political morality studs Fleming's prose – can perhaps be forgiven in light of the fact that le Carré's disdain for 007 arose partly from the fact that he knew the world of espionage intimately, having worked for both MI5 and MI6.

Although motivated by the same desire to make money, parodies are distinct from pastiches or imitations. Possibly the earliest example of Bond being mocked in print is a curious and brief one-page short story titled 'Some Are Born Great', which appeared in *Nursery World* in September 1959. A scene in which Bond is playing a tense card game soon evaporates into comedy when he is chided by his nanny for taking it too seriously. The nanny then proceeds to wonder what will become of him. Credited author

J.M. Harwood was none other than the Johanna Harwood given a script credit on the first two Bond movies.

Alligator was a novella-length Bond spoof written by Christopher Cerf and Michael K. Frith, editors of Harvard University's undergraduate monthly publication *Harvard Lampoon*. Sub-titled *A J*MES B*ND Thriller by I*N FL*M*NG*, it finds B*nd – as he is called throughout – investigating Lacertus Alligator and his organisation TOOTH (The Organization Organized To Hate). B*nd works for 'World-Wide Import & Export Ltd', where 'the few innocents who occasionally wandered in trying to import or export something were politely, but firmly, shot'.

Amusing stuff like this and a detailed knowledge of the Bond universe led to a stapled, thirty-seven-page publication becoming a critical success and a surprise bestseller. However, both it and a short-story sequel in *Playboy* in 1966 titled 'Toadstool' have disappeared into the folds of history. Despite the legal protection afforded parody, Fleming took action against the publisher. He may have had just cause: several reviewers noted that its humour was sometimes so subtle that *Alligator* read like an only slightly exaggerated Fleming novel.

Cyril Connolly also published a Bond parody – perhaps a natural extension of the fact that it was he whom Fleming had found mockingly reading out a passage of a Bond novel to a gathering of his wife's friends. Connolly's short story, 'Bond Strikes Camp', could almost be postulated as what is now called slash fiction, the Internet phenomenon wherein fictional cultural icons are portrayed in incongruous gay scenarios. However, in dressing Bond in drag to uncover a traitor who turns out to be an M intent on seducing him, Connolly was not motivated by whimsy but was making the point that the Cambridge spy ring had been homosexual. Although

Connolly and Fleming went way back, there is some evidence that there was a degree of malice behind the former's parody. Fleming neutered it slightly by buying the copyright for £100 before its first appearance in *London Magazine* in April 1963.

The Bond-movie cash-in game began in 1964, when the Carry On team almost inevitably decided to apply their saucy style to 007. In *Carry on Spying*, Charles Hawtrey played Charlie Bind, agent O-O-Oh! and sworn enemy of STENCH.

From there, vehicles exploitative of Bond – serious and comedic – came pouring out of the movie studios. In 1965 alone, there were over fifty spy-themed cinematic releases; in 1966 over sixty. Bulldog Drummond was even brought back to the screen as a consequence of Bond's popularity, completing a circle insofar as he was one of the characters responsible for Bond's existence. Another circle was completed by Drummond being played by Richard Johnson, once considered for the role of 007. One of the more bizarre Bond spoofs was 1967's *OK Connery*, a.k.a. *Operation Kid Brother*, a.k.a. *Operation Double 007*. It was not only stuffed with faces familiar from Bond films but secured the curious additional coup of engaging the services of Sean Connery's non-actor brother Neil for the lead role.

The films based on Len Deighton's aforementioned anti-Bond literary trilogy starred Michael Caine. Produced by Harry Saltzman, they inevitably boasted much of the creative personnel behind the Bond films. In *James Bond: My Long and Eventful Search for His Father*, Deighton revealed Saltzman told him that Saltzman's joint stewardship of the cinematic 007 meant that 'I am the only person in the world who won't try to make your working-class hero into some kind of James Bond.' Sure enough, *The Ipcress File*, *Funeral in Berlin* and *Billion Dollar Brain* (1965–67) were a sort of mixture of Bond and Saltzman's kitchen-sink films. The hero – nameless in the books, but called Harry Palmer in the films – was a laconic, bespectacled man with a hint of a cockney accent who worked out of dreary offices and spent much of his time form-filling.

Danger Man was one of the earliest of the television cash-ins. Made by production company ITC and broadcast on Britain's commercial television network ITV, it featured Patrick McGoohan as John Drake. The programme got progressively more Bondian after it debuted in 1960 and was even renamed *Secret Agent* in some territories, although the pompous puritanism of McGoohan rendered out of the question any sex quotient.

When McGoohan switched his attention to *The Prisoner*, ITC quickly replaced *Danger Man* with *Man in a Suitcase*, featuring the global freelance sleuthing work of McGill (Richard Bradford), a disgraced ex-US Intelligence agent. ITC, in fact, would specialise in shows that would probably never have existed without the template provided by Bond, among them *The Baron*, *Department S*, *Jason King*, *The Persuaders!*, *The Adventurer*, *The Protectors* and *Return of the Saint*. Another of their specialisms was the puppetry-oriented kids' TV shows created by Gerry and Sylvia Anderson. The two creative strands crossed with *Joe 90* (1968), a programme about a nine-year-old spy, and *The Secret Service* (1969), which featured a middle-aged vicar who moonlighted for governmental agency BISHOP.

September 1964 saw the television debut of *The Man from U.N.C.L.E.* It featured good-looking, gun-wielding characters with Fleming-esque names such as Napoleon Solo and April Dancer, who worked for a government agency that battled THRUSH (not the sniggering joke it seemed). Because of the obviousness of the cash-in, many are amazed to find out that the U.N.C.L.E. project originated with Ian Fleming. The Bond creator had in 1963 been approached by a Hollywood producer named Norman Felton about devising a globe-trotting secret-agent television series that would be a cross between Bond and the 'Thrilling Cities' articles Fleming wrote for *The Sunday Times*, which became his travelogue of the same name. After some preliminary work, Fleming changed his mind about participation, partly out of fear that it would use up his hardly plentiful ideas for Bond plots. Perhaps learning a lesson from the grisly business of the *Thunderball* lawsuit, Fleming willingly rescinded all rights in the property for the token sum of £1.

Running *The Man from U.N.C.L.E.* a close second as the most fondly remembered Bond TV take-off is *Mission: Impossible.* The CBS show debuted in September 1966 and featured the adventures of the Impossible Missions Force, a team of secret agents who took on Bondian madmen and organisations. It opened with an unforgettable, much-loved, frequently parodied gimmick: its agents would receive instructions about their missions on audiotapes that promptly self-destructed. As smoke rose from the tape, Lalo Schifrin's pounding, hook-stuffed theme music – as stirring as even the best Bond theme – kicked in.

Get Smart was an NBC (later CBS) television show that debuted in September 1965. That Mel Brooks was a co-creator will immediately give away that it was a vehicle that took up a notch or two *The Man From U.N.C.L.E.*'s twinkle-eyed approach into outright farce. The series lasted five seasons and bequeathed several catchphrases including 'Missed it by *that* much!' and 'I asked you not to tell me that!'

A more serious American spy show debuted in the same month as *Get Smart.* Some stations in the Deep South of the US banned

I Spy because it portrayed black secret agent Alexander Scott (Bill Cosby) working alongside white secret agent Kelly Robinson (Robert Culp) more or less as his equal. The two bickering, wisecracking agents posed as tennis-playing itinerants as they went about their Pentagon-mandated business.

The TV rip-offs did not really, contrary to assumptions, include *The Avengers*. Although the British show that debuted in 1961 may via osmosis have had some Bond DNA in its genome, by the mid-sixties it had set its face against any recognisably real aspects of the espionage genre. The bowler-hatted John Steed and his latest female companion in British intelligence work, Emma Peel, battled antagonists from no particular axis against backdrops so surreal that they might have been devised by Salvador Dalí.

Perhaps the most significant Bond imitation in either film or television came in the form of Mike Henry's Tarzan movies. The former NFL player appeared in three ape-man films, the first two of which – *Tarzan and the Valley of Gold* (1966) and *Tarzan and the Great River* (1967) – did the ostensibly impossible in making his jungle-based character look like a secret agent from civilisation. It was shocking – and to many laughable – to see a Tarzan who sported short hair, a suit and a briefcase boarding planes and helicopters, tussling with rich megalomaniacs and making Bond-like wisecracks.

Although the Tarzan series wasn't at the time the longest-running film franchise – that accolade belonged to Sherlock Holmes – it was the most successful. In retrospect, it can be seen that the advent of Bond marked the point where cinema audiences would no longer be satisfied with uncomplicated, wholesome fare like Tarzan. While the Bond franchise continued through thick and thin, Tarzan films began dwindling in number. Between 1918 and

1967, there were thirty-nine official Tarzan cinematic ventures. From 1970 to 2016 (almost as long a time period), there have been nine. The Mike Henry Tarzan can be posited as a moment in cinematic history where the other guy blinked.

9

CONTINUING THE LEGACY

On 23 June 1966 came the appearance of a coda to the Fleming Bond canon in the form of *Octopussy and The Living Daylights*. It was a slender volume of ninety-four pages containing merely two Bond short stories, both already published if not widely disseminated or even – in the world of segmented information that existed before the Internet – known of. It's precisely because of the Internet that, these days, such a volume would also automatically mop up '007 in New York' and 'The Property of a Lady', the other Bond short fiction then uncollected in volume form. While the latter story was added to the book when it went into paperback the following year, it took three-and-a-half decades for the New York story to also be hauled in.

'Octopussy' had been serialised in the *Daily Express* in October 1965 and in *Playboy* across March and April 1966. It's a tale in which Bond is, as in 'Quantum of Solace', merely a bit-player. However, it is on a far higher plane of quality than the latter work.

It's also odd, beginning with the fact that central figure, Major Dexter Smythe, feels like an older, decaying version of James Bond. An ex-British Secret Service man, he was once a 'brave and resourceful officer and a handsome man who had made easy sexual conquests all his military life . . .' He is now fifty-four, slightly bald, has a sagging belly and varicose veins. He also sounds a lot like Ian Fleming towards the end of the latter's life: domiciled in his beloved Jamaica, he enjoys underwater diving and continues to smoke and drink excessively despite two coronaries. Smythe's defiance of medical advice is due to the fact that he – in the first of several exquisite phrases herein – 'had arrived at the frontier of the death wish'. Tropical sloth, self-indulgence, widower status and guilt had worn him down to a state of 'spiritual accidie' – making him the third of Fleming's villains after Mr Big and Ernst Stavro Blofeld to suffer from this condition. The only thing that has lately kept him clinging to life is the anthropomorphism he has invested in the birds, insects and fish that inhabit the grounds of his villa, particularly a small brown octopus he has nicknamed 'Octopussy'. A couple of hours earlier, though, there had been an occurrence that made him realise even this circumscribed life was futile. The occurrence was a visit by one James Bond.

Flashback. When Bond states that he is from the Ministry of Defence, Smythe recognises it as a euphemism for the Secret Service. As the two men begin to talk, Fleming captures in Smythe the supplicatory, almost pathetic state of mind to which those with a guilty conscience are reduced: when Bond asks him if he minds if he smokes, 'Somehow this small sign of a shared weakness comforted Major Smythe.'

Bond's questioning leads to Smythe thinking back to the period immediately following the war. While employed cleaning up

Gestapo and Abwehr hideouts, the major had stumbled upon the existence of some hidden gold bars. He had found a pretext to pull in for questioning an Austrian mountain guide named Hannes Oberhauser. Once Oberhauser had acted as his escort to the mountain where the gold was hidden, Smythe had cold-bloodedly killed him as the only potential witness to his theft.

Shell-shocked by his distant past thus returning, Smythe tells Bond the whole story. He is curious as to why Bond volunteered to investigate following the emergence of Oberhauser's body from the glacier in which the major had dumped it. 'He taught me to ski before the war, when I was in my teens,' Bond replies. 'He was something of a father to me at a time when I happened to need one.'

We are brought back to the present. As he quests along the reef, Smythe is musing that Bond's advice that it will be a week or so before someone is sent to collect him is a version of leaving a guilty officer alone with his revolver. The major suddenly notices three bleeding pinpricks on his stomach and realises that a scorpion fish has stung him. It takes fifteen minutes for people to expire in agony from such wounds. Smythe's whimsical experiment with Octopussy turns now into the urgent resolve of a final act. In a state of delirium, he makes his way to the creature's lair. Octopussy is surprisingly friendly – but Smythe then realises it is attracted by his blood. He is dragged under as the octopus sets to work on his hand with its beak-like jaws.

The story should really have ended on that powerful and horrific note, but a subsequent short paragraph details how Smythe's body was discovered by fishermen; another, much shorter, one details Bond's assumption of suicide from Smythe's file, a sentence without which this would be the only Bond tale devoid of 007's point of view; and a final one almost spoils the story, suggesting as it does that the preceding events were pieced together via Smythe's autopsy, which would have been impossible.

Fleming wrote 'Octopussy' in July 1962 on an unusual mid-year visit to Jamaica. Michael Howard of Cape thought it better than any story in *For Your Eyes Only* but cautioned Fleming that such a Bond-light tale might provoke the same grievances as did *The Spy Who Loved Me*. The rescuing of the story by his literary executors from Fleming's metaphorical bottom drawer was a wise course of action, for 'Octopussy' is an intriguing and superbly crafted tale, and absolute proof that Fleming was more than capable – had he wanted – of branching out into different and supposedly more elevated fields of fiction.

Unfortunately for Fleming's legacy, the Bond movies were just about to plumb the depths of even low culture.

There was no Bond film released in 1966. The following year, though, there were two, for 1967 was the year that Charles K. Feldman finally got his adaptation of the first Bond novel to the big screen.

It wasn't worth the wait. The 1967 *Casino Royale* is the embarrassing deformed relative of the James Bond family locked away from public sight. Cherished by nobody, it rarely receives TV screenings. Ultimately, its value was deemed to be so low that in 2009 Sony – who had taken over ownership from original distributors MGM – made it available free of charge on YouTube. It was a sad conclusion to a saga that had started so promisingly with those glittering Ben Hecht scripts of the early 1960s.

In June 1964, shortly after Hecht's death, Feldman told the *Daily Mail* that his 'ideal man' to play Bond was Roger Moore. (Unknown to both Feldman and Moore, the actor had been briefly considered by Eon in the run-up to *Dr. No*.) 'I've had no approach from Mr Feldman yet, but this is a wonderful piece of news,' Moore was quoted as responding. 'I've always fancied myself as a Bond.' This means that, at a certain point in history, Sean Connery could have gone head to head with Moore in rival Bond pictures.

The idea of Moore was abandoned when it appeared Sean Connery was a real possibility. In the 12 May 1965 edition of *Variety* came the announcement of a joint United Artists–Columbia Pictures production of *Casino Royale* with Connery in his usual role of Bond. There have been some suggestions that Broccoli and Saltzman were ultimately deterred from this venture by the unpleasant co-production experience that was *Thunderball*. In Broccoli's version of events, however, Feldman kiboshed the project by demanding 75 per cent of the profits. Feldman said he himself was put off by the fact that Eon insisted that *Casino Royale* be the sixth Bond picture. As the unhappy Connery would by then be nearing the end of his Eon contract, Feldman would be able to approach him directly. Feldman did indeed do this, but is said to have baulked at Connery's terms of a million dollars.

Not necessarily after his Connery overture, Feldman signed one Terence Cooper to play 007, although contractually forbade him to tell anyone. A Northern Ireland native in his early thirties, Cooper was dark, imposing and handsome. Feldman – initially – would seem to have had considerable confidence in his ability to be something then almost inconceivable: a Bond actor who wasn't Sean Connery.

Cooper was not happy about his enforced idleness and the veil of secrecy over his casting. 'Do you have any idea how long that is to do nothing?' he complained to the press in early 1966 about his

two years of well-paid idleness. 'I'm an actor. I have to work.' No
doubt he would have been even more aggrieved had he known of
the overture made to Connery probably while he himself was under
contract. There was to be more heartache: Cooper did appear in
Casino Royale but only in a small, silly part as a British agent called
Coop. By then, the tone of the film had changed drastically.

Feldman could have opted to continue with his original plan
for a straightforward Bond picture. The character's proven cinema
track record guaranteed him a high budget. Ultimately, he and co-
producer Jerry Bresler were able to spend more money on *Casino
Royale* – $12 million – than was poured into either any previous
Bond film or the official Bond movie of the year of its release.

Amazingly, Feldman decided instead to spurn both the fine
scripts by Ben Hecht to which he owned rights and the convincing
leading man he had under contract in favour of a spoof movie
stitched together from scripts from multiple sources and starring
an ageing thespian. His rationale seems to have been no more than
spite over failing to get a deal with Eon or Connery or both. When
Feldman told *Time* magazine in May 1966 that he was planning
'the Bond movie to end all Bond movies', he didn't mean it in a
nice way. Four months later, Woody Allen – one of the stars of
the film – told *Look* that Feldman wanted to 'eliminate the Bond
films forever'. By making Bond seem ridiculous, Feldman felt he
could undermine the entire Bond industry. Accordingly, the only
major element that survived from any of Hecht's scripts was the
most risible one: that 007 was an inherited codename. It enabled
a comic-book plot strand whereby the Secret Service planned to
confuse the enemy by re-naming several spies 'James Bond'.

Jeremy Duns theorises of Feldman's reasoning for abandoning a
straight Bond picture, '"What's the point? Why would people come

to see it? It has to be something that's different." We're speaking from the hindsight of several people having played Bond. In the public's imagination, Sean Connery was James Bond and James Bond was Sean Connery.'

That the movie featured Peter Sellers was no small matter. Only three years before, he had turned in what is arguably the greatest movie-acting performance of all time with his multiple, massively varied roles in *Dr. Strangelove or: How I Learned to Stop Worrying and Love the Bomb*. Sellers, though, was apparently responsible for many of the things that went wrong in a shoot that – like that of *Cleopatra* before it and *Ishtar* after it – gave the picture a bad smell before it was even released. His bizarre behaviour included refusing to share a set with Orson Welles despite their being in the same scene, turning up late or not at all, commissioning lines from a third party to ensure he hogged the screen and walking out on the film before completion.

The rest of the cast is no less impressive. Long-time matinee idol David Niven is the 'real' Sir James Bond – something that from comments made by Feldman was not unrelated to the fact that Niven's younger self had been Fleming's choice to play his character. Orson Welles takes on the role of Le Chiffre. Woody Allen is 007's nephew Jimmy Bond. Ursula Andress is Vesper Lynd. Even the supporting players are a veritable who's who of British character actors, among them Geoffrey Bayldon, Derek Nimmo and Bernard Cribbins. Also no small deal is that top songwriter of the day Burt Bacharach provides the score (which spun off the hit Bacharach/Hal David single 'The Look of Love' for Dusty Springfield) and that the ultra-successful Herb Alpert and the Tijuana Brass perform the title music. However, a harbinger of disaster is that no fewer than five directors are listed: John Huston, Ken Hughes, Joseph McGrath, Robert Parrish and Val Guest.

The credited screenwriters are Wolf Mankowitz, John Law and Michael Sayers. However, *Catch-22* author Joseph Heller is rumoured to be one of the half-dozen people from whom Feldman commissioned a *Casino Royale* script following Hecht's abrupt death. In addition, both Allen and Sellers are believed to have written some of the sections in which they feature. The upshot of all this is a story sprawling across more than two hours wherein Jimmy Bond, who in the shadow of his uncle feels inadequate with women, hatches a plan to eliminate all men over four-foot-six. Bond is forcibly pulled out of retirement to help a Service in peril. It is at this juncture that, to sow confusion in the enemy ranks, all MI5 (*sic*) operatives are renamed James Bond – including the female ones. Card expert Evelyn Tremble (Sellers) is recruited to be another Bond. In one of the few resemblances to the book, he takes on Le Chiffre at baccarat with the object of cleaning him out. In the final section, everybody dies in an explosion.

An early indicator of what we are in for is the dwelling on the lions that run free in the grounds of Sir James's stately home. It serves no purpose, comedy- or plot-wise. The film is laden with such quirky longueurs. Although the picture buffoonishly goes up hill and down dale for laughs, the humour literally doesn't get better than the statement that M's wig is a 'hairloom'.

It should be pointed out, however, that, when it premiered on 13 April 1967, *Casino Royale* was a box-office success. A big promotional push was given what was a lavish, star-studded production. The success may have been partly caused by a misleading poster that featured a rear shot of a nude, splayed female with a montage of imagery from the film preserving her modesty. However, it is much more likely that, at this point in history, the very name 'James Bond' had an appeal that no amount of bad reviews or poor word of mouth could fully dispel. In Boston, there were riots when people were turned away from a free 4 a.m. screening.

Casino Royale did not succeed in Feldman's objective of destroying the Bond cinema franchise. The only long-term damage it did was to Feldman, whose heart attack during production he himself attributed to the stress of making the movie. His death in 1968 rendered *Casino Royale* his dubious epitaph.

The year's 'real' James Bond movie premiered on 12 June. Unfortunately, *You Only Live Twice* was scarcely less a parody than *Casino Royale*.

Lewis Gilbert took over the directorial reins from Young, for whom *Thunderball* was a finale. The theme song of *You Only Live Twice* is not that well known, and the choice of modish Nancy Sinatra to sing it soon seemed ill-judged when her star waned precipitously, but the music is a lovely lilting affair and Leslie Bricusse's lyric manages to work in the title phrase in an unusually uncontrived manner ('One life for yourself and one for your dreams').

When promoting *Thunderball*, Connery told *Playboy*, '. . . we've reached the limit as far as size and gimmicks are concerned . . . What is needed now is a change of course – more attention to character and better dialogue.' The fact that the opening shot of *Thunderball*'s follow-up is of a NASA craft just about to be swallowed up by a mysterious space vehicle shows that his hopes were in vain.

Perhaps it wouldn't have been so bad had Richard Maibaum been on board. This was the first Bond screenplay lacking his input. That the script was provided by Roald Dahl (Harold Jack Bloom has a credit for 'Additional Story Material') was a matter of a dispensed favour. Primarily a children's novelist, although also known for macabre adult short stories, Dahl had extremely limited cinematic experience. However, he was a friend of Ivar Bryce, whose brother-in-law had been helpful in easing the passage for *Thunderball* location shoots in the Bahamas.

Although most of the film is set in Japan, where signals indicate the appropriated space craft has ended up, the story bears little relation to Fleming's novel. Dahl's claim that the book consists of a travelogue unsuitable for translation to film might be true. However, his screenplay proceeds at the preposterous pitch at which it starts as he whisks Bond from one venue and adventure to another via ludicrous and often contradictory plot turns. Having placed the character in absurd but dangerous positions, he extricates him from them by ridiculous serendipity and preternatural intuition: more than once, an ally zooms up in a car in the nick of time. Meanwhile, the gadgetry is not self-parody but beyond parody: the world in Dahl's eyes is full of car-lifting magnets and trapdoors concealing metal chutes.

The warping of natural behaviour reaches a crescendo when Bond is taken up in the air by a villainess, who then drops a smoke bomb in the plane's cockpit, parachutes out and leaves 007 to what she hopes is a fiery fate. Why she didn't simply kill her captive on the ground and dispense with an aircraft altogether is a question with which Dahl doesn't detain himself.

Dahl also commits a cardinal sin. When Bond is handed a Martini that is 'stirred, not shaken', he responds, 'Perfect.'

There are some good points. Ken Adam excels himself. The villain's lavish HQ located inside a dormant volcano is awe-inspiring even by his sets' standards. We finally get to see Number One, and find out that his name is Blofeld, played by Donald Pleasance. There is a build-up to the reveal of Pleasance's face that is worth it for the shock of his bald pate and the disfiguring scar above and below his right eye.

During the making of *You Only Live Twice*, Connery veritably spat to interviewer Sheila Graham, 'The sooner it's finished the happier I'll be. I don't talk to the producers . . .' Connery had been granted bonuses and 5 per cent of profits by Eon, and Broccoli and Saltzman had in July 1966 even symbolically released him from his contract. That, though, wasn't enough for the actor. 'If they'd had any sense of fairness, they could have made me a partner,' he said. His basic fee of $50,000 for *Goldfinger* was eight times less than what he received for appearing in Hitchcock's *Marnie* earlier the same year. Moreover, he is reported to have received less cumulatively for the first four Bond films than Dean Martin – granted a healthy percentage of the grosses – had for Bond spoof *The Silencers*. Connery's disgruntlement was so severe that it led to his doing something inconceivable: walking away from the biggest movie phenomenon in the world.

The first attempt to further the James Bond literary heritage took a curious form. October 1967 saw the appearance of *The Adventures of James Bond Junior 003½*, 'a story for boys and girls aged 8-14', by R.D. Mascott.

James Bond Jr is not, as might be expected, the son of agent 007, but his nephew. The title therefore doesn't make any more sense than the existence herein of a Bond brother (David) never mentioned by Fleming. Nor that young James Bond has the nickname 003½ conferred on him by his housemaster: why would a civilian know the code number of a secret agent?

Highly unpromising though all this might be, the book is actually quite good. The narrative has dark, adult undertones and a gnarly descriptive style. Its only major problem for a Bond enthusiast is that it really has nothing to do with James Bond. The protagonist may be named after his uncle but he has never met him ('he was always on some mission or other'). Moreover, Young James's investigations of the mysterious goings-on at nearby Hazeley Hall, which involve him uncovering the culprits behind a gold bullion robbery, don't make him any different from any halfway resourceful protagonist from oodles of children's literature.

The 22 July 1967 edition of *The Bookseller* declared, 'Harry Saltzman plans to make a series of television films based on the book.' The series never materialised. Meanwhile, the book went quickly out of print and was seldom reissued.

The identity of the pseudonymous R.D. Mascott was a long-term secret, leading to conjecture involving names such as Roald Dahl and Kingsley Amis. In 2001, it was confirmed by the executors of the estate of the versatile British writer Arthur Calder-Marshall that he was the author.

The first adult Bond 'continuation novel' was commissioned partly because it was felt to be a good way of preserving Bond's pre-eminent status in a sea of imitators. It was Kingsley Amis who provided it after Glidrose had rejected as substandard *Per Fine Ounce*, written by South African thriller writer and former Fleming *Sunday Times* colleague Geoffrey Jenkins.

As the author of *Lucky Jim*, a novel considered to be part of the Angry Young Man literary trend in the UK of the late fifties/early sixties, Amis might be considered an unlikely chronicler of the adventures of a blunt instrument of state and establishment man. Certainly Ann Fleming thought so, predicting in an unpublished review for *The Sunday Telegraph*, 'we shall have a petit bourgeois red-brick Bond . . .' However, not only had his politics lately lurched to the right, Amis had demonstrated both considerable writing gifts and deep knowledge of the character.

Published in March 1968, Amis's *Colonel Sun* was issued under the pseudonym 'Robert Markham'. Raymond Benson explains, 'They thought if they were going to do a lot of books they were going to use the Robert Markham pseudonym for every author. [Also], Kingsley Amis didn't want his own name on it.' This house-name tradition was long-established, albeit in rather low-rent series such as Doc Savage. However, the identity of the real author was no secret, and reviews – and sometimes book covers – freely mentioned Amis's name. The Markham house name was never used again.

The book's action takes place the summer after the events in *The Man with the Golden Gun*. When Bond goes to visit M at his house, he finds himself in the middle of a kidnap plot. Bond evades his pursuers, and then has to follow the trail of the abducted M to Greece, where he slowly realises that Colonel Sun of the People's Liberation Army of China is planning to blow up a meeting of top brass from Soviet and African states and, via the resultant misunderstandings and recriminations, open up the Eastern Mediterranean to Chinese penetration.

It comes as a shock how all of Amis's witty mocking in *The James Bond Dossier* of Fleming's occasional bad writing or plot holes doesn't automatically translate into his being able to write as well as – let alone better than – the James Bond creator. Amis was a far more celebrated author than Fleming, but *Colonel Sun* is simply dull.

There is an additional problem. *Colonel Sun* was the first proof that reading a non-Fleming Bond story is an intrinsically strange experience. In its review, *The Sunday Times* declared that James Bond was so personal to Fleming that Amis's work 'doesn't ring true'. It would ever be thus. However well written or knowledgeable a Bond continuation novel, the reader will never be able to get over a vague feeling of impertinence and inauthenticity. As soon as the opening pages of this one, we feel that Amis is already stepping outside the established margins of the Bond literary canon: such an occurrence as the abduction of the head of the Secret Service seems more the sensational stuff of the Bond films. Fleming often took his character down unexpected, even illogical, avenues of course, but the instinctive feeling is that the creator is the only person who has the right to so transgress. Yet the continuation author is in a bind: attempting to avoid presumption leaves him merely with the option of pastiche, which so often tips over into formula.

Although *Colonel Sun* was a literary event by default, its sales were disappointing. Benson offers, 'I think it was too soon after Fleming's death to have another Bond author.' Aside from the necessarily one-off project *James Bond: The Authorized Biography* by John Pearson and two movie novelisations, there was no further sanctioned literary Bond activity for more than a decade.

Yet, ultimately, Amis's book was the first entry in what became a significant industry. Continuation Bond novels proliferated, as did spin-offs that include books for children about the junior Bond and even narratives from the perspective of Moneypenny. Such books now dwarf Fleming's original corpus by a factor of five.

Adjudging them all invalid for simply second-guessing Fleming would logically mean that a Fleming aficionado could never allow himself to enjoy any of the worthy Bond films not based on Fleming's original tales.

Uncomfortable as it may be to the Fleming fan or the Bond purist, with each passing year Ian Fleming's original Bond stories are increasingly reduced to the status of something akin to a taster for Bond's further adventures across the media.

AN UNCERTAIN ERA

O*n Her Majesty's Secret Service* was the first Bond movie whose soundtrack was in stereo. That, though, was hardly the main change.

At first, Eon toyed with the idea of a plot device wherein Bond underwent plastic surgery because he was too recognisable to his country's enemies. Such an idea sounds ludicrous now, but – the *Casino Royale* farce excepted – the wider public had never seen anyone else as 007. Presenting them with a new actor in the role was a worrying step into the unknown. Only slightly less outlandish was David V. Picker's suggestion of casting professional sportsman John Newcombe. He says, 'I thought, What an interesting idea: terrific-looking tennis player to become a movie star.'

Such bizarre ideas were a manifestation of the uncertainty that hung over James Bond, whether in book or movie form. Within the space of a few years, the Bond world had lost both Fleming and Connery. *Colonel Sun* had seemed to prove that there was no future for Bond novels without Fleming. The uncertainty about the viability of the cinema 007 without Connery would appear to be demonstrated by the fact that, following *You Only Live Twice*, there was a two-and-a-half-year gap before a new Bond film. Finally, after endless auditions and speculation, Eon bit the recasting bullet. It was announced that in *On Her Majesty's Secret Service* one George Lazenby was to inhabit the tuxedo and steer the Aston Martin.

Lazenby was, like Connery before him, neither of fine breeding nor English. Born in 1939 and raised in Australia, he had come to the UK in 1964, where he took up modelling. Although he was successful – reportedly earning £20,000 a year (astronomical for 1968) and becoming fairly recognisable from such things as a commercial for Turkish Delight chocolate – he had never spoken on film before. He was, however, handsome in Bond's conservative style. At a burly six-foot-two, he also looked as if he could handle peril. Also like Connery, he managed to suppress his natural accent enough to convince as a native of the same country as Elizabeth II.

Although some doubted the wisdom of recruiting a novice, Lazenby had been a sufficiently good actor to convince the seasoned Broccoli and Saltzman of his actually non-existent thespian background, something that so tickled Peter Hunt – who had graduated to director – that he said he insisted on him as the new Bond. (An alternative – and not necessarily contradictory – story is that Lazenby convinced Broccoli and Saltzman he was right for the part when during a screen test he accidentally broke the nose of stuntman Uri Borienko.)

Remarkably, with *OHMSS* the slightest of Bond books was turned into arguably the best 007 motion picture of all. The producers took such scenes as the assault on Blofeld's mountain lair and Bond's battle weariness when running from Blofeld's men and drew from them the excitement and pathos Fleming mostly failed to. The smaller scale necessitated by this particular story was complemented by a policy of avoiding the gadgets that Saltzman publicly pronounced 'overdone'. It all meant, ironically and by coincidence, that the newcomer got the classy Bond movie that Sean Connery had always wanted but been denied by two postponements, once because of the need to placate McClory by filming *Thunderball*, the second time because the latter's shooting overran so much it made impossible the filming of Blofeld's mountain lair at a clement time of year.

Lazenby does something different with his gun-barrel sequence, dropping to one knee as he fires his bullet. The wash of blood actually obscures him rather than presents him through a red haze, as had been the case with Connery.

The title sequence is a version of the opening of the Fleming book wherein Bond saves Tracy from suicide. As with Connery's first appearance, we are tantalised about the appearance of the new actor, here shown only in silhouettes and close-ups of his dimpled chin until the point where he introduces himself in the traditional surname-first manner. As an ungrateful Tracy zooms off in her car, Lazenby breaks the fourth wall to remark to the viewer, 'This never happened to the other fella.'

The now-unfamiliar lack of a lyric to the film's theme is due to the fact that John Barry and Leslie Bricusse couldn't find a way to work in that mouthful of a title. Instead, Barry devised an alpine horn-propelled affair that is both distinctive and stirring, if doomed to obscurity in the wider world by its lack of a vocal hook.

Mercifully, Richard Maibaum is back to produce a script proffering the authentic Bond, rather than an outsider's idea of 007. Getting an 'Additional Dialogue' credit is British novelist and Bond fan Simon Raven.

At first, everything seems gauche. Costuming is a problem throughout. Bond is variously shown in white suit, ruffled shirt, knee boots, sleeveless tweed cloak and even a kilt. Admittedly, the last two costumes are part of his Hilary Bray disguise, but they are effete departures from what we imagine Connery ever consenting to. The relationship with Moneypenny is all wrong: it is initially 007 who is the pursuer – even to the point of goosing her – while she is uninterested.

For the very first time, we see 007's office. Bond pulls from a desk drawer Honey Ryder's knife, Red Grant's garrotting watch and the 're-breather' used in *Thunderball*'s underwater sequences. As he does, music from the relevant films plays on the soundtrack. Similar reflectiveness informs the opening credits, in which we see heroes and villains from all of the five previous official Bond movies. Later, a midget cleaner will be heard whistling the title theme of *Goldfinger*. All this anxious self-referentialism is as desperate as the tagline of one of the film's posters, which insisted, 'This man *is* James Bond!'

Lazenby is a slightly stilted actor. However, the fault may be Hunt's: Lazenby has claimed that, apart from the final scene, he was only ever allowed one take. Hunt certainly creates his own problems. While it may be strange that he disdains for a luxuriant feel the fast cutting that, as an editor, he had helped pioneer in Bond films, it's not particularly an issue. What is, though, is his self-conscious and melodramatic employment of echoes, slow motion, jumped frames and incongruous reaction shots.

On the plus side, it is Hunt whom we have to thank for an insistence that the film return the character to his human roots: we see Bond surviving on his wits, not machinery, and reduced at times to a sweaty, exhausted state a world removed from his smugness of recent pictures.

No sooner have we been allowed to see Blofeld's face, than it is changed: Telly Savalas takes over the role from Donald Pleasance, who was thought not physically up to this script's tussles. Although the actors share a bald pate, the scar and the English accent are gone. Such are the exigencies of casting, of course, but, as Bond and Blofeld had met in the previous film, it is ludicrous that Bond's Clark Kent-like Hilary Bray disguise initially fools Blofeld.

Ruby Bartlett makes a refreshing change from Bond's usual cosmopolitan paramours. A pretty but gormless provincial, she is played delightfully by Angela Scoular. By the end, though, Bond has eyes only for Tracy. Few would blame him. Diana Rigg is transcendentally beautiful. Those assuming that the one-time Emma Peel had hopped on the same conveyer belt from *The Avengers* that brought Honor Blackman to the series were, according to Rigg, wide of the mark: she later asserted that her heavyweight thespian grounding had been considered necessary to cover up potential inadequacies in newcomer Lazenby.

The development of Tracy's romance with 007 is depicted in a very un-Bondian sentimental montage against a backdrop of a ballad Barry composed with lyricist Hal David, 'All the Time in the World'. It was a fitting finale to the career of the legendary Louis Armstrong, who sings it exquisitely. Curiously, it was not a hit in 1969, but did make the UK top three in 1994 on the back of its use in a commercial.

Coming hot on the heels of scenes of Bond and Tracy getting

married, the sight of Mrs Bond with a bullet in her forehead is genuinely shocking. Lazenby's horrified double-take at the sight of it is one example of his acting that is unequivocally good.

On Her Majesty's Secret Service premiered on 18 December 1969. The picture was considered by United Artists to be a flop, not least because the Stateside takings of $22.8 million were down by half on *You Only Live Twice*. Although the running time of 140 minutes – the longest Bond so far – reduced the number of showings cinemas could fit into a day, the rumour grew that *OHMSS* was a failure because of Lazenby and that this was the reason he did not return in the role. Interestingly, Broccoli himself never claimed this. In an interview he gave Stan McMann in 1971, Broccoli said, '. . . he's impossible . . . We would have used him again if we felt that he was able to cope with this big success that he had.' Broccoli was continuing to take this line in his autobiography, where he said Lazenby 'ruled himself out of the reckoning by behaving like the superstar he wasn't'.

There doesn't seem any question that Lazenby was a bumptious presence on the *OHMSS* set. Camera operator Alec Mills recalled how on one occasion the actor went horse-riding, keeping an entire crew waiting while simultaneously jeopardising production by risking injury. The 14 January 1970 edition of British newspaper the *Daily Sketch* carried an open letter to Lazenby from Rigg in which she alleged that during the shoot Lazenby's dresser threatened to hand in his notice, three chauffeurs left him within the space of a week, a member of the unit had to be restrained in the action of striking him after a crude outburst against one of the film's actresses and he had reduced Rigg herself to tears by threatening her with violence because of driving he considered inept. One thing Rigg didn't mention is the rumour that, when the last scene of the movie had been completed, she took the satisfaction of spitting in Lazenby's face.

However, when it comes to why Lazenby never appeared again as 007, the actor has always claimed that he was not sacked but walked away. For instance, in a 2010 interview with *popcultureaddict. com*, he said, 'I wanted to do the next one because they offered me a million dollars under the table which is probably ten million today, and I was offered any movie between the Bond movie that I wanted to do. So I looked at my manager and said "What's wrong with that deal?" and he said "No. You'll die doing Bond because it's over. It's finished."' Lazenby cites the ethos of the time for the conviction that Bond was passé. A film that outgrossed *On Her Majesty's Secret Service* in 1969 – and indeed all others – was *Easy Rider*. The biker road pic was the first mainstream counterculture movie and one that constituted a screw-you to the sorts of values that held sway in the milieux traversed by 007. 'Love and peace was in,' Lazenby said. 'Guys running around with suits and guns couldn't get laid. Honest to God. They thought you were a waiter or a cop or something.'

David V. Picker, though, seems to think it was out of the question that Lazenby could have been a long-term Bond. Told that 007 fans have voted *OHMSS* the best-ever Bond movie, he says, 'I couldn't care less whether they think it was the best or not. My interest was making commercial movies.' Of the film's grosses, he says, 'It was awful. They were very, very disappointing. It wasn't like nobody went, but when you're getting a series of movies that each one's getting bigger and bigger and suddenly you change one of the key elements, if not the key element, and the picture goes way the hell back, it's a disaster. If you don't solve the problem, it's over. You're not going to make a second picture with George

Lazenby, that's for sure.' As to Lazenby's claim that he was offered a seven-year contract, Picker shrugs, 'Well he was certainly offered options. But you're not obligated to exercise that option.'

Although he subsequently appeared sporadically in movies and television shows before doing well in real estate, Lazenby's name became a byword for short tenures and missed opportunities – e.g. Pope Benedict XVI is The George Lazenby of Popes; Paul McGann is The George Lazenby of Doctor Whos.

There are arguments to be made that *OHMSS* should have brought the Bond series to a close. One such argument was a temporary one. As the seventies dawned, some were dismissing Bond precepts as *sooo* sixties, an embarrassing reminder of the days when sex and violence were considered shocking.

The other argument was one that survived the novelty of twentieth-century years having a '7' as their third numeral. The Bond formula, it ran, was now overfamiliar, with no potential for profound development or refinement. Moreover, 007's values weren't being questioned only by the demographic of *Easy Rider*. The values of what was then called the Women's Liberation Movement dared to declare that Bond's ethics – which, unlike in the books, included gratuitously slapping around women – were not funny and not clever. It's certainly interesting how sleazy Lazenby now looks in an *OHMSS* scene where he is openly leering at a *Playboy* centrefold as he walks down a corridor.

While there have been good Bond films since, none of them have ever really done anything not seen in the series' first decade. Reconstructed them possibly, streamlined them maybe, reined them in perhaps, but a James Bond movie is a James Bond movie. The closest the series could come to transmutation was, in fact, *On Her Majesty's Secret Service*, the first film in which 007 says 'I love you,' excepting the phrase's deployment as code in *You Only Live Twice*. The human, vulnerable Bond seen in this film could – for his detractors – have ended a faltering franchise on a high and redemptive note.

In 1971, George Lazenby asked Broccoli and Saltzman for another chance as Bond. The producers rebuffed him. However, the return of Sean Connery for the next Bond film, *Diamonds Are Forever*, was just as humiliating for Broccoli and Saltzman as that knockback must have been for Lazenby. Moreover, the process involved in Connery's return was the start of the loss of Eon's autonomy, with it leading to United Artists taking a closer interest in Bond-movie production.

United Artists rejected John Gavin, Eon's choice as the new Bond, and insisted on the return of the only man whom it seemed the public would accept as 007. They did this by finally meeting Connery's pay demands. Broccoli always maintained that Connery's financial beefs were properly with United Artists, not Eon. Yet UA's David V. Picker tells a different story. Astounded to be told by Broccoli and Saltzman that they couldn't make an overture because they were on non-speaking terms with the actor, Picker flew to London for a meeting with Connery's agent Richard Hatton. The latter, Picker says, stated how much he appreciated UA getting involved and that, had Broccoli and Saltzman dealt with his client appropriately before, none of the problems between the parties would have taken place: while repeatedly renegotiating their own deals with UA, Broccoli and Saltzman had been dismissive of Connery's entreaties for a commensurate financial recognition of his role in the franchise's success.

'We weren't even aware of these problems,' says Picker. 'Unless the pictures went way, way over budget, we never got involved until they delivered us the movies and we distributed them. Richard was a gentleman. He was dealing with the producers. And it was only when finally he got so frustrated, as did Sean, that they came to me. I was able to save the franchise to do one more movie by offering him a deal to do pictures where he wasn't Bond so he could protect his own image in film. Harry and Cubby just did not handle it well.'

The deal that Picker agreed secured Connery an advance of $1.25 million (all of which he donated to a Scottish educational trust), 10 per cent of the grosses and funding for two non-Bond film ventures. These terms secured Connery a place in *The Guinness Book of Records* as the world's highest-paid actor. Connery also insisted on the right not to have to talk directly to Broccoli and Saltzman during the making of the movie, although Picker says, 'That was never written down. It was just an understanding. I have no idea whether they talked or not.'

Connery's victory, however, was somewhat pyrrhic. In the four years since his last outing, he had acquired grey hair, lines in his face and a double-chin in profile. His habitual Bond toupee now had to cover a much wider area and was, for the first time, unconvincing. His voice was also starting to acquire that slurred quality that would be much imitated by comedians. Whatever credibility there was to the idea of him either as a man of action or a Lothario was a remnant of the audience's lingering affection for the physical figure he had once represented.

Diamonds Are Forever premiered in the US on 17 December 1971. As with that of *On Her Majesty's Secret Service*, its pre-title sequence teases us a little, not at first showing us the face of the 'new' Bond actor. It contains one of the most famous of the series' lines, when

Bond says, 'There is something I'd like you to get off your chest' as he pulls up a woman's bikini top and strangles her with it until she yields up the whereabouts of Blofeld.

With Charles Gray, we have yet another manifestation of Bond's nemesis. He is a pleasing combination of sophistication (a cigarette holder) and menace (clipped, steely tones and a liquid stare). His appearance in the pre-title sequence seems to contain the film's one reference to Bond's grief over the murder of his wife in the previous film: 'Welcome to hell, Blofeld,' the agent crows as he buries the SPECTRE man in a sulphur bath.

Guy Hamilton returns to the director's chair. Richard Maibaum and Tom Mankiewicz share screenwriting credit. As in the novel, Bond is investigating the smuggling of diamonds, although an additional element is provided by the kidnapping of reclusive tycoon Willard Whyte (clearly modelled on Howard Hughes). In an example of the sort of novelty casting that would become common in the Bond film series, Whyte is played by Jimmy Dean, a country recording artist best known for his 1961 hit 'Big Bad John'. More murder and mayhem are attached to the diamond pipeline courtesy of Mr Wint (Bruce Glover) and Mr Kidd (Putter Smith) systematically eliminating elements of it.

These are certainly strong screen presences: Wint is effeminate but sinister; Kidd is hairy, buck-toothed and lugubrious. However, although the frankness about their sexuality was progressive at the time because risqué, it now comes across as reactionary. Their hand-holding in their first scene had the clearly intended effect of causing cinema audiences to whistle and whoop derisively.

The film is pacey and there are adroit segues between scenes, but before long we realise we are being wrenched back to pre-*OHMSS* Bond. A glib tone and nonsensical switchbacks mean we once again never worry for Bond's safety. The supposedly secret agent actually exploits his fame by slipping his Playboy Club membership card into a deceased villain's pocket, leading Tiffany Case to exclaim, 'My God, you just killed James Bond!' Blofeld turns out to be alive: Bond had killed a plastic-surgery-enhanced double, who himself has an exact double. Blofeld constitutes the end of the diamond trail, utilising the gems to concentrate laser beams from space to destroy submarines and missiles. All of this in a society that had only just developed the pocket calculator.

The producers and studio clearly felt that this stuff was what the public felt they had been deprived of last time out, but no one is going to be moved the way many were at the climax of the Lazenby film.

One thing the film does do well is mock the trashiness and cheesiness that then predominated in American culture. The gaudiness of Las Vegas, the insularity of many US citizens, the predominance of violence and the mirthlessness of comedy performers are all aspects of the States put under a merciless spotlight. That said, the film buys into the same culture's dramatic benefits with its scenes involving squealing tyres and whooping police sirens. One of the car chases contains an iconic Bond moment wherein 007 manipulates a vehicle through a narrow gap by driving on one side's wheels only; who knew you could do that by simply barking 'Lean over' at your companion?

Despite the fact that the coda is rather grisly – Kidd is immolated – the Bond series was beginning to lose its aura of sadism. Sam Peckinpah's blood-drenched Westerns and the cruelty-and-rape-punctuated likes of *Straw Dogs*, *A Clockwork Orange* and *Dirty Harry* (all 1971) were making even the worst Bond violence seem tame. This process was partly assisted by the increasingly light tone during the tenure of the next James Bond actor, but critics and cinemagoers in any case gradually became aware that it was never that prevalent. Across the history of the Bond series, sadistic violence or exultation in death – the killing of Dent in *Dr. No*, the torching of Kidd, the pressure-chamber scene in *Licence to Kill*, the eye-gouging in *Spectre* – can be counted on the fingers of one hand.

Diamonds Are Forever has a title song deserving of a better movie: Shirley Bassey gives her usual ultra-committed performance in a slinky creation (lyric by Don Black) that is one of the best known Bond songs.

During the summer of 1972, American cinemas played host to no less than a James Bond triple-bill: *Dr. No*, *From Russia with Love* and *Goldfinger*. United Artists and Eon Productions would seem to have been milking the last drops of revenue from Bond films while they remained a cinema-only phenomenon. The momentous first television screening of a James Bond motion picture occurred on 17 September 1972 as part of ABC's *Sunday Night Movie* strand.

ABC had agreed to pay $2.5 million each for the right to broadcast the seven Eon Bond films. Some have noted that the timing of the decision to sell TV rights occurred towards the end of the biggest upheaval in the franchise's history: the departure of Connery, the relative box-office failure of Lazenby and the sticking-plaster solution of the ageing Connery's temporary return. The series had, it could be argued, been losing its shine for the best part of half a decade. Roger Moore was due to start shooting his first Bond film the following month. Should the new 007 actor not prove a hit with the public, there were all sorts of dire consequences foreseeable. One was that the franchise might come to an end; another was that Bond TV rights would cease to command a theoretical premium price.

Those cineastes who felt television a vulgar medium were provided grist to their mill when ABC elected to make their inaugural Bond broadcast not the logical *Dr. No* but *Goldfinger*. Similar ammunition was provided by the cuts made to the third 007 flick. It being an era prior to the liberalisation of television content, the transfer from large to small screen meant a fundamental toning-down of sex and violence. In this case, this included the excision of the key moment when Oddjob is electrocuted. Moreover, the audience were denied an integral part of the 007 movie experience via the arbitrary omission of the gun-barrel sequence.

It would be another two years before Bond was seen on TV again, when ABC screened a bowdlerised *From Russia with Love*. From here on, though, Bond films would become a fairly regular ingredient of US TV, if in random sequence and with formatting that often outraged purists (*On Her Majesty's Secret Service* was screened across two evenings with scenes rejigged and narration added).

James Bond didn't reach the television screens of his home country until 1975. Says Picker, 'Well, British television doesn't like to pay a lot of money for movies.' ITV broadcast *Dr. No* on 28 October, repeated it a few months later and squeezed in three further films (in consecutive sequence) before the release of *The Spy Who Loved Me* in 1977, at which point they were contractually obliged to pause: they were not allowed to broadcast Bond when he was in the cinemas. Britain being more permissive than America, Bond films were subjected to less censorship by ITV. Moreover, unlike ABC, who tended to show Bond late in the evening, ITV saw Bond as family entertainment. This strategy was vindicated when the British television premiere of *Live and Let Die* on 20 January 1980 at 7.45 p.m. attracted an audience of 23.5 million, which makes it the most-watched film in British broadcasting history.

The prestige of Bond television broadcasts would be maintained for more than a decade after the first ABC broadcast. VHS or Betamax versions of Bond films would not be available to the public for rental until the early eighties, and not until the late eighties for purchase. Recording the TV broadcasts was hardly an option for most when blank video tapes retailed at something approaching £20.

Nowadays, before alighting on terrestrial television, Bond films go through lucrative tiers of extra-cinematic distribution not yet invented or popularised in the seventies: video/DVD, satellite, cable and pay-per-view. Once they do trickle down to that free-to-view plateau, their multiple repeats acquire them the immortality of moving wallpaper and a pleasant, lazy viewing option.

Embracing television did none of the long-term harm to Bond some at UA and Eon might have feared. Cinema audiences for 007 have held up even as revenue from television broadcasts daily pour in from around the world.

The process has also served to give 007 an enhanced cultural presence. Up until the 1970s and his arrival in living rooms, Bond was far less visible a figure than other fictional icons such as Sherlock Holmes, Tarzan, the Saint and even Napoleon Solo. The age of Bond ubiquity had dawned.

Asked if he is serious in his contention that his intervention with Sean Connery's agent saved the Bond franchise, David V. Picker says, 'Absolutely.' He uses the same word in response to the question of whether United Artists would have been happy for

Connery to make another Bond. He adds, 'He certainly could've. He chose not to . . . People would have accepted Sean as long as he wanted to play the role. And you know what you do if you're smart? You make him a little older.' Connery, however, seems to have simply treated the project as an exorcism and a quick money-spinner before moving on.

By now, Eon were evidently long past the point where they would consider only an unknown to play Bond. The success of the series made it a role that any actor would be honoured to be offered on a long-term basis.

Michael Billington, best known as Colonel Paul Foster in the Gerry Anderson TV series *UFO*, had been approached about playing Bond prior to *On Her Majesty's Secret Service*. For *Live and Let Die* he was given a screen test and a nod from his agent, and was 'stunned' when he failed to get the part. The closest he would ever come was his appearance as Soviet agent Sergei Barsov in *The Spy Who Loved Me* (1977).

With Billington rejected, the option of John Gavin – who'd already signed on the dotted line before Connery's return – was due to be picked up. Suave and handsome, Gavin certainly looked the part, even despite turning forty in 1971. He was also, unlike Lazenby, of vast thespian experience, having appeared in motion pictures since the late fifties, including roles in *Psycho* and *Spartacus*. He would, though, have to work on his English accent: he was a native of Los Angeles.

According to some, the only reason that Roger Moore and not Gavin became the next Bond is that Harry Saltzman insisted on an Englishman in the role – which, in point of fact, was a first. Gavin was paid off, his presumed disappointment assuaged by a rumoured $100,000 for precisely no work.

Not only had Roger Moore been considered by Eon for *Dr. No* and by Feldman for *Casino Royale*, something more concrete had been in the offing following *You Only Live Twice*. Had that movie been followed, as originally planned, by *The Man with the Golden Gun*, Moore would have been the new 007. As it transpired, the next film was delayed by military violence in the intended shooting location of Cambodia. By the time the decision was made to change the adaptation to *On Her Majesty's Secret Service*, Moore was engaged elsewhere. Eon and Moore were finally in sync for *Live and Let Die*.

Moore was born in 1927 in Stockwell, where he was raised. Despite his 'toff' tones, he is from working-class stock, the son of a policeman. Asked why his accent bears no trace of 'Sarf Lahndan', he says, 'I went to RADA where we were all taught to speak without a regional accent.' However, he appends, 'I don't know if I sound posh. I think of it as more of a flat accent.'

Moore began his career in movies, but his first proper success came on television, both sides of the Atlantic. *Ivanhoe, The Alaskans* and *Maverick* preceded a seven-year stint on *The Saint*. His being cast as Bond would instantly have struck many as somehow logical. Not so much because he was handsome, quintessentially English (or at least of the refined, ostensibly upper-middle-class stripe most non-Britons consider to be quintessentially English) and tall (six-foot-two, like his predecessors). Rather it was because his roles in *The Saint* and then *The Persuaders!* made him seem to the public a fixture of an amorphous action hero/espionage industry. Nonetheless, Broccoli had to appoint him over the misgivings of both Saltzman and United Artists. However, their suggestions – Burt Reynolds (mentioned not for the first time) and Steve McQueen – were risible. The studio even made an approach to

Clint Eastwood, who – to his credit – laughed at the idea, regardless of the honour conferred.

Moore was already forty-five on his appointment – making him four years older than Connery had been when *Diamonds Are Forever* was released. 'It didn't really bother me,' Moore shrugs of his advanced years. 'I was fit and looked after myself.' With regard to his approach to 007, he says, 'I read the books, of course, and the only line that stuck out was when Fleming wrote Bond didn't particularly like killing . . . I took that with me in my interpretation of the character. My Bond would rather kiss than kill.'

Moore's rather uncomplicated position as regards his profession is illustrated by his response to the question of whether he was hamstrung by simultaneously trying not to resemble Sean Connery and his own portrayal of Simon Templar. 'I play everything the same, so there's no great planning into making my characters different,' he bluntly states. 'I was conscious of not speaking with a Scots accent, and Guy Hamilton deliberately avoided having my Bond say lines associated with Sean's Bond, such as ordering a vodka martini, shaken, not stirred. I never said that line in any of my seven films. But otherwise I approached it like I did everything else.'

Richard Maibaum was never too impressed by Roger Moore. 'One of my reservations about Roger is that he is not the physical superman Sean made you believe Bond was,' he said. Maibaum also detested Moore's approach to the role: 'He does what I consider unforgivable: he spoofs himself and he spoofs the part.' On top of that was Moore's penchant for changing Maibaum's carefully crafted dialogue for double entendres.

As Maibaum was unavailable to script Moore's debut, he didn't have to endure this immediately. The screenwriting job on *Live and Let Die* went to Tom Mankiewicz.

Live and Let Die was released Stateside on 27 June 1973, not reaching the UK until just over a week later. This was symbolic, as it was the second successive Bond film set in the United States. In *Diamonds Are Forever*, the milieu of screaming sirens and gigantic car bonnets just made it another Bond-movie exotic backdrop, but a return to the same territory so quickly suggested something depressing and nationally emasculating: Americanisation of a property.

One could argue that the motivation to adapt to the screen the American-set *Live and Let Die* was not to make Bond just another *de facto* US cop drama but to hop a ride on the Blaxploitation bandwagon. However, that in itself was viewed by some as depressing, as it marked the first time that James Bond movies were following a trend rather than setting them. Eon decided that, because *Live and Let Die* was a Fleming story inordinately populated with black Americans, it would provide the ideal vehicle with which to join the trend kick-started by the jive-talking, Afro-sporting likes of *Sweet Sweetback's Baadasssss Song* and *Shaft*.

For the first time in the gun-barrel sequence, Bond is hatless. Moore strides purposefully and, when he spins, places his left hand on the wrist of his shooting arm. For the first time since (technically) *From Russia with Love*, 007 does not appear in the pre-title sequence. Instead, we have a montage involving the murders of three Secret Service agents.

Paul McCartney had clearly forgiven Eon for the *Goldfinger* line that dismissed the listenability of his previous ensemble. The title song is performed by his group Wings, the first occasion a *bona fide* rock act had been commissioned to provide a Bond theme. McCartney's weaving melody, adroit incorporation of the title phrase, unexpected reggae bridge and pseudo-improvisation (a little 'Say!' just before the line 'Live and let die') are all delightful, with the only blemish the tautologous 'in which we live in'. George Martin gave the song the orchestral swells appropriate for a Bond theme, and as a consequence was given the job of scoring the movie in the absence for the first time of John Barry (then busy working on stage musical *Billy*). Apart from a couple of gauche moments when his music works against the action, Martin does a good job.

Our first sight of Moore is in bed with an Italian lovely. He will later seduce Rosie Carver (Gloria Hendry), making her the first black Bond girl, before – conforming to the three-conquests grid then a staple of 007 films – moving on to female lead Solitaire (Jane Seymour). While his macho credentials are thus established, it's noticeable how much softer a Bond is Moore. His suits are of a lighter shade, he wears leather gloves, he is less muscly and less hairy. He seems slightly ridiculous in Harlem, where Connery – honky or no – would not have. Even the fact that Moore has light-brown hair and is uncommonly polite somehow makes him seem less of a man, unfair and irrational as that may be. He is undeniably handsome (albeit, like Lazenby, with a distracting mole). However, he is not smoulderingly sexy like Connery at his peak, but, rather, a smoothie, and furthermore a smoothie who – courtesy of the over-ripened tone of Moore's voice and his propensity to use the term 'darling' – can too easily tip over into being a smarmy creep.

Moore favours big cigars over cigarettes and bourbon over Martinis. He doesn't deliver the 'Bond, James Bond' introduction until twenty-three minutes into the two-hour film, when he meets Solitaire. (He tries to deliver the line to Mr Big as well and is met with the response, 'Names is for tombstones, baby.')

At first, it seems depressingly clear that this will be another Bond film whose precepts are that of the comic book. In the pre-title sequence, one of the agents is implausibly killed in the rarefied environs of a United Nations session, and furthermore by the method of transmitting something unspecified into his translation earphones. Mr Big (Yaphet Kotto) is a criminal intent on driving the Mafia out of the heroin business before moving in himself. However, the street value of the heroin with which he intends to flood the ghettos free of charge is over a billion dollars, making him similar to the spaceship-owning SPECTRE in already having so much money that one wonders why there is a need to strive so hard for more. An initial sense of Bond not being in peril is created by his reaction when Mr Big's goons are set to take him out and waste him: he smugly intones to Solitaire, 'Now, promise you'll stay right there. I shan't be long.'

On the plus side, Mr Big is the first freestanding movie Bond villain since Goldfinger. Moreover, things start hotting up in the final third. The moment when Bond stands on an artificial island surrounded by encroaching crocodiles is genuinely creepy and suspenseful. It's also amusing: its unexpected conclusion has him simply trotting to safety over some of the half-submerged creatures.

The drama of Bond fleeing the baddies in New Orleans via speedboat is counterpointed by the comedic outrage of the obese redneck sheriff J.W. Pepper as he watches him and his pursuers. As with Rosie Carver, one suspects that Pepper has been inserted to counter accusations of racism that might result from the predominance of black baddies, but it is a funny and a wonderfully over-the-top performance by Clifton James. The actual chase – involving speedboats working up enough velocity to sail over obstacles and across land – is skilfully and entertainingly directed by Guy Hamilton.

The coda action takes place on a train. The ending is new Bond territory. Baron Samedi (Geoffrey Holder) is in this version of the story a separate villain, not Mr Big's rumoured alter ego. Earlier in the film, he had mysteriously evaporated under Bond's gunfire. Now he is shown sitting on the train's bumper laughing in his inimitable maniacal way – and breaking the fourth wall by raising his hat to the audience. It provides a concluding note of ambiguity where previously Bond had always been shown as unmistakeably the victor. It's also something that belongs more in a supernatural movie.

Another difference in tone appears earlier. When 007 hijacks an aeroplane containing a flying pupil, the latter's 'Holy shit!' is the first profanity in a Bond film.

Some critics and fans detested Moore's softer Bond, but the picture's rentals of nearly $50 million meant it had done better than *Diamonds Are Forever*, even if the takings were still skewed away from the all-important US market towards the 'Rest of the World'. In short, *Live and Let Die* indicated that a recently creaking franchise had life in it yet.

With a proposed junior Bond novel series having fallen flat and the first adult Bond continuation novel also having been a failure, Glidrose Publications – as they were renamed in September 1972 – took several years to decide how to further exploit the valuable brand name they possessed. When they did, they used lateral thinking.

John Pearson had not only published the authorised *The Life of Ian Fleming* (1966) but had a high profile via his bestselling

Kray Twins biography *The Profession of Violence* (1972) and his award-winning novel *Gone to Timbuctoo* (1962). His *James Bond: The Authorized Biography* (some later editions spelt 'authorized' with an 's' and/or appended to the title '*of 007*') was published in August 1973.

The book – which began as a series of articles in *The Sunday Times* – resembles a grandiose version of what is today called fanfic. It mingles Pearson's anecdotes of meeting the real Bond (aged fifty-two, at odds with the Secret Service and about to be married to Honeychile Ryder (*sic*)) with vignettes depicting both Bond's childhood and his adult adventures in the field. Pearson also portrays Bond as an operative in the wartime missions guided by Ian Fleming.

Although few knew Fleming and the literary Bond better than Pearson, the experiment doesn't quite work. Not only is the prose made disjointed by its episodic structure, but there is a feeling of insubstantiality: the vignettes rarely assume the stature of even short stories. Moreover, the previously discussed presumption issue is intensified. For instance, the author takes it upon himself to pinpoint Bond's home as being in Wellington Square (one of a few real-life King's Road-adjacent candidates for 007's domicile) and even to project from Kissy Suzuki's pregnancy a son called James.

The book did reasonably well sales-wise, but, with Pearson spurning what he has said were vaguely held-out offers for him to write Bond continuation novels, 007's literary adventures were subsequently put into abeyance again.

At UA's insistence, Roger Moore's second Bond film followed quickly after his entrée, *The Man with the Golden Gun* premiering in both the UK and US on 19 December 1974.

Some reviews of his first Bond film were scathing. 'Will James Bond live on in the 1970s?' asked John Russell Taylor of *The Times*. 'Not much longer, if this episode is anything to go by.' Moore was unconcerned. 'I tried not to read what the critics wrote, as for every good review you're bound to get two bad or indifferent ones,' he reasons. 'I was employed to do a job, and they brought me back to do more after the first film, so nothing else bothered me.'

Although John Barry is back, the music is uninspired, a casualty, Barry claimed, of the UA-dictated short turnaround time. The title theme's Don Black-penned lyric is no more risible than that of *Goldfinger* but its instrumentation bops along like the introduction to a cheap made-for-TV movie. Matters are not helped by the fact that Lulu has nothing like Shirley Bassey's range.

Guy Hamilton was directing his final Bond picture. The script saw a reversal of the *Diamonds Are Forever* situation: Tom Mankiewicz wrote the first draft but was replaced by a returning Richard Maibaum.

Bond is removed from duties after a golden bullet embedded with '007' arrives at the headquarters of the Secret Service. With the tacit approval of M, Bond sets off to find Scaramanga so as to enable the resumption of his current mission of protecting a scientist called Gibson, who may have the answer to the world's energy problems – a topical issue in the wake of recent muscle-flexing by OPEC countries. The two stories implausibly dovetail when Scaramanga turns out to have been hired to kill Gibson.

Once again, the Bond series jumps on a media bandwagon, this time kung fu. Accordingly, the Jamaican setting of the book is swapped for Far East locations Macau, Hong Kong and Thailand. Although devotees will insist the early-seventies craze for martial arts was created by Bruce Lee, in point of fact most of the people who were swept up in the phenomenon – kids – couldn't get into Lee's X-rated films and were instead fans of the ABC television series *Kung Fu* starring David Carradine. *The Man with the Golden Gun*, therefore, was the first opportunity for many children of the period to see martial arts on the big screen. The prism through which they were able to view it, though, was a distorted one. Moore does not look physically up to the action as he is forced to participate in contests in a Hong Kong dojo.

Mary Goodnight (Britt Ekland) is one of Bond's squeezes in this film, and the distaff Secret Service agent plays quite a prominent role, even though she's often portrayed as a bubble-head. The other paramour is Andrea Anders (Maud Adams), and it transpires that she, not Scaramanga, had sent the golden bullet: she had wanted Bond – the only man whom Scaramanga speaks of as his equal – to rescue her from the gilded cage of her concubine state. Why she hadn't simply sent Bond a message instead is just one of an inordinate number of plot illogicalities.

It's not the expected Baron Samedi who is given an encore from *Live and Let Die* but Sheriff J.W. Pepper, who happens to be on holiday in Thailand with his wife. Pepper's recognition of Bond would have been bewildering to those who hadn't caught the previous film. In fact, when he states, 'You're that secret agent – that English secret agent, from England!' some will have assumed it merely a function of the fact that everybody on the planet now seems to know who 007 is. ('Your reputation precedes you,' a receptionist for the man who makes Scaramanga's bullets says to Bond.)

If the story is laughable, the high production values and quality stunts continue to impress. The highlight of the latter category is a remarkable river crossing where Bond makes a car perform a spectacular mid-air spin, even if it's slightly undermined by being accompanied by a buffoonish drooping sound effect.

Christopher Lee brings star quality to the role of Scaramanga, as well as a family connection: he was a step-cousin to Ian Fleming. His character's third nipple is impressively generated by the makeup department.

Bond doesn't always come across as likeable. The way he shoves a chid beggar into a river is distasteful, as is the extent to which he slaps around Andrea for information, as is his scorn for the politesse of martial-arts combat, but those things are nothing compared with the way he starts cracking jokes at Scaramanga just seconds after finding out that the latter has murdered Andrea. Some or all of this is apparently due to Moore deciding to harden up his Bond, but this new persona is scarcely less contemptible than the lounge lizard of his debut.

The Man with the Golden Gun has few fans. It was critically derided, and its worldwide rentals of $37.2 million made it the least successful entry since *On Her Majesty's Secret Service*. However, the Bond producers would shortly have worse problems than that with which to grapple. The year after the film's release, Cubby Broccoli and Harry Saltzman launched into a bitter legal dispute.

The enmity between them was longstanding. They had alternated main production duties on Bond films since *You Only Live Twice*. 'The tension between them towards the end of their partnership was not pleasant,' Roger Moore recalls of Broccoli and Saltzman. 'It boiled down to Cubby being content making Bond films, whereas Harry wanted to do more, and didn't really know when to stop.' Since he'd helped instigate it, Broccoli had devoted himself exclusively to the Bond franchise. The only exceptions were *Call*

Me Bwana with Saltzman and *Chitty Chitty Bang Bang*, which he produced on his own and which might almost be attributed to Broccoli's personal fondness for Fleming. Saltzman had produced worthy films such as the Harry Palmer trilogy, but his non-Bond ventures had left him $20 million in the red.

Broccoli later claimed that Saltzman had broken the terms of their partnership agreement by pledging to Swiss banks 100 per cent of Danjaq to cover liabilities racked up by his non-Bond production work. As ever, Broccoli's claims are open to question. Saltzman's assistant, Sue St John, painted a less sinister picture: Saltzman had wanted to buy the company Technicolor and had simply pledged his own Danjaq shares to his creditors as collateral on the deal. Ultimately, Saltzman tried to sell his Danjaq shares but matters were complicated by the fact that both Broccoli and United Artists had a veto on the parties who would thereby become partners in Bond-film productions. Meanwhile, Saltzman – presumably for reasons of personal hostility – didn't want to sell his half to Broccoli. As a consequence, the alternative story goes, the debt went unpaid for so long that Saltzman's creditors attempted to take control of Danjaq.

The closing credits of *The Man with the Golden Gun* might have read 'James Bond will return in The Spy Who Loved Me', but over the course of much of the next two-and-a-half years – as a follow-up failed to materialise – that began to seem more hope than promise.

DING-*DONG*!

In December 1975, the impasse in Bond film world was ended when United Artists bought Saltzman's 50 per cent share in Danjaq.

Saltzman subsequently rather dropped off the public radar. He would be reduced to a position of penury – literally having to sell his wife's jewellery – although was probably less concerned with that than his wife's terminal illness. His name appeared in the credits of just two further films: *Nijinsky* (1980, on which he was executive producer) and *Time of the Gypsies* (1988, co-producer). He concentrated instead on the chairmanship duties of his theatrical production company H. M. Tennent. He died of a heart attack in September 1994, by which time Saltzman had made his peace with Broccoli.

The fact that his name has not appeared in a Bond film's credits for over four decades has artificially diminished Saltzman's role in the franchise's success. Not only did he do the original deal with Fleming, it should be noted that in the early days of the film series he seems to have been by far the more visible and influential of the two partners. Certainly, from Fleming's discussion of the burgeoning Bond motion-picture industry in his private correspondence, one could be forgiven for not knowing that Broccoli was even involved.

Although Broccoli now had to carry the entire production burden of a franchise, from Roger Moore's point of view the development was a good thing. 'When Cubby resumed production alone, there was a very different, more relaxed atmosphere,' he says. 'It was largely the same crews, so there wasn't any huge overnight change in that respect. Cubby just wanted to make the biggest and best film he could and that's all we focused on.' With *The Spy Who Loved Me* – whose London premiere was on 7 July 1977 – many felt Broccoli achieved that objective.

That Broccoli opted to adapt *The Spy Who Loved Me* was surprising. The novel had something of a bad smell because of Fleming's known displeasure with it, but, more importantly, the author had contractually insisted that it not be adapted. This meant that for the first time – notwithstanding the Bond films' increasing departure from their source novels – Eon were working from scratch. According to Broccoli, Eon even had to negotiate long and hard with the Fleming estate just to get the right to use the title.

Broccoli claimed that a total of fourteen writers were ultimately used. Among them are reputed to be Sterling Silliphant, John Landis and Anthony Burgess – an Oscar winner, a future superstar director and an acclaimed literary novelist respectively, a breathtaking list of talent that seems merely to demonstrate how difficult Eon were finding the unparalleled situation of not being able to lift anything from a Fleming novel. Broccoli claimed that he and his wife Dana rewrote the whole story with all the scripts spread out on the floor. None of which explains why the only screenwriters listed in the credits are Maibaum and Christopher Wood. Nor why Gerry Anderson was given an out-of-court settlement after claiming similarities with a treatment he had once devised at the request of Saltzman for an adaptation of *Moonraker*. Nor why there is an almost farcical overarching resemblance to *You Only Live Twice*, also helmed by this film's director, Lewis Gilbert. Moreover, Tom Mankiewicz claimed that he did a 'big rewrite' but agreed not to claim credit because Broccoli was worried that an additional non-Briton officially working on the picture would mean it was no longer eligible for Eady Plan benefits.

Eon had taken the peculiar decision to film Moore's first two Bond films in standard aspect ratio, something they had spurned since *Goldfinger*. The reversion to widescreen for *The Spy Who Loved Me* necessitated a new gun-barrel sequence. This time Moore wears a tuxedo. The sequence would be used through the rest of Moore's tenure, although the background colour would change each time.

The pre-title sequence is possibly the most fondly remembered of them all. With both Soviet and British submarines going missing, the respective powers call up their best agents. In a genuinely delightful plot twist, Russia's Agent Triple-X turns out not to be the hairy-backed man in bed to whom we cut but the woman underneath him, Major Anya Amasova of the KGB (Barbara Bach). Meanwhile, Bond is recalled from a mission in Austria. He flees Russian pursuers in an Austrian ski chase before tumbling off a cliff to his apparently certain death. Several silent seconds pass as his tiny figure spins in the air. Then the 'James Bond

Theme' blares in triumph as a parachute with a Union Jack design unfurls from his backpack. The combination of surprise, relief and patriotism (tied in with that year's Silver Jubilee celebrations) had some British audiences whooping as if American. It's both over the top and stirring, and in that sense is much like the rest of the film.

The title is not worked into the script in any way. It also seems to find its way into the theme song only as an afterthought, featuring not in the title or the chorus but in a verse. 'Nobody Does It Better' – sung by Carly Simon, written by Carole Bayer Sager (lyric) and Marvin Hamlisch (music) – is additionally a modest pop tune rather than a widescreen anthem. It shouldn't, therefore, work, yet it is very pleasing.

It was, though, a last hurrah for Bond themes – a shocking fact considering that three-and-a-half decades have since passed. The reasons for the decline of the Bond theme are varied – the recruitment of fashionable pop stars who insisted on co-writing, the departure of John Barry, the adoption of cacophonous or soporific modern recording technology, the self-consciousness of young composers weaned on Bond . . . Bizarrely, the one person during this period to manage to write a Bond theme of high quality had not actually been recruited to do so: Spandau Ballet's pulsating 1983 hit 'Gold' – composed by the band's guitarist/keyboardist Gary Kemp – showed far more understanding of the prerequisites of a Bond theme than any of the latter-day limp film anthems.

Hamlisch also provided the film's score, as John Barry, in a dispute with the UK taxman, was refusing to work in his home country. Hamlisch had scored the ultra-successful stage musical *A Chorus Line* and garnered Oscar nominations for his music for *The Way We Were* and *The Sting*. However, his work here is a little ham-fisted, and his choice of pulsating rock instrumentation not in Bondian tradition, Wings notwithstanding.

Maurice Binder's title sequence consists of silhouettes of naked females doing gymnastics on the barrels of giant guns, leading to many split-second semi-convictions in cinema seats of having seen something explicit. These titles are also notable for being the first to feature Bond himself.

Shipping magnate Karl Stromberg (Curt Jürgens) is swallowing up armed submarines with his supertanker *The Liparus*. He lives in a gargantuan submersible sea platform called *Atlantis*, from where he intends to use the captured subs to destroy corrupt civilisation and start afresh on the seabed. Strangely, his webbed hand is easily missed and its implications not explored.

Stromberg was originally Ernst Stavro Blofeld but, in yet another hiccup in an extended production, the reappearance of SPECTRE had to be abandoned as a consequence of a legal challenge by Kevin McClory, who pointed out that the ten-year licence that he had granted Eon to use the evil organisation had now elapsed. Also expired was the ten-year period in which McClory had agreed with Eon that he would refrain from remaking *Thunderball*. He was currently actively developing a new Bond project, provisionally called *Warhead*.

The syndicate that had underpinned all but one Connery movie would now not be seen in an official Bond picture until both McClory and Broccoli were long dead. It's quite surprising to realise that, although SPECTRE is felt by many to be synonymous with 007, Blofeld never crossed swords with Bond in an Eon production over a period of three decades and that the character as played by Roger Moore, Timothy Dalton and Pierce Brosnan never once mentioned him.

Stromberg's henchman is Jaws (Richard Kiel), a silent behemoth (his paw looks huge on Moore's face in fight scenes) with a gimmick weapon (teeth made completely of steel – perhaps the faintest echo from the book of the villain Horror, who had steel-capped teeth). The clownish allusion in Jaws' name to Spielberg's blockbuster movie of two years previously is a gesture of deference one can't imagine occurring in the series' triumphalist early days.

The doe-eyed, softly spoken Agent XXX is not particularly physical, getting male minions to do her violence for her. She would have been made a much steelier character in a modern Bond picture. Bond and Anya are instructed by M and his Soviet counterpart, General Gogol (Walter Gotell), to team up to deal with the common threat. Their screwball-comedy romance comes to an end when Anya realises it was Bond who killed her lover: he was one of the skiers chasing 007 in Austria.

Their confrontation has a real pathos even before Anya announces that, as soon as their joint mission is concluded, she will kill him. Bond seethes, 'In our business, Anya, people get killed. We both know that. So did he. It was either him or me.' It is Moore's finest piece of acting in the series, and proof that he was not the mannequin many – including himself – have posited him as. Asked if he would have liked to have been able to demonstrate his range in Bond films more often, he responds, 'Well it's always nice to have more than just the one line of, "My name is Bond, James Bond" to say.' However, he adds, 'Though I'm not sure they'd have wanted to stretch my acting range too much.'

A returning Ken Adam constructed the largest soundstage in history to accommodate the submarine bays of *The Liparus*, on which Bond and the crew of the captured British submarine do gun battle with Stromberg's men. The set was not, as is the norm, pulled down after shooting wrapped but remains standing as the 007 Stage of Pinewood Studios, albeit rebuilt twice after fires. Rentals from other productions meant that it eventually paid for itself.

Among the gadgets in the film are a Lotus Esprit car that is already futuristic-looking without turning, as it does, into an undersea vessel equipped with missile-firing capabilities. It became the most iconic Bond car – and most sought-after Bond toy – since the Aston Martin DB5. It was designed by Derek Meddings, a special-effects supervisor who specialised in miniature models – he was a veteran of Gerry Anderson's various Supermarionation TV series – and who had joined the Bond/Eon family during the production of *Live and Let Die*.

For the first time, the American market proved receptive to a Roger Moore Bond movie. The grosses of *The Spy Who Loved Me* were the highest of any Bond film to date, even if not inflation-adjusted. For Broccoli, the film proved that he could carry the franchise forward on his own. For the public, *The Spy Who Loved Me* confirmed finally that Roger Moore was now properly, unequivocally James Bond.

That same year, another attempt was made to continue the James Bond literary heritage. It wasn't, however, the idea of Glidrose. Instead it was Eon who had the audacious notion of commissioning a novelisation of the film of *The Spy Who Loved Me*.

Novelisations were big business at the time. With the video industry in its infancy, the only way for most of the public to re-experience a recent movie was to go and see it again at the cinema. Consequently, every major motion picture of the time had a tie-in book. That is, every major motion picture not based on a literary work.

That would, at first glance, rule out *The Spy Who Loved Me* as a candidate for such treatment. A second glance, however, would reveal the fact that *The Spy Who Loved Me* was not based on a book. It being the first Bond movie not even to retain a fragment (possibly excepting Jaws) of its theoretical source, it made a sort of sense – albeit a convoluted and mercenary one – to issue a book with the careful title *James Bond, The Spy Who Loved Me*. Unusually for a novelisation, it was issued in hardback, albeit in the same year as a paperback edition.

Peter Janson-Smith, then chairman of Glidrose, recalled to *commanderbond.net*, 'We had no hand in that other than we told the film people that we were going to exert our legal right to handle the rights in the books. They chose Christopher Wood . . . and they decided what he would be paid.' Speaking to *universalexports. net*, Wood himself said of the task of novelising the film he had co-written, 'At first I was daunted by the idea of . . . trying to combine Fleming with the much larger-than-life movies . . .' However, 'Writing the books gave me the chance to put in things that had not appeared in the movies – and improve (I hope) some of the things that had.'

Reaction from fandom was favourable, while the wider buying public sent the paperback into the top ten of the UK best-sellers list.

The *New Statesman* commissioned a review from the last person to have written a proper Bond novel. Kingsley Amis's assessment was mixed. He said, 'Mr Wood has bravely tackled his formidable task, that of turning a typical late Bond film, which must be basically facetious, into a novel after Ian Fleming, which must be basically serious. To this end he has, by my count, left out nine silly gadgets and sixteen silly cracks . . .'

Although he allowed that 'the descriptions are adequate and the action writing excellent', Amis felt there was a fundamental problem with the project that no amount of either adequate or excellent writing could rectify:

> What nobody could have cut out is the element of second-sight contingency planning (or negligence) that gets by in a film, indeed is very much part of the style of these films, but obtrudes in a book. Your enemy has an explosive motorbike sidecar ready to launch at your car in case he's forgotten to kill you for certain and in secret a few minutes before. In case that misses, he has already aloft a helicopter fitted with jets and cannon. Your car is submersible in case you meet such a helicopter while driving on a coast road. In case you submerge your car he has a midget submarine waiting. In case he has you have underwater rocket-launchers . . .

Roger Moore's original Bond deal had been for three films. Following *The Spy Who Loved Me*, therefore, new contract negotiations were in order. That Moore decided to ask for increased remuneration was, in the wake of the commercial triumph of his latest 007 picture, understandable. However, it nearly scuppered his chances of resuming the role. Although stories abound of Cubby Broccoli's personal generosity, so do tales of his parsimony. When, for instance, no less a figure than Catherine Deneuve approached Broccoli about playing Anya in *The Spy Who Loved Me*, Broccoli refused to meet her fee. In a December 1976 *Los Angeles Times* article, it was stated that Broccoli also refused to meet the demands of Marthe Keller and Dominique Sanda. Boasted Broccoli, 'The money I've saved by not using a well-known actress I spent on that marvellous ski stunt.' He therefore wasn't going to easily accede to Moore's demands. One also wonders whether at the back of his mind Broccoli was beginning to worry about the fact that Moore was now on the brink of his half-century.

In the end, Moore did sign up, but on a one-off basis. The fact that Moore continued to decline to sign contracts for more than one Bond at a time meant that there would be further showdowns over money across the rest of his tenure. 'Not at all,' Moore responds when it's suggested that this led to repeated, unnecessary brinkmanship. 'I never discussed business with Cubby, and he never with me. That was left to agents and lawyers.' That Moore ultimately appears to have always had his pay demands met does seem to suggest that Eon had learned a lesson from their conflicts with Connery.

The end credits of *The Spy Who Loved Me* had stated that James Bond would return in *For Your Eyes Only*, but that plan changed around 1977, when *Star Wars* enraptured the public. Handily, the only Bond novel not yet adapted to the big screen lent itself to a fashionably star-speckled backdrop.

Moonraker, therefore, premiered in the UK on 26 June 1979 as the third Bond movie of the last four to shamelessly jump on a bandwagon. The results of such cynicism had so far been mixed but worldwide box-office grosses of $202.7 million showed that it certainly worked in *Moonraker*'s case. If that was the only way Eon measured success, everything was fine. Unfortunately, Moore had followed possibly his best Bond picture with probably his worst.

Christopher Wood has the sole writing credit, although Broccoli claimed that Mankiewicz and director Gilbert worked on the story too.

The pre-title scene depicting a large vessel being hijacked feels groanworthily reminiscent of both *You Only Live Twice* and *The Spy Who Loved Me*. In 1979, though, it could be said to be ahead of the curve in one respect: the vessel in question is a NASA space shuttle – herein also called Moonrakers – which in real life wouldn't be formally launched until 1981.

Bond meets Holly Goodhead (Lois Chiles) when he goes to the California mansion of Hugo Drax (a subdued performance by Michael Lonsdale), who builds the Moonrakers for America. (Britain's involvement comes from the fact that the missing shuttle has been lent to it by the US.) The beautiful but no-nonsense Dr Goodhead is a qualified astronaut on loan from NASA (she will also transpire to be a CIA agent), but, introduced to her, Moore exclaims, 'A woman!' This reaction would have felt less oily in 1979, when women were not so common in the workplace, but Moore is beginning to seem like a dinosaur in more ways than one. Liver spots are beginning to appear on his hands and he is a vision of clubland in his blue blazer and flannels. British viewers would have half-expected him to exclaim, 'Ding-*dong*!' – the slavering catchphrase of senior, upper-class, comedy acting lech Leslie Phillips.

When Bond is sitting in a centrifuge trainer, a huge spinning contraption that simulates the crushing inertial force produced by rapid acceleration into outer space, a Drax minion proceeds to sabotage it. As he spins helplessly, we are provided a glimpse of vulnerability rare for Moore's Bond, who looks distressed when he realises he can't quip or punch his way out of this one. Finally able to bring the machine to a halt by improvising with a Q-supplied gadget, he staggers from the machine, angrily pushing away Holly's comforting hands.

Now suspecting Drax, and having uncovered evidence that Drax has an operation in Brazil, Bond makes his way to Rio, where an attempt on his life is made by Jaws, who just happens to have been offered employment by a second megalomaniac with whom Bond has wound up in conflict. After another attempt to kill Bond – this time on a cable car – Jaws is rescued from the rubble by a bespectacled girl in plaited pigtails. She never speaks but is named in the credits as Dolly (Blanche Ravalec). It's at this point that the film tips over from merely the nadir of self-parody into tut-provoking idiocy: the two fall for each other on sight and instantly walk off hand in hand to the accompaniment of Tchaikovsky's overture *Romeo and Juliet*.

When the action moves to the Amazon, another attempt is made to bump off Bond by the indefatigable Jaws. The secret agent escapes it by abandoning his boat at the edge of a waterfall and swooping off on a detachable hang-glider. Conveniently, he alights in the immediate vicinity of a Mayan temple being used by Drax to house his space shuttles, into which 007 makes his way almost without breaking stride. This is a perfect example of the oleaginous timbre of the film, Bond slithering effortlessly from country to country, ancient splendour to ancient splendour, providential lead to providential lead, gadget to gadget, expressing no surprise or wonder as he does.

Inside, Bond witnesses Drax launching a series of space shuttles. 'What exactly are you up to here, Drax?' demands Bond, which at least makes a change from the villain's usual unprompted exposition. What Drax is up to is planning to wipe out life on Earth and transport via his Moonrakers some beautiful young chosen ones to a new outer-space Eden. Drax, naturally, has sufficient wherewithal to have built and launched a space station the size of a city and, naturally, has done so undetected. The hijacked Moonraker was actually nabbed by Drax because one of his own developed a fault.

Bond and Holly are whisked off to the space station. The American government sends up a marine squadron, resulting in a massed laser-gun battle in vacuum. Also floatingly taking place in zero gravity is Bond's final-stages lovemaking with Holly. An unknowing Q informs the White House and Buckingham Palace, 'I think he's attempting re-entry.'

Moonraker's necessarily high budget motivated Eon to solicit massive amounts of product placement. One particularly unsubtle example comes in a scene wherein a car crashes into the mouth of a flight stewardess depicted on a billboard emblazoned with a well-known British Airways slogan. Product placement in Bond movies – which had started with *Goldfinger* – would shortly become so ferocious that it even contaminated areas outside the action: the opening credits of *Licence to Kill* artlessly featured a beauty taking pictures with a camera pointedly made by Olympus.

The soundtrack saw the return of John Barry. While his score is fine, the melody to the title song is featureless and Hal David's lyric works in the title word rather awkwardly. Not even Shirley Bassey – returning to perform her third Bond theme – can do much with it.

Listed as executive producer of *Moonraker* was one Michael G. Wilson. He, in fact, was a lawyer by training. His strange switch in careers is explained by the fact that he was also Cubby Broccoli's stepson. As well as his production role on every Bond movie since, he co-wrote scripts for a period.

This might smack of nepotism and insularity. Roger Moore has certainly publicly noted that a dual role of producer and scriptwriter was a conflict of interest. However, the concentration of power in the hands of the Broccoli family engendered by

Saltzman's departure may well be the explanation for James Bond's enduring position in the culture. Saltzman and Broccoli was a combination that had worked well up to a point, but the fact that the two men ultimately fell out indicates how precarious partnerships can be. And, if those two were unable to see things the same way, what implication did that have for harmonious relationships among the eventual respective familial heirs to their 007 rights?

With there now being only one non-studio set of heirs to those rights, the situation became less complicated. It became even less complicated in 1986 when the studio element was erased from the ownership picture by Broccoli buying out UA's 50 per cent share of cinema Bond.

That the James Bond franchise is – uniquely in motion-picture history – a true family business has meant a certain guarantor of care. Bond films have not been made perfunctorily, carelessly or grudgingly by hired studio hands. Instead they have been crafted by people whose application has gone hand in hand with the subconscious apprehension of the responsibility of birthright. This and an inevitable element of sentimentality creates total conscientiousness. This is not the same thing as saying that all Bond films are outstanding – as *Moonraker* itself emphatically demonstrates. It is the reason, however, that no Bond movie has ever been a true commercial flop. The family ownership has meant the type of careful nurturing and updating never granted to any other film property.

The dynasty is set to continue. Whether Barbara Broccoli's daughter Angelica is interested in following in her mother's footsteps is yet to be seen, but Wilson's son Gregg has been working as an associate producer since *Skyfall*, his other son,

David, works on ancillary rights and niece Heather is employed in publicity.

The sealed protection granted Bond films by the status of family property will only be jeopardised when the character falls into the public domain, as has done a comparable precursor icon, Sherlock Holmes. In Canada, which unusually stuck to the Berne Convention dictates of death-plus-fifty-years, that situation came into existence at the beginning of 2015, a half-century on from Fleming's passing. It was quickly exploited by ChiZine Publications, who in November of that year published a crowd-funded anthology of new Bond stories defiantly titled *Licence Expired.*

The small amount of new copyright freedom regarding 007 is not restricted to books. Theoretically, anyone can now make a Bond movie in Canada, although it could not be distributed outside those shores except to countries with similar copyright limits. Moreover, that film would have to be strictly based on Fleming's Bond. Any incorporation of elements of Bond exclusive to the films would be actionable. In the USA, Fleming's Bond could be in the public domain in 2034, seventy years after Fleming's death, although legislators in the States have a habit of stretching and making exceptions in copyright law. In Britain, it will be 2039 that third parties will be free to make even a Bond movie that sidesteps Eon hallmarks. The perilous business of avoiding litigation may even come down to making sure to call the Secret Service's cover name Universal 'Export' rather than 'Exports'.

With *Moonraker*, Christopher Wood was once again asked to provide a novelisation of a Bond script on which he'd worked. The result was another book with a title carefully delineating it from its putative Fleming source: *James Bond and Moonraker* (1979).

Following that book, Eon abandoned the novelisation approach. The reason possibly lay with the fact that Glidrose felt more books-of-the-film would conflict with their planned new Bond novels. If so, there is an element of injustice, for it does seem logical to conclude that it was the success of the Wood novelisations that prompted Glidrose into reviving continuation Bonds.

John Gardner was not as illustrious a name as Arthur Calder-Marshall, Kingsley Amis or John Pearson, but with him Glidrose finally alighted on a writer able to further James Bond's written chronicles to the long-term satisfaction of the public. (Wood has said he would have been interested in writing an original James Bond novel but wasn't asked.) Gardner had been a successful novelist since the mid-sixties. He had proven himself adept at both Bond pastiche (while valid thrillers in their own right, his Liquidator novels were, by his own admission, 'a complete piss-take' of 007) and continuing a longstanding literary franchise (he had produced novels about Sherlock Holmes's adversary Professor Moriarty). Gardner later wrote:

> What I wanted to do was take the character and bring Fleming's Bond into the Eighties as the same man but with all he would have learned had he lived through the Sixties and Seventies . . . Most of all I wanted him to have operational know-how: the reality of correct tradecraft and modern gee-whiz technology.

Gardner's new Bond – hair flecked slightly with grey, now working directly for M after the disbandment of the double-O section, a moderate drinker, a low-tar-cigarette smoker, a Saab 900 Turbo-driver, a Walther PPK refusenik – made his first appearance in *Licence Renewed* in mid-1981. His adversary was Anton Murik, a disgraced nuclear physicist intent on extorting $50 billion in diamonds in exchange for returning to the custody of the authorities six hijacked nuclear power stations. The updatings were bound to irritate some aficionados, but, regardless of those, the book is curiously flat, with Gardner confused about whether it is the literary or cinematic Bond he is portraying and proffering ritualistic and perfunctory sex scenes.

Despite this, Gardner's take on Bond 'took' and he remained the official James Bond author for fifteen years. During that time, his take changed, whether it was by Bond's switch from a Saab to a Bentley Mulsanne Turbo, the mention of 'precautions' as sex became more hazardous with the rise of AIDS or the creeping upwards in violence levels, which it had been agreed at the beginning would be moderate. Some changes were definitively devolution. The consensus is that Gardner's Bonds began to steeply drop off in quality at the halfway point of his tenure, while his determination to age Bond with the times began to result in the timeline difficulties Fleming spent his last few books trying to untangle. Gardner also had Bond suffer the indignity of no fewer than three rejected marriage proposals.

Gardner's books sold well – especially in the US – and, if the serious reviews were thin on the ground and the reception of fandom mixed, this was no more than Gardner expected when he took on what he termed 'a no-win situation'. He published fourteen 007 books of his own devising – the same number as did Ian Fleming (including the latter's short-story collections). He also wrote novelisations of the films *Licence to Kill* and *GoldenEye.*

He gave up the reins not because of illness, as has sometimes been reported, but because, 'I had already had my fill of Bond . . .'

Around halfway through Gardner's run, Jonathan Cape ceased being the continuation Bond-novel publisher, with the franchise switching to Hodder & Stoughton. From what Gardner said, he would have been well advised to bail out around the point when Cape did. He told *universalexports.net*, 'Should have stopped at six . . . The Bond books are formula writing and that doesn't improve anyone's technique.'

Nonetheless, Gardner left literary Bond in a far better state than he had found it, when it had been so reduced in stature that only novelisations of bastardisations of Fleming's work met with any public favour. He also served notice to the masses that there existed a vision of James Bond more thoughtful and nuanced than the one being purveyed in the films.

For the next Bond movie, John Glen took over the reins from Lewis Gilbert. Although a novice director, he settled in for a record-breaking five pictures, all in succession.

With all the Fleming Bond novel titles now exhausted, Eon turned to the short stories. The script of *For Your Eyes Only* is actually a conflation of 'For Your Eyes Only' and 'Risico'. Mixed into that is a section of the *Live and Let Die* novel unused – like much of its source – by the film of that name.

'We figured it was time Bond headed back in a more realistic direction,' Michael G. Wilson told *The Hollywood Reporter* in 1980. The new, gritty direction for Bond was touted as a reaction to *Moonraker*'s timbre. Now that Bond had gone into space, the expansion of the fanciful that had been increasing exponentially ever since Q's first gadget could go no further – Bond was hardly going to travel to the moon or Mars. Others, however, have suggested that United Artists were more concerned with ballooning budgets than realism. Certainly, Ken Adam – once lionised for his grand visions, now marginalised for his extravagance – had lately found life increasingly difficult. *Moonraker* was his last Bond.

There is indeed far less technology in *For Your Eyes Only* – which premiered in the UK on 24 June 1981 – than had been seen in any Bond picture since *On Her Majesty's Secret Service* a dozen years before. However, this is nothing like the gritty espionage proposition Wilson was suggesting. At this point in history, at least, it was not possible to put on general release a largely gadget-free, often static Bond film like *From Russia with Love*.

In the pre-title sequence, Bond is picked up in a Universal Exports helicopter, but the helicopter is remotely taken over by somebody with murderous designs on 007. That person is an anonymous bald man whose face remains unseen as he strokes a white cat. Eon are pushing at the margins of the intellectual property laws to include somebody who, though not formally identified, is unmistakably Blofeld, the object being to deliver a screw-you to McClory and assert how little the franchise now needs the criminal organisation once central to it. Blofeld is these days confined to a wheelchair, an unexplained development apparently solely engineered to enable Bond to scoop him up with the 'copter's landing skids and drop him down an industrial chimney to his certain death.

The music accompanying the pre-title sequence is grisly. John Barry was originally retained but dropped out, with the reasons disputed. Bill Conti, who stepped in, sadly doesn't provide something as glorious and transcendent as his 1976 theme music to *Rocky* but instead a self-conscious funky soundtrack made all the worse for its using contemporary synthesiser instrumentation, which was suffocating and weedy then and is dated now.

Conti's title song (lyric by Michael Leeson) is half-decent, but, though it has a sumptuous melody, it suffers from that aforementioned electropop construction, as well as the fact that it's sung by Sheena Easton. Recruiting Easton could be described as the Nancy Sinatra Syndrome: like Sinatra, Easton was currently famous but of limited vocal range. Nonetheless, Easton's petite beauty gained her the accolade of the first artist to be seen singing in a Bond credit sequence.

For the first time, Bond's briefing is not given by M. Bernard Lee, who had played him in all eleven official Bond movies so far, died during production and, as a mark of respect, Eon rested the character. Instead Bill Tanner (James Villiers) is tasked with telling 007 that a British Intelligence boat has been sunk along with its precious cargo of the Automatic Targeting Attack Communicator. As ATAC is used to communicate with Polaris submarines, it is vital that it be retrieved before the Soviets get their hands on it. The story, though, focuses not on the USSR but freelance killers hired by it, proffering dialogue about 'détente' along the way. The scriptwriters tasked with this half-hearted departure from the series' disinclination to tackle the Cold War are Michael G. Wilson and Richard Maibaum.

In keeping with a grimmer outlook is the moment when Bond kicks over a cliff a car containing a man who has killed a colleague. Yet the action also includes some underwater fisticuffs that are comical for the fact that the character attacking Bond is encased in a submersible suit that makes him look like a cross between Robby the Robot from *Forbidden Planet* and the Michelin Man.

There are respectable parts of *For Your Eyes Only* – the

commando attack on Kristatos's opium operation has a refreshing straightforwardness and even nobility – but the film falls awkwardly between the stools of fantasy and realism.

And indeed comedy. *For Your Eyes Only* ends with a scene wherein impersonator Janet Brown plays British Prime Minister Thatcher as she telephones Bond to thank him for performing his duties for his country, only to get through to a parrot who subjects her to such entreaties as 'Give us a kiss.'

When in 1980 United Artists ran into financial difficulties with the famous flop *Heaven's Gate*, not even the revenues generated by their mega-successful James Bond, Rocky and Pink Panther franchises could save them. In 1981 they were absorbed by MGM. The longtime Bond distributors subsequently decided they wanted Eon to go back to 'spectacle' Bonds, which they considered the more bankable kind. In acquiescing to UA, Eon abandoned the elements of grittiness they had made a virtue of incorporating into *For Your Eyes Only*.

Moore, meanwhile, was, as usual, being strategically coy about returning. Eon were as usual negotiating with Moore's agent while ostentatiously interviewing and screen-testing other actors. One of those actors was Lewis Collins, seen as SAS man Peter Skellen in 1982 action movie *Who Dares Wins* but most familiar as Bodie from the late-seventies/early-eighties UK television espionage drama *The Professionals*.

Something about Lewis – his dark good looks, the cruel cut of his mouth, his sardonic manner, his real-life passing of SAS courses – suggested for many Bond fans the real thing. Moreover, a real thing for the modern age. Had he transported across to Bond the high, unkempt fringe and black turtlenecks he wore as Bodie, it would have made 007 a contemporary figure without sacrificing his essential nature. Additionally, the fact that Collins was in 1982 only thirty-six suggested someone who could have been credible as Bond for a decade. However, it seems that, despite two meetings with Broccoli separated by a couple of years, he never came close to landing the role. Collins recalled of the first interview that Broccoli 'found me too aggressive . . . When someone walks into their office for the most popular film job in the world, a little actor is bound to put on a few airs.' Collins arouses wistful comments among 007 aficionados such as, 'Best Bond there never was.'

Having spurned that opportunity, Eon agreed terms with Moore once again and James Bond resumed the process of growing old disgracefully. Times two. While Eon set about filming *Octopussy* with Moore – aged fifty-five upon its 6 June 1983 London premiere – production on Kevin McClory's own new Bond picture was proceeding, with Sean Connery – aged fifty-three when it was premiered in Los Angeles on 6 October 1983 – returning as 007. For a period it seemed the two elderly agents would be going head to head at the cinemas.

Even in 1983, the word 'Octopussy' sounded obscene, and perhaps it will never be entirely free of its patina of sniggering rudery. However, as with Pussy Galore, with repetition it lost some of its how-can-they-get-away-with-it? quality.

The *Octopussy* film incorporates the plot of the Fleming short story only in a couple of lines of dialogue. The screenwriters rely instead on the story 'Property of a Lady', as well as the usual new material. George MacDonald Fraser, author of the Flashman novels, wrote a first-draft script, which was then taken over by the team of Maibaum and Wilson.

For the first time, men (other than Bond) appear in the title sequence. The title theme is a mediocre John Barry/Tim Rice pop song called 'All Time High', sung by Rita Coolidge. This time it's understandable that the lyric doesn't use the film's title.

The new M actor is Robert Brown, who had previously played Admiral Hargreaves in *The Spy Who Loved Me*. Although there was a tradition of recurrence of actors in different roles in Bond pictures, this had deliberately never been applied to Bond girls. Maud Adams, seen as Andrea in *The Man with the Golden Gun*, breaks that mould in being cast as *Octopussy*'s titular female lead.

The latest in a flurry of tainted Fabergé eggs has come up for auction at Sotheby's. Bond follows the trail to India (cue the novelty casting of tennis player Vijay Amritraj), where he works out that rogue Russian general Orlov (the glowering Steven Berkoff) is supplying exiled Afghan prince Kamal Khan (Louis Jourdan) with the eggs and other historical Russian treasures in a convoluted plan to undermine faith in Western atomic deterrents. Orlov intends to plant a nuclear bomb in a West German US Air Force base, using the travelling Octopussy circus as his unwitting courier.

The Octopussy circus is owned by a woman who happens to be the daughter of Major Dexter Smythe. It's rather nice that, through her dialogue, a distillation of the excellent 'Octopussy' short story makes it into the screenplay, although it is completely immaterial to the film's plot. Even the way it gives the picture a title is tenuous, not to mention warped: 'Octopussy' was the pet name of Smythe – a leading authority on octopi – for his daughter. (This, understandably, renders Bond speechless.)

The plot recycles a surprising amount from the *Goldfinger* film. We have already seen a pre-title sequence and a golf-course scene reminiscent of that Connery flick by the time Bond defuses the bomb with seconds to spare – although the screenwriters do at least resist the temptation to stop the digital countdown at '007'. Dignity issues lie in other areas: sundry examples of silliness include Bond performing his heroics in a clown costume he adopts to blend in on his arrival at the Octopussy circus; neutralising the danger posed by a tiger by successfully ordering it to sit in a way deliberately redolent of TV dog-trainer Barbara Woodhouse; and swinging on vines to the aural backdrop of a Johnny Weissmuller Tarzan yodel.

The climax at least merits its place. Bond, pursuing Khan, jumps on his private plane as it takes off. The consequent aerial photography as Khan tries to get rid of his irritant – spinning the plane and sending out a minion to battle with him – is hair-raising.

When Bond uses one of Q's video gadgets to zoom in on the cleavage of a female assistant, it demonstrates that what was once thrilling sexual libertarianism is, two decades after the first Bond movie, increasingly what Q describes herein as 'adolescent antics' and what the world would soon term political incorrectness. The antiquated ambience is not helped by the fact that the India depicted is one of snake charmers, sword swallowers, firewalkers and people who take naps on beds of nails.

Octopussy contains the series' first comments about Moneypenny's vintage, itself a cheek considering Moore's increasingly lined and leathery face. Like the fact of death having necessitated a new M, these are signs of a passing regime.

When *Never Say Never Again* received its premiere exactly four months after *Octopussy*, it meant that for the first time since 1967 two new James Bond pictures had hit the cinemas in the same year.

Kevin McClory – billed as executive producer – was now a background figure, having licensed to Jack Schwartzman permission to produce the remake of *Thunderball*. This followed several years of legal wrangling with the Ian Fleming estate, financed by Danjaq and UA. Significantly, Schwartzman had practised as a show-business lawyer. The financing he secured for the picture was deliberately diffuse – three banks and twenty-six distributors across the world – so as to make it difficult for any litigant to cut off the money supply. However, a final challenge aimed at stopping the film's distribution was defeated only because production was so far advanced that it was deemed that it would be unfair and impracticable to halt it – a symmetrical echo of the reasons McClory had been unable in 1961 to stop the dissemination of the *Thunderball* novel.

Norman Wanstall – now happily employed as a plumbing and heating engineer – was brought out of moviemaking retirement to work on the film. He recalls, 'A friend of mine was the assistant to the American editor and he said, "Sean is a little bit peeved that all the people he remembers are gone. We thought perhaps if you came back at least he'd know that someone who'd won an award and been on all those early ones of his . . ."' Wanstall agreed to do it as a favour to his friend.

Wanstall recalls, 'I never got to know Sean [before] because of the fact that [the] dialogue editor is the one that always works with the actors . . . He introduced himself to me. He came into my editing room and we had a chat. I thought that was great.' It was about the only thing related to the project about which Wanstall had positive feelings. 'It was a very unhappy film. I wish I'd never done it. The script hadn't been thoroughly written. This guy came over from America who was the money man and he caused all sorts of disruptions . . . He was a really weird guy. The first night he arrived, he threw an ashtray through a window.'

Moreover, 'The director said, "Norman, we're making a spoof." I thought, "Christ, do you mind?"' Yet the fact that Dick Clement and Ian Le Frenais – a writing team notable for television comedies such as *The Likely Lads* and *Porridge* – did some script-doctoring work does suggest that the film was intended to have more than a smidgeon of comedy.

'There was so much discussion, always discussion,' Wanstall says of rough-cut screenings. 'I remember sitting and hearing them talking at the back. Sean was on the executive as well. I wanted to turn round and say, "Why are you talking about that? There are far, far more important things you should be discussing." It was like a bunch of amateurs. I hated it all.'

Connery had been involved in the project from an early stage, co-writing in 1976 a script with Len Deighton and McClory. It would appear that at that point he was interested only in scriptwriting and perhaps producing the film. By the time the project went ahead, Connery had changed his mind about starring. If he was embarrassing as Bond in *Diamonds Are Forever*, he is now pitiful: slurry-voiced, dewlappy, creased, crinkled and waxen, with unnaturally neat grey hair. Yet all of the female characters are instantly smitten by this apparition.

Nevertheless, the knowledge that to many only Connery was 007 prompted McClory/Schwartzman to agree to a jaw-dropping fee for the actor of $5 million plus a percentage of the profits. Frankly, they would have been better advised to sign up Lewis Collins. Not only would this have saved money and secured a more credible lead actor, but the motivational power behind both McClory and Collins wishing to extend a screw-you to Cubby Broccoli should not be underestimated.

Despite all of that, *Never Say Never Again* constitutes a better 007 swansong for Connery than *Diamonds Are Forever.*

The film's title was the result of an exasperated comment from Connery's wife Micheline about the fact that he had reneged on his vow that he was finished with Bond. It's almost worked into the script's final lines. It does feature in the lyric of the theme song, written by Alan and Marilyn Bergman and sung by Lani Hall. Unfortunately said theme song is an awful, soporific affair, which – like much of the rest of Michel Legrand's jazzy, good-time soundtrack – works against the action.

The film is directed well by Irvin Kershner, a prestigious name from his having recently directed *The Empire Strikes Back.* (Kershner was also the first non-Briton to direct a Bond cinematic release.) Veteran Lorenzo Semple Jr provides the screenplay.

It might be assumed that it wouldn't matter much who was writing the script, but Semple forcibly pushes at the margins of the original legal agreement that McClory's Bond rights extended only as far as remaking *Thunderball.* The banishment of Bond to a health farm and the hijacking by SPECTRE of two nuclear warheads constitute the broad framework retained from *Thunderball,* but just about every other detail is changed. The depiction of Britain as a declining, cash-strapped power, however, is probably as much a nod to reality as a manifestation of a desire to differentiate the movie from its predecessor.

Max Von Sydow is ridiculously miscast as Blofeld, managing to make the character something that none of the actors who had played him previously had: avuncular. Fortunately, he is not on screen much, with the role of central baddie given to the reasonably good Largo (Klaus Maria Brandauer).

Edward Fox plays a man who has inherited the title and job

of M and has nothing but contempt for Bond. Only the crisis of the hijacked weapons causes him to reactivate the double-O section he had disbanded. Domino is played by then-newcomer Kim Basinger. Bond's colleague Nigel, a bumbling oaf smitten by secret-agentry, is drawn overly comically by Rowan Atkinson. Half a decade later, Atkinson's Bond spoof began appearing in credit-card commercials. The role would eventually be expanded and transferred to the big screen under the name *Johnny English*.

This is a Bond film largely without gadgets, and is all the better for it. A lengthy fight at the health farm between Bond and a burly would-be assassin is well choreographed and real-looking (not least because Bond spends much of it running away). It also has a hilarious payoff: when Bond hurls a beaker of liquid into his antagonist's eyes, it causes agony; Bond looks at the label on the beaker to find it is his own urine sample.

There are the usual Bond-movie absurdities – for instance, a character is bumped off by SPECTRE by the method of a snake being thrown into his moving car when he could have just been discretely shot in private. Generally, though, the film is enjoyably down-to-earth, even if its climax is a little disappointing: in place of armies of battling frogmen is the undramatic sight of Bond turning off a timer.

As well as being a better picture than the official Bond movie that year, *Never Say Never Again* achieved grosses of $160 million, which were only $23.7 million less than those of *Octopussy*. It was, though, a dead end. With his Bond rights consisting simply of endless *Thunderball* remakes, McClory hardly held a long-term bankable commodity, especially without the novelty and sentimentality attached to one last hurrah for Sean Connery. Not that it stopped his Bond-related efforts.

After *Never Say Never Again* – if hardly as a consequence of it – Sean Connery barely looked back, becoming the hugely successful and diverse actor he had always wished to be. *Highlander, The Name of the Rose, The Untouchables, Indiana Jones and the Last Crusade, The Hunt for Red October, Medicine Man, Rising Sun, The Rock* and *The League of Extraordinary Gentlemen* – among others – all added to his reputation and/or his bank balance before he retired in the mid-noughties.

In addition, of course, is the fact that for a certain generation Connery will always be the only man they can ever take fully seriously as the celluloid 007.

The next Eon Bond movie was *A View to a Kill,* premiered in San Francisco on 22 May 1985.

In collaboration with John Barry, Duran Duran provide a theme song in their usual style of pounding rhythm, shrieking slabs of synth and whined, nonsensical lyrics, and they lazily dispense the title line only in a verse. This lack of quality didn't stop it becoming a UK No. 2 and US No. 1, an all-time chart high for Bond themes that was the ultimate fulfilment of the vision of cultural cross-fertilisation that had first motivated Eon to get such *zeitgeist* popsters to sing them.

Richard Maibaum and Michael G. Wilson's script is nominally based, of course, on 'From a View to a Kill'. However, it wasn't just the title that was tweaked: there is no resemblance to Fleming's short story in a tale that has Bond uncovering and frustrating a scheme by Max Zorin (Christopher Walken) to flood California's Silicon Valley so as to raise higher the value of the holdings of his own Zorin Corporation.

The villain's female cohort is May Day, played by high-cheekboned pop chanteuse Grace Jones. She and Duran Duran are deliberate tilts for the youth market, but neither disguise the fact that the main cast creaks with age. In the early stages, Bond forms a not-exactly dynamic duo with Sir Godfrey Tibbett, played by sixty-three-year-old Patrick Macnee. It's rumoured that a bald spot on the left of his crown had always necessitated that the makeup department augment Moore's hair. If so, they did a good, non-detectable job. However, little can be done about the fact that, when Moore widens his eyes in this film, it makes for an alarming sight.

The end credits declare 'James Bond will return', but this time fail to say what the next film will be. This may have been down to the prosaic fact that Eon were running out of titles from the Fleming canon. However, it could also be read as symbolic.

The film was Moore's swansong. With it being inevitable that any replacement of Moore would be considerably younger, the age gap between the next Bond and Lois Maxwell – eight months older than Moore – would make their flirtatious banter unsustainable. Accordingly, Maxwell was informed that she would not be invited back to reprise the Moneypenny role she had owned since 1962.

Although the $152.4 million receipts of *A View to a Kill* showed that Eon had not been holed below the waterline by *Never Say Never Again*, a new era was dawning for Bond, and, like all new eras, it was one shot through with sad farewells and hurt feelings. Whether Moore's departure was voluntary is, as usual for the world of Eon, something on which recollections divide. Broccoli claimed in his autobiography that Moore was shocked when Eon indicated they were going to make a change. Moore's version of events doesn't necessarily contradict that story in terms of facts, but does suggest a different complexion. 'I hadn't really wanted to make *A View to a Kill*,' he says. 'I felt I was getting a little long in the tooth and would have been happy to stand aside after *Octopussy*, but I agreed to do one more. Afterwards, both Cubby and I agreed it was time I hung up my Walther PPK. There were no tears, no tantrums. We both realised it was the right time, that's all.'

From this end of history it's possible to see Moore as a uniquely ungritty Bond. It's a measure of the actor's perspective on his film career that he would not consider this assessment in any way a slight, even if he doesn't seem to quite agree with it. 'Each actor plays to their strengths,' Moore reasons. 'Mine is always a light, fun style. Brosnan played it lighter than Dalton, but that's all to do with the times, the scripts and what audiences want and expect. When Jason Bourne arrived, that changed things – audiences liked and wanted an edgier, tougher, rougher Bond . . . and Daniel was the perfect casting. But, had they cast a Daniel Craig type in 1995, I'm not so sure the series would still be here. Pierce had it right for his time, and so did the others.'

One thing can't be disputed. Moore managed to consistently please audiences across the course of a dozen years and during that time was primarily responsible for the hardly small achievement of sustaining the world's most successful film franchise.

A FRANCHISE
IN PERIL

In late 1985, Raymond Benson proposed to Glidrose a James Bond stage play.

Live theatre was just about the only form of media in which 007 had not made an appearance. Perhaps because of this, Glidrose proved agreeable to the idea. It transpired that the only Fleming work that could be adapted to the play format was *Casino Royale*: Eon owned all other Bond-related performing rights. The fact was attended by a certain serendipity, as *Casino Royale* was the only existing 007 tale that lent itself to the stage.

Benson spent two to three months turning the narrative of the novel into a nine-scene play script. 'I was paid, and we did [a] staged reading of it off Broadway,' he recalls. This February 1986 reading saw Ed Clark play James Bond. 'I thought it went very well,' says Benson, 'although nobody from Glidrose was there to see it. Shortly after that, they just decided, "We don't want to produce this." I think they may have gotten pressure from Eon not to do a James Bond stage play.'

The play will probably never have a professional performance again. Explains Benson, 'Since then, Glidrose has sold all their *Casino Royale* rights to Eon and so Eon now owns my play.'

In August 1986, Eon announced the name of the first new James Bond in fourteen years.

Like Moore prior to him and Pierce Brosnan after him, Timothy Dalton was cast as Bond after previously not taking up the role. In his case, Dalton had level-headedly turned down the part of 007 in his mid-twenties, bemusedly pointing out to a Broccoli displaying a surprising lack of judgement that he was far too young. He had another meeting with Broccoli circa 1980 at a point where Moore actually publicly stated, 'I won't do another Bond.' Dalton's varied pre-Bond career encompassed the films *Agatha* and *Flash Gordon*, the TV series *Centennial* and Shakespeare stage productions.

Dalton was a slight risk, although not because of his Cheadle background – he had the received pronunciation to be expected of an alumnus of RADA, if with a Northern tinge. Rather it was because, although certainly attractive and tall (yet again, six-foot-two), he was almost equine, almost androgynous, almost sibilant and almost forty, the last of these suggesting the potential for only a short tenure. (Possibly even over forty: his birth in North Wales was in either 1944 or 1946, according to which source you believe.) Nonetheless, Eon signed him to a three-picture deal.

Dalton's youth (compared with Moore) and sophisticated thespian hinterland played a large part in the decision to recalibrate the Bond series. *The Living Daylights*, which premiered in the UK on 29 June 1987, was a return to more thoughtful, down-to-earth Bond fare.

The screenplay was another collaboration between Maibaum

and Michael G. Wilson. (The latter's stepsister Barbara Broccoli joined the Eon team at this point as associate producer.) That such a high-quality screenplay is the work of a pair responsible for the recent Moore travesties is quite astounding.

Dalton's gun-barrel walk is brisk-paced and stylish (and not just for his tuxedo), after which we have a pre-title sequence that provides a perfect introduction to the new Bond. A double-O training exercise on Gibraltar is sabotaged by an unspecified villain and ultimately leaves Bond battling with an assassin in a jeep, from which he cannily allows his parachute to drag him as it hurtles off a cliff into the sea. He steers his parachute towards a pleasure boat and surprises a bored rich woman by dropping in and demanding to use her phone. 'Who are you?' asks his bikini-clad host as she takes in his body. 'Bond, James Bond,' naturally comes the reply. Bond tells Exercise Control he will report in an hour. When the woman proffers him a glass of champagne, 007 appends into the mouthpiece, 'Better make that two.'

After such an exciting and likeable introductory sequence, it's a little disappointing that we are then in the midst of an anaemic song performed and co-written by A-ha, whose synth pop stylings are hardly the stuff of Bond themes, even if they are provided assistance by John Barry.

The Living Daylights turned out to be John Barry's swansong. He was too ill to provide the score for the next film and would never contribute another, the result of disenchantment with his experience working with A-ha and an overarching feeling of staleness. He told his biographer, Eddi Fiegel, 'It started to be just formula, and once that happens, the work gets really hard.' A fitting valediction is provided by the fact that Barry secured a cameo in *The Living Daylights* as an orchestra conductor.

The film incorporates much of the Fleming short story of the same name as a jumping-off point. This time, Bond's reason for not killing the beautiful gunwoman – here named Kara Milovy (Maryam d'Abo) – is that he realises she is not a trained killer. She is the blackmailed pawn in a game by fake defector Georgi Koskov (Jeroen Krabbé), which ultimately leads via Tangiers to Afghanistan, with arms- and opium-dealing pocking the trail.

The climax of the film contains the most gut-churningly exciting piece of Bond action in a decade or more, as the agent tussles with a villain while hanging out of the back of a mid-air plane, inside of which a bomb is ticking down to detonation.

Bond informs a fellow agent that all Stradivarius cellos have individual names, but, other than that, the insufferable know-all persona of the Moore era is nowhere in evidence, replaced by a grim professionalism, brusqueness and rough-hewn humanity. The script features the first-ever profanity from the film Bond himself in the shape of 'horse's arse'. Dalton's Bond smokes cigarettes and, for the first time since the Connery days, orders a shaken-not-stirred vodka martini.

There is, though, no return to Bond's rampant licentiousness. In recent years, AIDS had ensured that the promiscuity traditionally celebrated in Bond films had become not a byword for sexual enlightenment but potential death. Because of this, Eon did as much as feasible in a Bond picture to rein it in, restricting 007's conquests to two. (Moore's tally had been similarly low in recent years, but more likely as a function of a fear that for a man of his age such exertions appeared a little unseemly.)

Although a standard length of just over two hours, *The Living Daylights* could have been shorter: an early protracted fight sequence which doesn't even involve Bond would not have been missed. However, it's a quality film, one that strikes a good balance between gritty espionage and larger-than-life spectacle.

Ominously, the territory in which *The Living Daylights'* performance was mildly disappointing – and made it the lowest-grossing Bond since *The Man with the Golden Gun* – was the United States. The rumblings of discontent in American accents were already beginning.

Licence to Kill, the James Bond film that premiered in the UK on 13 June 1989, saw Bond turn his attention to the menace of Latin American drug cartels. Pockmarked, murderous cocaine baron Franz Sanchez (Robert Davi) served as Bond's new nemesis.

A Bond picture not named after a book written by Fleming was a step into the unknown. It soon, though, became unremarkable and irrelevant. *Licence to Kill* was a good one with which to start: it was by now an instantly recognisable shorthand for the Bond character and series. Ironically enough, the title was a compromise dictated by the fact that the one originally preferred – *Licence Revoked* – was comical to Americans because it was a familiar term for a punishment for driving offences.

Public discourse has always stated that Eon's original contract with Fleming gave them the right to adapt his books, existing or future. The fact of using a new title means, then, that at some point the contract was renegotiated to allow Eon to place Bond in adventures unrelated to anything of Fleming's devising. The irony of all this is that *Licence to Kill* is, in reality, based to a large extent on Fleming prose: more unused parts of *Live and Let Die*, with a pinch of 'The Hildebrand Rarity'.

That it took three people – Narada Michael Walden, Jeffrey Cohen and Walter Afanasieff – to write the vapid title song (sung by Gladys Knight) becomes even more risible when one learns that a cut of the publishing had to go to John Barry because it used part of the melody of 'Goldfinger'. Michael Kamen wrote the rest of the score. The fact that he provided the music for *Die Hard* (1988) gave ammunition to those who claimed that this film marked a decision by Eon to tilt the Bond series towards the grimy, informal ambience of both that movie and *Lethal Weapon* (1987). Another apparent manifestation of this determination is that 007 is seen – unconscionably – in jeans.

When Sanchez murders Felix Leiter (David Hedison), the authorities – for reasons legal and geopolitical – decide not to pursue him. The vengeance-minded Bond goes rogue and for the first time has to operate without Service backup. Cue a narrative in which the violence is unprecedentedly gruesome: villains variously get blown up – literally – in a depressurisation chamber, sliced in machinery and burnt alive. Also unprecedented is the profanity: 'shit', 'ass', 'piss off', 'bastard' and 'bullshit' all feature. The consequence was that *Licence to Kill* was the first Bond picture not to receive a family-viewing rating. American censors passed it 'PG-13'. In Britain, it was given a '15' certificate. This had the inevitable knock-on effect regarding its box-office takings.

The Wilson–Maibaum story is unfortunately literally half-and-half. About an hour into the two-hour running time, Q turns up like a throwback to the type of normal Bond picture we were just beginning to forget existed. He has been dispatched by an order-bucking Moneypenny (Caroline Bliss, reprising her young, slightly irreverent and bespectacled interpretation from *The Living Daylights*). From this point, what has been a muscular espionage thriller becomes ridiculous. There are improbable gadgets, absurd plot twists (after being shown arduously breaking out of Sanchez's base, Bond effects an unseen, unexplained break back in) and impossible physical stunts (the vehicle-on-one-side trick from *Diamonds Are Forever* is repeated, but this time with a petrol tanker). One wonders whether this division of quality is due to the fact that a Writers' Guild strike meant that, after collaborating with Wilson on the story, Maibaum had to leave him to write the screenplay of *Licence to Kill* on his own.

His vendetta takes Bond from Florida to the fictional country of Isthmus (for which Mexico stands in). No primary shooting was done in the UK, however: the Eady Plan, which Eon had long taken advantage of (and sometimes taken the piss out of) had been abolished.

The closing credits feature an anti-smoking disclaimer. No one had doubted that Connery looked cool with a cigarette hanging from his lips when the world first saw his face in *Dr. No*, but the world was a more complicated place than in 1962. The fact that modified Lark cigarettes are used herein by Bond to detonate explosives because their manufacturers Philip Morris paid for the privilege raised legal issues regarding TV broadcast rules. After questions were asked in the House of Representatives, the health warning was added to prevent the loss of US television screenings.

The box-office performance of *Licence to Kill* was disappointing in the mild way that of any Bond picture can be – it was only the world's twelfth highest-grosser that year. However, this time MGM/UA's seeming willingness to downplay success in territories outside the United States could not be dismissed: *Licence to Kill* had for once failed to perform in the usually loyal United Kingdom, where receipts were down by a third on the hardly spectacular ones for *The Living Daylights*.

Had things been proceeding as normal in Bondland, perhaps

the studio's disgruntlement with the performance of his two films would at this point have forced Timothy Dalton out of the Bond role. We'll never know. There followed six wasted years in which legal issues prevented Eon shooting more Bonds.

September 1991 saw the debut transmission of *James Bond Jr.*.

This animated television series was made by Murakami-Wolf-Swenson, previously responsible for, among other things, *Teenage Mutant Ninja Turtles* and *Alvin and the Chipmunks*. That Michael G. Wilson was billed as one of the creators was significant: the cartoon's producers had licensed only the right to extrapolate from the screen James Bond.

Although back in 1967 it had been Glidrose who enabled the publication of *The Adventures of James Bond Junior 003½*, the similarly titled projects were not only unrelated, but the Fleming Estate were keen to distance themselves from the new endeavour. They vetoed any events or names from Fleming's work that hadn't been used in the films. This may or may not have had something to do with the rumour that the entire project was an attempt to undermine yet another putative McClory Bond project, this one a series of animated Bond adventures. A more plausible impetus for the project, though, was a desire by Eon to keep open the 007 revenue stream in the likely protracted absence of James Bond films. Although *James Bond Jr.* was fairly short-lived, merchandise was plentiful. As well as a Marvel comic, it spun off six novelisations and two video games. It also inspired board games, toy cars and action figures.

The episodes were twenty-two minutes long, designed to run half an hour including commercials. Each featured the goings-on at Warfield Academy, an English prep school for the children of Secret Service organisations around the world. Among those resident is Q's grandson, IQ, and Gordo Leiter, son of Felix.

As with *The Adventures of James Bond Junior 003½*, the hero is, in fact, not the son but the nephew of agent 007. As a personality, Bond Jr bears little relationship to his uncle aside from his privileged background and his catchphrase ('The name's Bond, James Bond. [Pause.] Junior.') It could be argued that his gelled, upright hair and big-tongued trainers were fashionable among the character's late-teenage peer group, but so were many other things that at least had something of Bond's traditional suaveness. Moreover, Corey Burton, who voices Bond Jr, gives the character an accent that never quite suggests Englishness. James Bond himself was not seen in the sixty-five broadcast episodes.

In between classes, Bond Jr is constantly trying to thwart the plans of SCUM (Saboteurs and Criminals United in Mayhem), which organisation employs villains familiar from the films, including Jaws, Goldfinger, Oddjob and Dr No (the last in his lesser-known green-skinned incarnation). Like his uncle, Bond Jr gets involved with plenty of pretty girls possessed of outlandish names, but naturally there is no sex either in the double entendres (Marcie Beaucoup, Terri Firma, Haley Comet) or the relationships.

The animation, as with many American TV cartoons of the era, is adequate but stilted. It would have been nice if the makers had raised their sights a little and aimed for the quality of TV animation classics like the intelligently scripted seventies *Star Trek: The Animated Series* (Filmation) and the noir-ish nineties *Batman: The Animated Series* (Warner Bros. Animation). But, then, fallback buck-spinners do not usually lead to great art.

In 1992, Dark Horse took over the franchise for James Bond comics. This outfit seemed to constitute that elusive thing: a publisher who looked with proactive enthusiasm on the Bond property they had licensed.

Over the preceding three decades, James Bond comics had remained thin on the ground. There were Bond comics in Japanese, Swedish and Spanish, but – fairly or unfairly – foreign-language material tends to be discounted in English-speaking Western countries. British hardback Christmas annuals gave rise to a few mid-sixties Bond comics pages, but a once-a-year proposition was a world removed from a regular title.

That in the 1980s Marvel acquired the licence to publish Bond comics was exciting – they had long overtaken DC as the premier American comic-book publisher and their 1977 adaptation of *Star Wars* was phenomenally successful. Deflatingly, though, the upshot was not a monthly Bond title but merely special edition, single-issue adaptations of the movies *For Your Eyes Only* and *Octopussy*. Perhaps it was because the company already had a hero in its universe who was a manqué 007: Nick Fury, Agent of S.H.I.E.L.D.

Play Value's 1985 'James Bond 007 Adventure Storybooks' – *Blackclaw's Doomsday Plot* and *Storm Bringer* – were for a very young readership. Moreover, they seem to have been markedly unsuccessful: two further titles in the series were advertised but appear never to have been released.

The franchise then passed to Eclipse, who issued an adaptation of *Licence to Kill*. Later in 1989, they delivered something of a Holy Grail: a James Bond comic that both contained original material and lasted longer than one issue. *Permission to Die* was published in the prestigious and newly modish graphic-novel format. Written and illustrated by Mike Grell, its first two parts at least were reasonably well received by fandom, not least because the informed Grell modelled his Bond on Hoagy Carmichael. However, issue three – which dribbled out two years later – was received as the afterthought it felt like.

The cover-date calendar year of 1992 saw Marvel publish twelve titles of what still wasn't quite a regular, *bona fide* Bond title. Instead, *James Bond Jr.* was a comic based on the titular TV series. It featured a combination of episode adaptations and new stories.

A variety of writers and illustrators were responsible for Dark Horse's fifteen Bond comics, which ranged from a one-off to a four-parter. Quality and creator perspective naturally varied (in *Serpent's Tooth*, Bond tussles with a genetically revived dinosaur), but this mattered less than the fact that, during their four-year ownership of the licence, Dark Horse published more Bond comics/graphic novels than had all previous English-language Bond comic publishers combined. Moreover, there was an adult-oriented sensibility to their publications that allowed such things as nudity, thus giving them a flavour of Fleming.

This flurry of Bond comics activity came to an end with the expiry of Dark Horse's licence, after which it wasn't even back to business as usual but something worse. Topps took over the licensing rights in time for the publication of a three-part adaptation of the 'comeback' Bond movie *GoldenEye*. The project was a catastrophe. The first issue duly appeared, cover-dated January 1996, and was of high quality. Yet issues two and three were seen only in a very small, privately printed run sold at comics conventions. The racy style of artist Claude St Aubin seems to have delayed the second issue, and the momentum lost while approval was being sought from Danjaq kiboshed not only the remaining two issues but a putative regular Topps Bond title. Once again, it provoked the thought that James Bond comics were cursed.

A case in point: in 2008, Puffin published a graphic novel adaptation of Young Bond novel *Silver Fin*. Although it was award-nominated, a mooted line of further Young Bond graphic novels never materialised.

All was silence again until 2014, when Dynamite Entertainment were announced as the new 007 comic licensees. The New Jersey publisher's stated plans revolved as much around the wider Bond universe as 007 himself. They spoke of their line – which started in November 2015 – portraying not just the adventures of the mature Bond, but a younger, pre-*Casino Royale* 007, as well as exploring the lives of Bond-supporting characters and villains.

It may, though, be too late for Bond to finally prosper in comics the way he has in almost all other media. The medium is no longer the big component of the childhood experience it was when Bondmania was at its apex in the mid-sixties. Any twenty-first-century parent will tell you that their kids spurn comics for video games.

The six-and-a-half-year gap between *Licence to Kill* and the next Bond movie was more than double the length of any previous hiatus.

As might be expected, the reasons for the interregnum in the most successful film series on the planet were serious. In 1988, while filming *Licence to Kill*, Timothy Dalton told fan magazine *Bondage*, 'My feeling is this will be the last one. I don't mean my last one. I mean the end of the whole lot.' He was clearly in the loop about something not yet on the public radar. It reached that public radar on 8 August 1990, when Cubby Broccoli put Danjaq up for sale. Broccoli's asking price has been reported as anything from $166 million to $200 million, but either way he found no takers, possibly because of the perennial financial problems of the studio with which the Bond property was intertwined.

While the companies swooping on the increasingly troubled MGM were partly attracted by the value of the Bond franchise, the attraction was not reciprocated. Particularly vexing to Danjaq was the fact that when in 1990 Italian financier Giancarlo Parretti bought MGM through his company Pathé Communications Corporation, he did not actually have the $1.2 billion selling price and got around that problem by pledging to creditors access to MGM assets, prominent among which was the Bond series. Broccoli felt that there would ensue a cheapening of the Bond series by the selling of TV rights at bargain-basement prices. Danjaq sued to prevent the deals going ahead. The stasis meant that MGM couldn't afford to fund a Bond movie, and, because they held an exclusive licence to do so, it meant nobody could.

Ultimately, Danjaq was taken off the market. Public comments by Michael G. Wilson suggest that putting it up for sale had only been a tactical manoeuvre designed to establish a value for the Bond franchise, but in 2012 Bond documentary *Everything or Nothing* Barbara Broccoli claimed that the move was her father's anguished response to the conviction that his final few years would be spent in law courts.

Even without the problems with the distributor, things were awry with cinema Bond. The increasingly ailing Broccoli had left the day-to-day operations of Danjaq/Eon in the hands of his stepson and daughter. Their market research was showing that young male cinemagoers were only vaguely aware of James Bond. Possibly related to that fact is that the year 1990 saw John Glen and Richard Maibaum informed they would not be working on a Bond film again. An unnamed Eon employee even gracelessly claimed in *Variety* that the eighty-year-old Maibaum was a 'has-been'. (One wonders what said employee felt about the vintage of Cubby Broccoli, born a month prior to Maibaum.)

Then were other reasons to believe that the world had left James Bond behind.

In December 1989, American president George H.W. Bush had declared the Cold War to be over. *Licence to Kill* had been the only Bond film not released while the Cold War was running and it had flopped. The assumed connection between the two facts was dubious for more than the reason that the film Bond had never quite been a Cold Warrior. Nonetheless, the general public perceived 007 as a character predicated on tensions between the West and the USSR, a geopolitical alliance that had been dissolved at the end of 1991.

It wasn't only politically that Bond seemed old-fashioned. *True Lies* (1994) was the latest in a line of movies that were felt to have stolen Bond's thunder. That the protagonist secret agent was a married man grappling not just with bad guys but the problems caused him by his troubled teenaged daughter made Bond's perennial tomcat lifestyle look shallow, even undignified. The greater realism granted cinema espionage by Harrison Ford's Jack Ryan films also gave pause.

Accordingly, even when the legal issues had been resolved, there were postponements to and rewrites of the next Bond picture that indicated the occurrence of much agonising.

There was also a clear-out among Bond staff, onscreen and backstage, whether it was through death, retirement or the new recalibration changing times had made necessary. As well as Glen and Maibaum, never to be seen again in Bond credits were Maurice Binder, Bob Simmons, Robert Brown, Caroline Bliss, John Grover (long-term editor) and Alec Mills (long term cameraman/director of photography/cinematographer). The biggest change, though, was the man playing 007.

Whenever he has been asked, Timothy Dalton is always careful to give the impression that the decision for him to vacate the Bond role was his. For instance, in 2014 he told Scott Meslow of *theweek. com* that Broccoli said to him, 'There's no way, after a five-year gap between movies that you can come back and just do one. You'd have to plan on four or five.' Dalton said he declined: 'I thought, oh, no, that would be the rest of my life. Too much. Too long.'

Yet United Artists executives Jeff Kleeman and Alan Ladd Jr, when spoken to by authors Matthew Field and Ajay Chowdhury, bluntly communicated the message that Dalton departed at the insistence of the studio. 'The Dalton Bonds had not performed significantly well at the box office,' said Kleeman. 'We were trying to introduce Bond to a new audience. It seemed counterintuitive to what we were trying to accomplish to continue on with Timothy at that point.' Eon were probably powerless in this: some had noted that the studio's marketing of *Licence to Kill* could be viewed as half-hearted or, if one was really inclined, sabotage.

Dalton brought a trademark to his Bond – pulling the top of his tuxedo jacket across to a Velcro attachment to create a ready-for-action turtleneck effect – but wasn't really in the role long enough for his tenure to constitute an era. However, in his short occupancy, he brought a much-needed vigour and merciful absence of smugness to the James Bond series. Most of each of his films was better than any Bond picture of the previous decade.

It is in terms of legacy, though, that his brief reign has had the greatest impact. When Dalton made his Bond entrée, an increasingly digital world was just beginning to use the term 'reboot' to refer to the function of restarting a computer. The term was yet to acquire the wider meaning of a fresh beginning for a long-running but waning media property. However, a reboot is precisely what Dalton gave cinema Bond. His urgent, intense and naturalistic portrayal has set the trend for the two subsequent Bond actors, and of course such a portrayal dictates the timbre and quality of scripts. That the farcicality and the complacency that began to set into the Bond series from around 1965 onwards are now, apparently permanently, things of the past is largely due to Timothy Dalton.

Even as the days of a Bond-film family atmosphere started to come to an end, Danjaq and Eon became even more of a clan affair as Barbara Broccoli climbed the ranks to join her stepbrother as producer. Michael G. Wilson at this point relinquished any further formal role in screenwriting.

Martin Campbell became the first new Bond director in a decade-and-a-half. He was probably best known for his television work, including *Reilly, Ace of Spies* (whose real-life protagonist Sidney Reilly has been suggested by some as a prototype for Bond) and the acclaimed 1985 BBC drama series *Edge of Darkness*. His 1994 science-fiction motion picture *No Escape* starring Ray Liotta made little money but won many fans, including John Calley of UA/MGM, who recruited him.

The new Bond film would be called *GoldenEye*. Although given a consultancy credit, Campbell reports that a 'very ill' Cubby Broccoli played no active role in the film's production.

The preparation stage of the movie was almost certainly the

most intense since that for *Dr. No*. On that movie, the franchise was being birthed. Here it was being given a rebirth. Eon and their distributor were cognisant of the fact that, for really the first time since that debut, they could not rely on an audience being automatically there for the latest Bond instalment. 'There was certainly a lot of publicity about, "Is Bond past its sell-by date?" because the gap had been so long, and was it so relevant in the nineties and should they be making another Bond?' says Campbell. A drastic change of tone was deemed necessary. Campbell: 'What we did was two things. One, we had a female M, which was a big change, and, secondly, we have a scene between M and Bond where she calls him a dinosaur, a relic from the Cold War, et cetera, et cetera. So we kind of addressed it so she spells it out in a way that perhaps the audience might be asking themselves . . . We had to drag it well into the nineties.'

Another change was the absence of smoking on the part of the hero. Campbell says, 'Smoking was a big issue at the time with kids who go and see Bond. I had no problem with him not smoking and I probably was part of that decision.' However, the director dismisses rumours that he demanded the absence of cigs because he was virulently anti-smoking: 'If you believe the press, then good luck, mate.' This finally brought Bond's physical prowess into line with reality: anybody with the fag habit depicted in the Fleming books and many of the Bond films would have been a wheezing wreck after a few seconds of fisticuffs.

Another manifestation of the uncertain new era in Bond films was the limited resources available to the director. Campbell recalls, 'Everybody felt a little bit of trepidation at whether it was going to be successful, which translated into being a little careful with the budget.' Nonetheless, one staple of the deluxe Bond production process remained: multiple units shooting simultaneously across the globe. Campbell: 'We had a unit in Switzerland shooting some of the action there, we had a model unit, we had a third unit shooting bits and pieces. What I would have to do is endless storyboards.'

GoldenEye's script is credited to Jeffrey Caine and Bruce Feirstein from a story by Michael France. The reality is less clear-cut than politics and Writers' Guild attribution rules would suggest. Campbell recalls, 'I had the Michael France version, then it was Jeffrey Caine, Kevin Wade – who's the guy that wrote *Working Girl* – came on for a period of four weeks, and then it was Bruce Feirstein who came on, did a lot of work on it.' Campbell also says he contributed 'a lot' to the scripts, although also says, 'I can't write. All I can do is comment, so I have absolutely no problem with the credits at all.'

Campbell says he would 'absolutely' have taken the job if Dalton had still been in the Bond role. However, with Dalton gone, Campbell had the privilege of being involved in the casting of the new 007. 'The Broccolis are terrific,' he says. 'Barbara and Michael are probably the best producers I've worked for. It's all discussions, it's all very democratic.'

Liam Neeson has said that he was 'heavily courted' at this juncture to play Bond but turned down the role at the insistence of his wife-to-be. From that point there seems to have been little agonising about offering the role to Pierce Brosnan. 'Pierce was pretty obviously the number-one choice,' Campbell reveals. 'We saw other people, but frankly I think in all our minds we knew it was going to be Pierce.' Of those 'other people', he notes, 'I hate to say it, I can't even remember who we saw.'

Brosnan was born in County Meath, Ireland, in 1953 and raised in London from the age of ten. The reason that the casting process was pretty much a one-horse race is that Brosnan had actually been awarded the Bond role once before. Brosnan made a name for himself during the eighties in the lead role of the blatantly Bond-esque NBC television series *Remington Steele* and was offered the part of Bond when *Remington Steele* was cancelled in 1987. In a sickening twist of fate, the publicity the Bond offer generated caused *Remington Steele* to be revived and Brosnan had to turn down the biggest film role in the world to fulfil his obligations on a programme that had just one further, and somewhat half-hearted, season in it. Subsequently, Brosnan appeared in more than one Bondian television commercial. He also had discussions about playing Bond with that perennial spectre (as it were) at the feast Kevin McClory: one of McClory's fleeting, straw-grasping, lawyer-frustrated plans to exploit his ownership of a corner of the Bond universe was a live-action Bond television series.

Brosnan was on the cusp of thirty-five when first slated to play Bond. He was forty-two when *GoldenEye* was premiered in LA on 13 November 1995. Ironically, Brosnan doesn't suffer for being older, despite his crinkly forehead. Although a little wide of cheek, he has lustrous black hair, piercing blue eyes and a flawless, chiselled profile. He also inhabits with poise the well-cut suits provided by wardrobe, even if he is slightly stiff in his gun-barrel sequence, where – dressed in a tuxedo – he ends with knees unbent.

Despite all the changes, it was decided that one thing at least must stay. 'Bond was legendary for delivering an opening sequence that took your breath away,' Campbell explains. 'We just felt it was part of the iconography and it was essential that we did that. I suppose the only difference was that our prologue in *GoldenEye* was the beginning part of a story.'

In the tradition of Bond films latching onto the latest crazes, the pre-title sequence includes a bungee jump – although that up-to-the-minute note loses its logic when we learn that this is a flashback to nine years previously. Bond uses this method to effect entry to the Arkangel Chemical Weapons Facility, USSR. Inside he is met by 006 – Alec Trevelyan, played compellingly by Sean Bean. The two embark on their plan to blow up the facility, making this one of the few genuine Cold War passages in the Bond films. A captured Trevelyan shouts out that Bond should finish the job. Taking him at his word, 007 flees the imminently exploding building.

Although this film endeavours to be a bit more realistic than some Bond fare, that there are limits to this objective is illustrated by the fact that Bond loses his ticket out of enemy territory when he falls from an aeroplane about to take off, but then catches up with it by calmly freefalling. In the same unlikely vein is the fact that Bond subsequently engages in a road duel with a fiery young woman who by coincidence is one of the villains behind the case he is assigned to crack. Said woman is Xenia Onatopp (Famke Janssen), who smokes oversize cigars and murders men during sexual congress by squeezing the life out of them with her thighs.

The theme song is disappointingly limp. Tina Turner sings a mid-tempo, unmemorable composition by U2's Bono and The Edge that – like the theme of *Thunderball* – seems to confuse the title with a quality possessed by Bond. The first non-Binder title sequence since 1964 is provided by Daniel Kleinman, who delivers visuals in which the usual slinky female silhouettes symbolically walk over hammers and sickles and topple statues of communist icons.

Although now out of titles of Fleming books, Eon keep intact a thread to Bond's creator. GoldenEye – as it is rendered here – is brought into service as the name of a secret space-based weapon that creates a radiation pulse that leaves enemies vulnerable by destroying their communications.

Rapidly advancing technology is also represented in the proliferation of modems and the fact that Secret Service headquarters is full of gleamingly hi-tech banks of equipment and massive screens, the latter a quantum leap from the almost patently cardboard sets of M's and Moneypenny's offices that had been pretty much unchanged since the start of the series.

Then there is political correctness. There are several feminist put-downs of Bond, even as the film glorifies the macho behaviour such comments supposedly ridicule and undermine. 'You are just trying to show off the size of your [pause] ego,' notes a female colleague of Bond's competitive driving. Moneypenny (Samantha Bond) is not interested in Bond romantically and suggests that his comments to her 'could qualify as sexual harassment'. Most seismically, Bond's boss (Judi Dench) is a woman. This development does not feel gimmicky. Although David Spedding was then chief of MI6 – named as Bond's employers for the first time – it was now perfectly plausible to portray the organisation as headed by a female: Stella Rimington had been director general of MI5 since 1992.

It was also of course more interesting in a dramatic sense. The writers pulled out all the stops on this score to create this exchange between M and Bond:

M: You don't like me, Bond. You don't like my methods.
You think I'm an accountant, more interested in numbers
than your instincts.
Bond: The thought had occurred to me.

M: Good. Because I think you're a sexist, misogynist dinosaur, a relic of the Cold War . . . If you think I don't have the balls to send a man out to die, your instincts are dead wrong.

Although a little manufactured, the repartee was destined to both instantly draw attention to the refreshment of the franchise and go down as one of its most famous pieces of dialogue.

A yet further sign of a new era is a layer of postmodernism. When Bond meets his CIA contact Jack Wade (Joe Don Baker), he dutifully chants his assigned greeting, 'In London, April's a spring month,' only to be met with the response, 'Oh, yeah? What are you – the weatherman? For cryin' out loud. Another stiff-assed Brit with your secret codes and passwords.' On a grimmer note, Trevelyan says to Bond, 'I might as well ask if all the vodka martinis ever silence the screams of the men you've killed. Or if you find forgiveness in the arms of all those willing women for all the dead ones you failed to protect.'

Yet, though the world has changed around him, Bond remains the same. His unapologetic womanising, speeding and relish for battle gives him an incorrigible charm that counteracts the disapproval. His patent decency and humanity, meanwhile, puts into context assumptions about his value system.

Trevelyan turns out both to be alive and to have been working for the Soviets since the incident in the pre-title sequence. That he blames 007 for the disfigurement of his face that resulted from Bond's destruction of the Arkangel facility is fairly standard Bond movie motivation. More nuanced stuff comes with the revelation that he is the son of Lienz Cossacks, a Russian group who worked for the Nazis in World War II, surrendered to the British and were then handed over by them to Stalin. This is something for which Trevelyan wants revenge, hence his plan to bring financial chaos to Britain with GoldenEye.

Trevelyan makes an excellent opponent. Physical and strategic equals through their identical training, he and Bond are like good and bad bookends. They also have similar domestic hinterlands: both are orphans. In 006 stating that Bond lost his parents in a climbing accident, the films are finally incorporating the biographical details first laid out by Fleming in the *You Only Live Twice* obituary. The familiarity of the two men means Trevelyan is one of the few villains who don't address 007 as 'Mr Bond'.

GoldenEye took $350.7 million, making it the highest-grossing Bond film yet by around $150 million. Although part of *GoldenEye*'s outstanding success could conceivably be put down to the public's joy at the return of a long-absent pleasure, it set the trend for Brosnan Bonds. It had taken him a long time to secure the exalted position of incumbent, but Brosnan found himself in the gratifying position of being instantly accepted as 007.

The man who had first approved the casting of Brosnan as Bond will have been pleased that he finally got to see him do well in the role. It was the final Bond-related triumph of Cubby Broccoli's life. On 27 June 1996, six months after the premiere of *GoldenEye*, Broccoli died of a heart-related ailment at his Beverly Hills home.

The fact of the cinema Bond being a family business has meant that his name has not died with him. The credits of every Bond film now begin – and presumably will ever after – with the phrase, 'Albert R. Broccoli's Eon Productions Ltd. Presents . . .'

THE DINOSAUR
LIVES AGAIN

Politics and cinema weren't the only things that had changed in James Bond's absence. The technology and financial potential of video games had advanced considerably in that time. Of Rare's 1997 *GoldenEye 007* for the Nintendo 64 computer console – the first Bond video game of any real sophistication – Raymond Benson reveals, 'The video game made more money than the movie.' From here on, video games would constitute a substantial plank of the Bond merchandising operation.

For a third of a century after Bond entered the world, the closest thing to a video game remained the good old board game. *James Bond Secret Agent 007* was the first one, manufactured by Milton Bradley in 1964, a proposition involving numbered squares and plastic miniature figurines. The fact that set into the board was a clock with an hour hand that moved would actually have been considered by both kids and adults of the time to be fairly hi-tech.

The next jump forward was a role-playing game of the type that became very popular in the eighties, with *Dungeons and Dragons* the iconic success story of the genre. In Victory Games' *James Bond 007*, released in 1983, the actions of players were dictated initially by a roll of a die, then their own instincts, with the designated Games Master determining whether their actions were correct by reference to provided scenarios. That several supplements and additional adventures were added to the 'basic set' over the following four years is testament to the fact that *James Bond 007* was a superior example of its kind (it won multiple awards) and sold accordingly (it easily outstripped its espionage role-playing competitor, TSR's *Top Secret*). A classy product was completed by high-quality cover art.

Victory's licence came to an end in 1987, with licensor and licensee failing to agree terms for an extension. There have been no similar products since, the role-playing games market having been (like that of comic books) all but obliterated by video games. (Four 1985 James Bond Find Your Own Fate books in the Ballantine series of that name operate on a similar premise, but don't quite count: one person chooses different plot outcomes.)

Not that video games were initially anything to write home about. Angelsoft's PC games *A View to a Kill* (1985) and *Goldfinger* (1986) were marketed when home computers were still in the silicon Stone Age. These text-based adventures required proxy Bonds to type at the blinking cursor proposed solutions to their current situation, using the traditional article-less idiom ('Put clip in gun'; 'Open door'). Such stuff seemed fun before the days of graphical user interfaces, PC multitasking and competent graphics cards, but today appears qualitatively indistinct from role-playing games, interactive books or, indeed, reformatting your hard drive.

James Bond 007 (1983) constituted a series of generic

tableaux wherein a vehicle fired missiles at other objects to the accompaniment of tinny 'Choo! Choo!' sound effects. In *A View to a Kill* (1985), Bond was a matchstick figure identifiable only via 'The James Bond Theme' playing in the background. In *The Living Daylights* (1987) he had evolved into a sprite comprising a collection of different-coloured pixels. *Live and Let Die* (1988) was a step forward from these sideways-scrolling propositions, containing approximations of that film's speedboat chases in a first-person format (the player facing the action). Significantly, though, it started life as a non-Bond endeavour. What turned an ordinary video game into something to do with Bond was still a matter of names, music, copyrights and gentlemen's agreements with the player.

The N64 *GoldenEye 007* game was a first-person shooter, meaning the player killed baddies with the gun that was poised at the bottom of his screen, supposedly in the player's/Bond's hand. Its quality in terms of gameplay, graphics and sound was almost unrecognisable from the sideways-scrollers and platform games that had preceded it, not just in Bond games but in video games *per se*. For the first time in decades, Bond was ahead of the curve. With video-game critics talking about *GoldenEye 007* in terms of best game ever and close to perfection, it picked up the Game of the Year award from the Academy of Interactive Arts and Sciences. Its 8 million sales up to 2001 made it history's biggest-selling video game. As it retailed at over $60, this meant serious profits. The game also had the supplementary beneficial effect of making Bond an icon for a teenaged demographic to many of whom he had hitherto been only a peripheral cultural presence.

The first Daniel Craig-related Bond game was *Quantum of Solace* (2008). By now, such was the quality of the graphics that, in the parkour scene transported from the 2006 *Casino Royale* film, 007's climb up the crane was more stomach-churning than in the film itself, while the Bond avatar (face permanently visible despite first-person orientation, and entire body occasionally observable) was often almost indistinguishable from the real Craig.

Because in video games the player controls the action, James Bond had now become the blunt instrument Fleming had originally foreseen – a blunt instrument, furthermore, often in the hands of children. However, Eon's family-oriented approach at least meant Bond games were not allowed to stray into the vicious and disturbing types of violence seen in products like *Grand Theft Auto*.

James Bond video games are an aspect of the Bond phenomenon that is in some senses 'invisible'. The extent of their success – and the depth of their profitability – makes little or no impression on generations who simply don't play video games. This includes even many older Bond fans who otherwise make a point of being cognisant of Bond's impact on the culture. Yet, though it may be a quasi-underground phenomenon, it is real and hugely important. The care and cost devoted to the video-game market is demonstrated by the fact that Bond screenwriter Bruce Feirstein was hired to write several of them.

Nineteen eighty-four saw the publication of *The James Bond Bedside Companion* by Raymond Benson, a Bond fan since the age of nine. It won the Edgar Allan Poe Award for Best Biographical/Critical Work. During the course of his research, Benson met Peter Janson-Smith, head of the board of Glidrose. This latter connection would transpire to be fateful.

'We stayed in touch,' Benson says. As well as the *Casino Royale* play,

Benson 'did little odd jobs' for Glidrose over the next ten years. 'They would send me [John Gardner's] manuscripts from then on and I would find continuity Bondian universe mistakes and they'd get them fixed.' The fact that in the mid-eighties Benson wrote two James Bond computer games – *A View to a Kill* and *Goldfinger* – would no doubt also have played a part in the momentous telephone call made to him by Janson-Smith in November 1995. Benson: 'He called me and he just said, "Raymond, John wants to retire from doing Bond. We wanted to know if you'd like to give it a shot." It was just offered to me on a silver platter. I couldn't believe it.'

While it was a given that Benson knew the Bond universe better than most, he was not a published novelist. However, Janson-Smith had seen his unpublished first novel. Benson explains, 'They figured they could guide me through writing that first [Bond] novel.'

Smith explained there were certain hoops through which Benson had to jump. 'I had to come up with an outline of a story on spec that, first, they would approve and then both the British publisher and the American publisher would approve. So I did the outline and then I had to write the first four chapters on spec. Same approval process. Then I got this contract.'

Naturally there was a conversation about the approach Benson would be taking towards his version of 007. 'I had actually suggested that we do period pieces and set them back in the fifties or sixties. Peter said, "No, we want to stay in sync with the movies," because at that time they had just rebooted the movies again with Pierce Brosnan and *GoldenEye* was a huge hit. I said, "Well I want to keep the character of Bond the same." John Gardner had gone politically correct. I said, "I want him to have all of his vices intact.

I want him to smoke again, and drink a lot and sleep with a lot of women." They said, "Yeah, that's fine. Just make it work within the context of the 1990s." They only said, "Make 'em like the movies and make M a woman."' Benson adds, 'We just don't talk about his age. We just say, "Well he's a little older and wiser" and that's it.'

Something that caused controversy was the fact of Benson's American origin. Even Benson admits he had always previously assumed that his nationality made it impossible for him to write Bond continuation novels. 'I was being vetted,' he says of the inevitable cultural gaffes. 'They corrected a lot of stuff in the first couple of books.'

The first Bond fiction Benson published was a short story, 'Blast from the Past', which appeared in *Playboy* in January 1997. This was his idea, he being keen to revive the Bond short-fiction tradition that had died with Fleming. Benson's debut Bond novel was *Zero Minus Ten*, published the following April. It revolved around terrorist events in Hong Kong – a topical subject given the handover to China that year of the then-British territory.

Benson had to be careful about things that might cause problems between Glidrose and Eon, whom he describes as 'feuding cousins'. For instance, he ignored Bond-film continuity in his novels: 'If you put anything in that was only in the films then you could get in trouble.' For related reasons, Benson didn't use SPECTRE and Blofeld in his books, even though Glidrose owned the literary rights to them. As an alternative, Benson created The Union. He describes this outfit, which appeared in a trilogy of books, as 'like the working-class SPECTRE'.

Like Gardner before him, Benson also wrote novelisations of the Bond films. 'I had to kind of switch,' Benson says. Of how the novelisations differed from the 'real' Bond books, he explains, 'He had more lines that were jokes, witticisms, that I wouldn't have had in my books.' Asked if his novelisations sold better than his other Bond fiction, Benson says, 'I don't think so, because usually they were just in paperback. They did have a small print run in England of hardcovers that sold to collectors.'

By this time, video recorders had achieved wide penetration of the home market and James Bond films were available to rent cheaply, thus reducing the market for the book of the film. Ultimately the market would be destroyed. Benson: 'It's now being shifted more and more to novels of video games. I actually enquired about a novelisation for *Skyfall* and the people at Ian Fleming Publications just said that they and Eon decided that they're not going to do novelisations any more. They didn't think it was worth it.'

Benson was productive in his tenure as a Bond scribe, with six novels, three novelisations and three short stories to his name. 'The whole seven years while I was doing Bond, it was a roller coaster,' he says. While the workload may have been offset by the fact that the entire job was a fantasy come true, there were some real downsides: 'I got death threats from some fans, mainly because I was American.'

Pierce Brosnan's second Bond outing, *Tomorrow Never Dies*, premiered in London on 9 December 1997.

Inevitably, Martin Campbell had been asked back. He says, 'I remember thinking, "Well just how many control rooms can I blow up?"' This would transpire to be the complication of Eon's new policy of engaging the services of 'worthy' directors: their artistic-mindedness made them disinclined to repeat themselves. Roger Spottiswoode, a man who had veered from the wildly populist (*48*

Hrs, Turner & Hooch) to the highly worthy (*Under Fire, And the Band Played On*), directed a film written by Bruce Feirstein.

The film's title is the first with absolutely no connection to Bond's creator, save a vaguely Fleming-esque ring. That it is not mentioned in the film is a consequence of the title's farcical origins. Chief villain Elliot Carver owns a newspaper called *Tomorrow* and a fax informing MGM of potential titles, among them *Tomorrow Never Lies*, was misread.

The title song by Sheryl Crow is only half-decent, and Crow doesn't have the range to do justice to her own creation. The film is scored by David Arnold, who had recently been successful with a Bond-music tribute album called *Shaken and Stirred*. John Barry himself was so impressed by it that he concluded Arnold was the heir apparent and recommended him to Barbara Broccoli. Arnold would score five Bond pictures in a row.

Although the beginning of the story shows tensions between the West and China, the mutual suspicion has been deliberately orchestrated by Carver (Jonathan Pryce). After decades of obsequiousness towards the Soviet Union while simultaneously being relaxed about offending their fellow human-rights abusers the Chinese, the Bond series is now being sycophantic towards Beijing. As with *The Spy Who Loved Me*, Bond ends up working with an attractive female operative from the other side, in this case Colonel Wai Lin (Michelle Yeoh).

Jonathan Pryce does not quite have the menace to be fully effective as a Bond villain, even if he is put in the Nehru suit traditional for a main Bond baddie. Also not quite convincing is his motivation, which is less psychopathy or personal enrichment than the expansion of his media empire. However, he does provide an amusing moment when he mocks Wai Lin by throwing self-defence shapes while issuing such things as 'Hi-yaa!' The moment mocks the very chopsocky traditions that the film elsewhere exults in.

Unusually, Bond's sex life comes back to haunt him. It transpires that he once had a fling with Paris Carver (Teri Hatcher), wife of the villain. When he greets her, she responds by slapping his face. As with the last film, Brosnan's Bond is portrayed driving his Aston Martin DB5 for leisure and a BMW for work. Bond switches from a Walther PPK to the new model, the P99.

Brosnan is ever more comfortable in the role of Bond. Moreover, he is noticeably more hollow of face, the loss of those slightly bulbous cheeks removing just about his only physical flaw.

Bruce Feirstein and the team of Neal Purvis and Robert Wade provided the screenplay for *The World Is Not Enough* – premiered in LA on 8 November 1999 – from a story by Purvis and Wade. British director Michael Apted was known primarily for classy fare such as *Agatha*, *Coal Miner's Daughter* and *Gorillas in the Mist*.

The film's title is of course a link to Fleming even if the invocation of what Bond explains as a 'family motto' is rather contrived and irrelevant to the plot.

The pre-title sequence lasts for nearly a quarter-hour and is a good one, involving a mass fight in Switzerland and a boat chase in London culminating in Bond tumbling from an exploding hot-air balloon onto the Millennium Dome, a new and spectacular fixture on the capital's skyline. The chase sees Brosnan executing underwater the tie-adjustment that he made his urbane Bond trademark.

The so-so title song is by David Arnold and veteran Bond movie lyricist Don Black, and performed by the group Garbage.

Q introduces Bond to a 'young' man he is grooming to take over from him upon his retirement. This stripling turns out to be the sixty-year-old John Cleese, who – as might be imagined with the ex-Monty Python member – plays it for laughs. Q tells Bond, 'I've always tried to teach you two things. First, never let them see you bleed.' 'And the second?' asks Bond. 'Always have an escape plan,' responds Q, at which point he starts slowly disappearing via hydraulics into the floor. Bond watches impassively the departure of the man he had driven to distraction so many times. Desmond Llewelyn was the only actor to have played opposite every Eon Bond from Connery through to Brosnan.

Elektra King (Sophie Marceau), the film's chief villain, has devised a scheme to create a nuclear blast that will have the effect of increasing petroleum prices, from which she will benefit as heiress to an oil empire. She is in league with Renard, who would be an excellent villain even without Robert Carlyle's fine acting chops. An ex-KGB man, he is both walking dead, due to a bullet slowly worming its way through his brain, and superman, consequence of the brain deterioration rendering him immune to pain.

M is uncharacteristically right in the heart of the action. Having failed to engineer M's death at the beginning (a revelation that comes in a twist-laden plot), Elektra tricks her into coming out to her base, where she puts her in a cell and torments her with her impending demise. M improvises an escape every bit as inspired as the ways 007 usually gets out of a fix.

Although Brosnan's films have reined back on the graphic violence, Bond movies are getting ever more daring in other ways, such as Moneypenny's patent dildo allusion when Bond presents her with a cigar in an aluminium case: 'I know exactly where to put that.' (For the record, she throws it in the dustbin.) Meanwhile,

Elektra is shown closer to (lingering) nudity than a character has ever been seen in a Bond movie.

Die Another Day – premiered in London on 18 November 2002 – coincided with the fortieth anniversary of the Bond film series. Accordingly, it contained references to every single one of the previous Eon Bonds, making for a fascinating parlour game for 007 aficionados. Among them are Giacinta 'Jinx' Johnson walking out of the Cuban surf with a bikini-and-knife-belt combination redolent of Ursula Andress in *Dr. No* and a character jumping out of a plane with the aid of a Union Jack parachute. There is also a nice tip of the hat to both Fleming and the real James Bond: at one point, Brosnan idly examines a copy of *Birds of the West Indies*.

In the gun-barrel sequence, the bullet is seen coming towards the viewer. It's one of the few moments in the film where computer-generated imagery (CGI) – first used in a Bond film in *GoldenEye* – is employed adroitly.

The pre-title sequence sees Bond infiltrate a military base in North Korea. The latter is the 'safe' national villain that the series has lately been looking for. Nonetheless, Colonel Tan-Sun Moon (Will Yun Lee) – who is trading arms for 'conflict diamonds' – is a rogue element of whose decadence his father, a general, disapproves. After the usual explosive fisticuffs, Moon disappears into a waterfall and is presumed dead, while Bond is dragged off to a North Korean prisoner-of-war camp. The title sequence for the first time actually furthers the plot: vignettes show Bond being tortured in captivity.

As was largely becoming the norm, the rearrangement of 'The James Bond Theme' is overly playful and modernistic. This is carried over into the opening credits. The title song is written and performed by Madonna (who also plays the role of fencing instructor Verity). It is very techno, with much robotic voice distortion.

Bond's fourteen months in a cell leave him long-haired and bearded – and in fact not too dissimilar to how the newly hippiefied George Lazenby turned up for the premiere of *On Her Majesty's Secret Service*. When he gets back to Blighty after a prisoner exchange, Bond finds that M suspects him to be the person who betrayed the operation. Bond goes rogue to clear his name.

When Bond shaves off his beard and cuts his tresses, a new restyling of Brosnan is revealed. His hair is both less groomed than in the previous film and noticeably greyer. While it's admirable on one level that Brosnan doesn't bother to dye his locks, it is unfortunately the case that in some shots he is, looks-wise, less impressive than Toby Stephens, who plays villain Gustav Graves.

To absolutely no one's surprise (the pre-title sequence put him on display too much for him to be so quickly dispensed with), Moon is not dead. However, it definitely is surprising that he is now Graves, an English businessman who is debonair, vastly wealthy and emphatically white. The transformation has been effected by DNA therapy involving the replacement of bone marrow. This and the fact that a side effect of said treatment is Moon's being unable to ever sleep makes *Die Another Day* an outright science-fiction picture, not to mention unutterable nonsense. Other examples are the virtual-reality glasses that enable agents to be engaged in training exercises and – most notoriously – the invisible car furnished Bond by Q. Or should that be screenwriters Neal Purvis and Robert Wade? It seems to suggest that the absent Bruce Feirstein – involved in the scripts of the three other Brosnan films – was a steadying hand. The film's fanciful tenor certainly doesn't sit easily with the reputation of director Lee Tamahori, a

New Zealander most renowned for the socially conscious, local-colour piece *Once Were Warriors*. Nor does Tamahori direct it well, employing self-conscious effects such as blurred slow motion normally the preserve of first-year film students.

When Bond meets up with Moon again, he quips, 'So you lived to die another day.' Moon retorts, 'I chose to model the disgusting Gustav Graves on you . . . That unjustifiable swagger, the crass quips, the self-defence mechanism concealing such inadequacy . . .' What he fails to explain in his postmodern tirade is how he could possibly have planned his fake death when the arrival of an enemy agent was an unforeseen event. Moon has constructed the Icarus satellite, whose solar magnifying powers he intends to use to create a single Korean state run by the totalitarian North. When he and Bond end up tussling on an aeroplane in mid-air, Moon is swept into one of the jet's engines – a grisly, convincing scene that is one of Tamahori's better moments.

Brosnan's Bond breaks his no-smoking rule in this film by indulging in a cigar or two, but, as he is in Cuba, he can perhaps be excused. It is while on that Caribbean island that Bond teams up with Jinx, an employee of the National Security Agency pursuing similar leads. Halle Berry – the woman playing Jinx – is a classy proposition: she won an Oscar that year for her role in *Monster's Ball*. The days of a trade-off between ski stunts and top-drawer Bond-girl actresses would appear to have died with Cubby Broccoli.

Moneypenny doesn't actually have a real scene with Bond, only interacting with him via the virtual-reality glasses, the second time using them to fantasise about Bond ravishing her. It's almost as though Eon knew this would be Samantha Bond's farewell, so were free to destroy the frosty disdain she had always shown Brosnan on screen.

Also appearing for the last time is John Cleese as 'Quartermaster'. (So is that what 'Q' meant all these years?) The comedy turn that his appearances constituted had no place in the new, severe Bond era just around the corner.

It has to be said that – even leaving aside death threats from the more intense end of the fandom spectrum – Raymond Benson's tenure as James Bond continuation novelist was not universally well received. Naysayers objected to his graphic violence, paucity of internal monologues, clunky insertion of research material and sex scenes that made Bond resemble less a sensualist than a horny schoolboy.

Others praised his deep knowledge of Bond history and capacity for crafting an easy beach read. That his original contract was renewed supports Benson's assertion that Glidrose and the publishers were 'very happy' with his books. However, additional comments by him indicate the reason why his contract was not renewed for a second time: 'I inherited the marketplace from John Gardner. When John started, the first four books were bestsellers, but starting with the fifth one, the sales just settle into this niche thing because they were just, "Oh, another year, another Bond book."'

If things had not changed at Glidrose, that niche audience might have continued to satisfy those overseeing Bond's literary affairs. However, in 1997 Ian Fleming's literary estate came fully back into the ownership of his family for the first time since 1964. With the purchase of Booker's holdings, Glidrose now became Ian Fleming Publications (IFP), but the new name was only the start of the changes, one casualty of which was Benson, who says, 'They decided they were going to stop doing the Bond novels on a yearly basis and do some other things for a while.'

Although Benson maintains an interest in James Bond, he admits that a thing of the past is the fanboy attitude that was the impetus behind *The Bedside Companion*. 'I used to collect the books and the posters and the toys and all the shit, and I don't any more,' he says. Because he's seen 'behind the curtain'? 'I think it's that, and I'm a bit jaded. I've moved on to my own stuff.'

With the literary adult Bond put in abeyance, IFP initially decided to reinvigorate the name of the man in their company title. Benson: 'When they stopped my books, it was right before the fiftieth anniversary of *Casino Royale*. The very next year, they reissued all the Flemings and really set about for the next two years exploiting the original Flemings.'

Following that, while they mulled over what to do with the Bond continuation novels, IFP took not just one but two unusual steps in furthering Fleming's legacy. They decided on lateral angles: a series of books about the adventures of a young James Bond and another about the escapades of Miss Moneypenny.

Both approaches seemed counterintuitive. The idea of a young Bond had already been tried in two separate failed projects spaced a quarter-century apart. The Moneypenny idea, meanwhile, involved pitching Bond to the demographic that had seemed least susceptible to the character down the years: women. As if to compound the apparent contrariness, the projects were launched with what would appear to be unseemly confidence: the first instalments in each series appearing within seven months of each other in 2005. In both cases, however, IFP were vindicated.

The man chosen to helm the Young Bond series was musician, author and actor Charlie Higson. His approach was not the nephew-conceit copout of the previous 'junior' projects, but instead chronicles from the 'real' James Bond's childhood, starting at the age of thirteen. Higson stuck to the time period established by Fleming, depicting Bond's schooldays as being in the 1930s. Although the facts established by Fleming's novels prohibited making young James a teen agent, grounding for his future career is provided by mentor Uncle Max, an ex-spy. One thing established by Fleming, though, was worked around, namely *The Times* obituary's assertion that he attended only two halves (terms) at Eton.

In first book *SilverFin* (March 2005), Higson never rises to the elegance of Fleming, but his prose, dialogue and scene-setting are competent. However, his leisurely style – the books are unusually long for children's fiction, and, unlike the Mascott book, the text is not leavened by illustrations – doesn't work in the way that it did for Fleming: the intrigues of a school cross-country run, for instance, are essentially not that enthralling. Moreover, it has to be said that the Eton stuff can't help but work against the series: this is stultifyingly privileged terrain.

Sales were good enough for *SilverFin* to be followed by *Blood Fever* (2006), *Double or Die* (2007), *Hurricane Gold* (2007) and *By Royal Command* (2008). The fifth book was the end of a natural cycle. James was by now fifteen, leading not just to difficulties with identification among younger readers, but problems regarding the inevitable sexual feelings of a boy of that age.

Curiously, while sex may have been banished from the picture as inappropriate for the intended demographic, the violence in the Young Bond books was quite high. In *Double or Die*, Higson created a literally decreasing villain: a man who came away from each fight minus a body part.

The author of *The Moneypenny Diaries* was not Kate Westbrook, as the covers had it, but Samantha Weinberg, who used a conceit whereby it was suggested that Miss Moneypenny was a genuine person whose forty leather-bound diaries had been discovered after her death by her niece, Westbrook. Weinberg was an award-winning journalist and nonfiction author, but she had never written a word of fiction before. She was a fan of the Fleming books, if not an obsessive one.

Weinberg opted for the first name Jane as a plain and common-place juxtaposition to the unusual, polysyllabic Moneypenny. For Moneypenny's backstory, Weinberg opted for an African colonial one like her own. Like Higson, Weinberg decided to keep within the timeframe of Fleming's books.

There is an overarching but slight awkwardness to the series' concept in the fact that the Moneypenny who has become iconic to the public is, in the books, not very prominent, nor particularly important to Bond. Leaving aside that minor anomaly, Weinberg is true to her stated mission of using the Fleming, not the Eon, universe as her touchstone.

Bond is a key, though not overwhelming, figure in the first and third of the Moneypenny Diaries series. In *Guardian Angel*, published in 2005, he is the shambling wreck to which he was reduced after Tracy's death in *On Her Majesty's Secret Service*. Moneypenny, on the other hand, is made central to the Cuban Missile Crisis. *Secret Servant* (2006) again revolves around a genuine historical incident, this time the scandal of the defection of Kim Philby. In *Final Fling* (2008), Westbrook's contemporary attempts to uncover the reason for her aunt's death in 1990 parallel historical chapters in which Moneypenny helps Bond try to flush out a mole in the Service. On the final page, Westbrook is told that a character she met earlier on – an elderly man living on a Scottish island with an impressive capacity for holding his liquor – is in fact the real James Bond. Weinberg also published a pair of Moneypenny short stories.

The covers of the British editions of the *Moneypenny Diaries* trilogy were rather 'chick-lit'. Moreover, the books were rendered generally unexciting by their lack of forward momentum and their passive voices, structural conceits and intrinsic inability to do anything other than fill holes in existent narratives. However, *The Moneypenny Diaries* was a less trashy, more Fleming-faithful and more enjoyable proposition than many had predicted.

THE BLONDE
BOMBSHELL

In 2003, a Quentin Tarantino interview in the *New York Daily News* electrified parts of the James Bond fanbase. 'Someday I'm going to get the rights to do *Casino Royale*, the first James Bond novel, and do it the right way,' the film director said.

Not too many people had bothered thinking about *Casino Royale* in film terms since the 1967 Charles K. Feldman adaptation had made it synonymous with failure and farce. These comments, though, reminded people that, just because *Casino Royale* had been made once, it didn't mean it couldn't be made again. It also made them realise that, in the right hands, it could be transformed. Through the likes of *Reservoir Dogs* and *Pulp Fiction*, Tarantino was one of the world's most celebrated cinema stylists. Should he prevail in his intent, it might actually lead to one of the best Bond movies of all.

In fan magazine *Bondage* in 1989, Michael G. Wilson said of the film rights to *Casino Royale*, 'United Artists bought out Charlie

Feldman's rights and Columbia owns the rights in common, so they're in a Mexican standoff.' That Mexican standoff was solved by MGM, effectively the new owners of UA, triumphing in a Bond-related court case in the 1990s. Its story is tortuous and almost inevitably involves Kevin McClory, that perennial thorn in Eon's side.

In 1997, Sony Pictures Entertainment announced they were to start a rival Bond series predicated on the assertion of McClory that, as effectively the creator of the signatures of the cinema Bond, he held rights that extended further than remakes of *Thunderball*. That Sony had inherited through takeover whatever rights Columbia had to *Casino Royale* could be said to slightly bolster the idea of a rival franchise: that was at least two Bond films. UA/MGM and Danjaq made a legal challenge to this plan, pointedly purchasing the worldwide distribution rights to *Never Say Never Again* as they did ('We have taken this definitive action to underscore the point that the Bond franchise has one home and only one home – with the collective family of United Artists, MGM, and Danjaq'). An injunction was obtained closing down production on McClory's latest putative *Thunderball* remake, *Warhead*, a.k.a. *Warhead 2000*, for which McClory had made noises about recruiting Timothy Dalton that were almost certainly news to Dalton.

The arcane out-of-court settlement that came on 30 March 1999 involved franchise horse-trading whereby Sony dropped their Bond claims and ceded to MGM their rights in *Casino Royale*, but emerged with rights previously held by MGM to make Spider-Man movies. McClory was left out in the cold. The question of which studio had really won became moot in 2005, when MGM was subsumed into a consortium headed by Sony. Consequently, the new version of *Casino Royale* wound up being co-produced by MGM and Sony holding Columbia.

However, the Sony–MGM settlement seems to have given MGM only distribution rights to *Casino Royale*. That remake rights were a separate issue is illustrated by the fact that Tarantino's comments about wanting to do *Casino Royale* came after the 1999 legal settlement. Martin Campbell, who ended up directing the remake, told the *Daily Express* in 2002, '. . . after a long battle, the Broccolis suddenly got the film rights to the first Bond novel *Casino Royale*, despite Quentin Tarantino bidding against them.' Eon seem to have won that bidding war by 2004. Tarantino then embarked on a campaign to persuade Eon to let him be the director of their version of *Casino Royale*, and took that campaign into the public arena. In April of that year, he revealed to *Sci-Fi Wire* that he had talked to Pierce Brosnan about adapting the book. Tarantino said of the notion of Eon hiring him, 'Let's – just this one year – go my way and do it a little differently . . . I won't do anything that will ruin the series.' Brosnan weighed in on Tarantino's side, telling the media, 'He's got a cutting edge . . . Someone like Quentin would be magnificent.'

Brosnan had proven himself a different kind of Bond actor when in 1990 his disapproval of French atomic tests in the South Pacific caused the cancellation of the French premiere of *GoldenEye*. While that particular incident was probably beneficial – bolstering the notion of a modernised 007 – his flirtation with a man with whom they had only recently been in a bidding war may have been a step too far for Eon. Could Tarantino be the reason they decided not to engage Brosnan's services again? Martin Campbell, the man who did end up directing *Casino Royale*, says not: 'Frankly I've never heard that. You generally hear that sort of stuff.' One thing not in dispute is that the decision was a shock.

Pierce Brosnan had made *Die Another Day* after his initial three-picture deal had expired. As it had done $456 million worldwide, it wasn't too surprising that Eon initially gave every public indication that the option on Brosnan's services would be taken up again. However, sometime in 2003, the powers-that-be in 007 World began publicly humming and hawing over the issue of Brosnan's continuing. In September, for instance, an MGM spokesman said of the issue of the actor's presence in the next film, 'Once we get a director then I think we can get into casting.' In 2004, while filming *After the Sunset*, Brosnan was stunned to receive a call from his agent telling him that it had been decided by Eon not to continue negotiations with him.

That Brosnan was asking for what Eon and/or MGM considered too much money has been mooted as a reason for the actor's departure. Campbell has a different theory: 'There was a feeling from the Broccolis that perhaps the previous Bond, they'd gone a little bit too fantastical with it. They thought it needed a complete rethink tonally and I think then they got the idea of doing *Casino Royale*, simply because they wanted to reboot. And of course *Casino* is a prequel to everything, so I think Pierce's age put him out of the running.'

Whatever the reason, the upshot was that Brosnan was unequivocally the first actor to leave the Bond role involuntarily. Brosnan told Bruce Kirkland of the *Edmonton Sun*, 'I accepted the knowledge after 24 hours of being in shock.'

Whatever the temporary element of humiliation in his exit, Brosnan can, in the clear light of day, look back with pride on his 007 legacy. His Bond managed to successfully combine the grittiness seen in Dalton's films with the larger-than-life spectacle that – for good or ill – the public has come to expect of the franchise. There was also even an element of providence in his dismissal: as a consequence of it, he was the first long-term Bond who did not go into a protracted decline in either his physical appearance or the quality of scripts he was given.

Of being enticed back to Bond to direct the new version of *Casino Royale*, Martin Campbell explains, 'Again: new actor, whole new tone to Bond. We wanted to go back to the tone of the books.'

There was, though, a bit of an issue with this particular book. 'Nothing happens,' Campbell says of Ian Fleming's *Casino Royale*. Naturally this is not literally true, but there were multiple problems presented by the book's lengthy passages of baccarat and other elements that would make for nothing but a longueur in the context of a motion picture. He says, 'We put the whole beginning of the story in with a lot of action, we had that airport sequence with a lot of action, but the real problem was there came suddenly this point where three sections of the movie were broken up into card games and the question was, "How do you hold the audience's attention?" That was a big worry. What I realised was, it's not the game itself: it's the guys playing the game that is really the secret to it. So I just had to cover the hell out of it basically and get as much tension into those games as I possibly could.' An additional solution was the shuffling-in of action during the game: 'It's broken up a little bit by the sequence where he gets poisoned and the sequence in the stairwell where the guys that Chiffre owes money to attack him.'

The previous franchise reboot that inaugurated the Brosnan era had gently mocked the series' signatures. This reboot quite ferociously pulled them apart and reassembled them, not necessarily whole. It also dispensed with levity. This Bond was far too grim a figure for even gallows humour. Characters with double-entendre names were also out of the question.

While Brosnan's Bond was an updated one, it was still recognisably a part of the same franchise as the Roger Moore films. The new Bond was so dark in tone as to make one wonder what somebody who enjoyed, say, *Octopussy* might have got out of him, raising questions as to whether the reboot was working against the Bond films' notional audience. 'I don't remember discussing that with them,' Campbell says of the producers. 'I think they just trusted their judgement. That's what Barbara and Michael do. There were no long discussions about who's likely to see this, does it alter the demographics.'

Five months before the release of *Die Another Day*, a rival espionage film series featuring another agent with the initials 'JB' – CIA operative Jason Bourne – had released its opening instalment. A sequel followed in 2004 and a third was now in preparation. Based on novels by Robert Ludlum, the Bourne films spurned stylisation for grit and featured a protagonist riddled with insecurities and uncertainty. Many suspected that the new brooding Bond timbre constituted a deliberate quest not to be left behind by Bourne. While Campbell concedes that the Bourne films were 'probably subconsciously an influence', he denies that Eon nudged him: 'The Bourne films are terrific but they're so different really. Bond is a fantasy figure, Bourne is a very realistic figure.'

Casino Royale was to take Bond back to the days when he was earning his stripes (or, rather, his double-O number). More than two decades previously, Richard Maibaum and Michael G. Wilson had contemplated making the first post-Roger Moore Bond movie an origin story. Their vision of a reckless young naval officer who acquires a maturity through secret-agent work was vetoed by Cubby Broccoli, who considered the appeal of Bond to be founded on the very opposite of such callowness. Now the confluence of acquiring rights to the very first James Bond story and the determination to scale back the fantasy provided the impetus and opportunity to revive that origin-story concept.

Along with this intoxicating resolve for a new direction, though, came logic-related headaches. The most pronounced of these resulted from the decision to retain Judi Dench as M. Reasons Campbell, 'If you think of M, God she'd be about ninety. You've still got her as M even though she's been in all those other movies as well, which presumably happened after this movie. We said, "Look, if you start applying that logic it'll never work."' Thus was brought about the most audacious of all the recalibration decisions: to make the film a 'hard' reboot. *Casino Royale* resets the clock, effectively pretending that all other James Bond films never happened. Unencumbered by previous Bond continuity, the writers now had almost unprecedented freedom.

It was perhaps incongruous that Eon hired Purvis & Wade for the project. As well as the derided *Die Another Day*, the writing pair were responsible for the subsequent Rowan Atkinson Bond spoof *Johnny English*. That and their technology orientation did not suggest that they could get with *Casino Royale*'s naturalistic programme. However, Campbell says that it can't be inferred that there was something wrong with the first draft from the fact that 'Paul Haggis did an extensive rewrite on it.' He says, 'It was mainly the character parts. The love story, all of that with Vesper was the key to it all, and that's what Haggis is marvellous at doing. He did a complete sweep through the script.' Purvis & Wade and Paul Haggis (note the legal distinctions as regards collaboration created by ampersand and 'and') created a story that, while it sang with love for the cinema Bond, also stayed true to his grittier literary roots. The result was easily the best 007 picture since the sixties.

Few would have predicted this from the incredulous reception that greeted the announcement in October 2005 that the sixth Eon James Bond was to be Daniel Craig.

As before, Campbell was involved in the casting of a new Bond. 'Because of the tone change, it was a little more difficult to actually focus in on who was going to play Bond, whereas with Pierce it was very obvious,' he recalls. In the end it came down to two actors. One was Henry Cavill, a square-jawed, almost impossibly handsome twenty-two-year-old who has since gone on to fame by playing Superman and Napoleon Solo. Campbell: 'He was close. He did a very good test, but the consensus was he was a little too young for Bond.' Born in March 1968 and raised on Merseyside, Daniel Craig was a fine actor, notable for his appearances in *Lara Croft: Tomb Raider*, *Perdition* and *Layer Cake*. However, his thespian chops were no more the issue than the fact that he was 'only' five-foot-eleven. What aroused the ire of long-term Bond fans and inspired a tidal wave of Internet protest was that Craig was (1) strawberry blonde and (2) not straightforwardly handsome.

Blonde was a big problem not simply because of the issue of tradition (even if Moore was not that much darker in his early Bond films). Fairly or unfairly, blonde hair is synonymous with lack of gravitas. Moreover, while Craig is hardly unattractive, his face is a bit wide, his eyes are somewhat small and his nose is not exactly chiselled. He simply did not conform to the standard pattern of male beauty that had always been embraced by the Bond series and without which, it was assumed, Bond's ladykiller status would not be believable. Moreover, while he had the requisite clipped accent, Craig's rough-hewn air did not suggest a denizen of casinos, exclusive gentlemen's clubs and fine restaurants. It hardly helped that, when Craig was introduced as the next Bond, a dramatic arrival on board a speedboat at a media conference was undermined by his looking like a wimp because Britain's pedantic health-and-safety laws required him to wear a life jacket over his suit.

A further problem arose when the fact was made public that *Casino Royale* would be an origin story. Although Craig was the first actor under the age of forty to play Bond since George Lazenby, he had a been-around-the-block mien. Previously one of his few plus-points for his naysayers, it now seemed to make a nonsense of the idea that he was to play a rookie.

Campbell recalls, 'They slagged him off something terrible. "We've got a blonde guy, he looks like President Putin." The usual British press negative reaction.' Craig has admitted he collapsed into a depression for twenty-four hours over the reaction to his casting. Campbell: 'I must say to his credit, he came in one day when we were filming very early on and I said to him, "You obviously don't read this bullshit on the Internet and so forth?" He said, "Yep. I read every bit of it. I need to, because I know all the crew have read it and everybody else. I just like to keep up to date." But it never affected him. He just pushed through it. He didn't care.' The only thing Craig did seem to care about was his craft. Campbell: 'He took it very, very seriously. He had something to prove, Daniel.'

Although the mounting costs of shooting in the highly industrialised countries saw filming transfer to Prague, Campbell had freedom in matters fiduciary. 'It was good,' he says of his funding situation. 'I think the budget was 150 [million dollars], which we came in on budget, and I think with tax reductions it came to 134.'

One indication of a change of style is the fact that Campbell opens *Casino Royale* in black-and-white. Explains the director, 'It's bleak, it's Prague, it's in the past. The other thing was, I wanted the first colour on the screen to be the blood running down the top of the frame [from] the rifle barrel, which gave a terrific contrast.' In this noir-ish pre-title sequence, Bond is shown killing treacherous section chief Dryden (Darwin Shaw). He has been dispatched to do so by M.

It is revealed that acquiring the double-O status takes two kills, and Dryden is Bond's second. This is in keeping with the two kills that earned Bond the status in the original novel, although is not in keeping with the altered meaning of the term: Double-O can hardly mean a licence to kill if one has to kill to earn it.

The first kill – an accomplice of Dryden – is shown in flashback and involves Bond spinning and shooting, which forms the gun-barrel sequence. 'I tried to make it the origin story of the gun barrel,' explains Campbell. 'So, when the bad guy is picking up the gun, that is the gun barrel he's about to kill Bond with and Bond shoots him first, and that becomes the stylised blood coming down the top of the frame.' This is the first occasion that the gun barrel sequence follows, rather than precedes, the pre-title sequence and the first occasion that it is not accompanied by 'The James Bond Theme'. As it takes place after a vicious fight in a toilet, it's also the first in which Bond is open-collared.

The credits state, 'Based on the novel by Ian Fleming' – amazingly, the first time this formula of words has ever been used in the franchise. Said credits are knowledgeable, being based on

Ian Fleming's playing-card cover design for the first edition of the book. Notable for their absence among the battling silhouettes, gun motifs and cascades of spades, clubs, hearts and diamonds are the traditional slinky, underclothed female figures. It's rather a pity that this is accompanied by 'You Know My Name', a piece of featureless rock by Chris Cornell, written in collaboration with David Arnold, although the latter at least adds some impressive production swells and punches.

While the book's characters and overall structure are maintained, various tweaks and updatings are applied. Le Chiffre is gambling away not the funds of SMERSH but the capital of terrorists and insurgents, to whom his unnamed organisation is a private banker. The location of the central card contest is moved to Montenegro, while baccarat is jettisoned for poker. The latter is not only a game more readily understandable to the masses but one that gives rise to intrigue about Le Chiffre's 'tell' – a physical tic that gives away when a player is bluffing about his hand. The objective of the Secret Service/MI6 (as they are alternately called) wiping out Le Chiffre is not to cause financial problems for the enemy but to put the man in a position of such danger that he will take up MI6's offer of sanctuary in exchange for providing information on his organisation, which is believed to be connected to the 9/11 attack.

Although since Brosnan's debut we have become used to the dialogue and character interplay being modernistically sceptical of the series' traditions, values and nomenclature, this film takes it much further. M, for instance, says to 007, 'I would ask you if you could remain emotionally detached but I don't think that's your problem, is it, Bond?' Bond says, 'Vesper? I do hope you gave your parents hell for that.' Vesper herself (Eva Green) is the very opposite of the drip the character constitutes in the original book. She is an HM Treasury official who provides the funding for Bond to participate in the poker game. (When she introduces herself with, 'I'm the money' and he responds, 'Every penny of it,' it is the closest the movie comes to including M's secretary, absent for the very first time.) Vesper is disdainful of Bond. After Bond has sneered at her for trying to compensate for her beauty with masculine clothes and a prickly manner, which he suspects undermine the very chances of the promotion she is trying to assist, she responds with her own theorising: 'By the cut of your suit, you went to Oxford or wherever and actually think human beings dress like that. But you wear it with such disdain, my guess is you didn't come from money and your schoolfriends never let you forget it . . . hence the chip on your shoulder. And since your first thought about me ran to orphan that's what I'd say you are . . . And that makes perfect sense, since MI6 looks for maladjusted young men that give little thought to sacrificing others in order to protect Queen and country . . .' She also turns Bond-girl objectification on its head: 'You think of women as disposable pleasures rather than meaningful pursuits. So, as charming as you are, Mr Bond, I will be keeping my eye on our government's money – and off your perfectly formed arse.'

Campbell says that this soliloquy was deliberately an equivalent of M's misogynist-dinosaur speech from *GoldenEye*: 'It was a real reality check for Bond. And that of course is why he admires her, because she's got the balls to do it.' Of course, we know this is all hogwash on one level – Bond will get this ice maiden into bed and the series will continue on the same path of sex, violence and breast-beating it always has. Moreover, whatever realism is in evidence, Bond will never be depicted wearing glasses to read his top-secret documents or unable to achieve an erection when trying to seduce Bond girls. However, it's all a far cry from the unchallenged swaggering of Connery and Moore. Moreover, it's the sort of stuff that makes even the once cutting-edge Brosnan films already seem slightly tame and antiquated.

Despite the predominant realism, the first chase scene – set in Madagascar – involves, as ever for Bond films, supreme athleticism, preternatural reaction time, incredible fearlessness and the heedless endangerment of many innocent bystanders. It exploits current interest in Parkour, the street sport that involves the use of public fixtures as climbing frames, with 'free running' superstar Sébastien Foucan cast as villain Mollaka. It's an indication of where the franchise is now heading that Foucan's breathtaking facility is juxtaposed with Bond's occasional hesitancy and clumsiness.

The film is an even better trainspotting opportunity for Bond aficionados than *Die Another Day*. For instance, when Bond follows a clue on Mollaka's phone to Nassau, he participates in a card game with his accomplice Dimitrios (Simon Abkarian). The prize he ends up winning is a 1964 Aston Martin (although with a left-hand drive appropriate for the Bahamas). Another example is M calling Bond a 'blunt instrument'.

Later on, another Aston Martin – a modern DBS model – is provided 007 by M. The handguns, communications equipment and defibrillator in its concealed trays are the picture's only significant gadgets. Campbell says that, if discussion turned to anything 'a little too silly or fantastical', it would be jettisoned. Nevertheless, Craig's Bond is a bit of a whizz with IT.

Despite Craig's seriousness as an actor, he was turned into a piece of cheesecake by his appearance in a pair of bathing trunks on a Nassau beach. The relevant scene involved his striding in surf in a manner reminiscent of Ursula Andress emerging from the water in *Dr. No*. 'Ironically, it was never even thought of as that,' says Campbell. Nonetheless, Eon and/or Sony seemed to take great delight in distributing to the press pictures from the scene in advance of the film's release, almost as if to silence those who had questioned Craig's beefcake credentials. 'Well, why not?' Campbell shrugs. 'He looked pretty good. Daniel had done four months' working out.' Also going some way towards assuaging the doubts of those who felt him not Adonis-like enough was Craig's restyled bristly hair, magnetic blue eyes and self-possessed presence.

When we see him taking the trouble to thank waiters and croupiers, and stand up for ladies, we note that, although Craig's 007 is blunt and unsmiling, he is good on small courtesies. The lack of finesse detected by Vesper doesn't quite sit with the fact of Bond relishing caviar or his complicated proprietary dry-martini recipe. (The instructions Bond gives the barman for the drink that will become The Vesper come almost word-for-word from the book. Half the gamblers at the table instantly ask for one of these intriguing-sounding concoctions.)

Le Chiffre is played brilliantly by Mads Mikkelsen. The effect of his dead, impassive face and unnerving stare is made even more powerful by the makeup department, who give him one milky eye, from which a medical condition causes blood to weep.

Another indication of the hard reboot is the resurrection of Felix Leiter. Jeffrey Wright is not, incidentally, the first black actor to play the CIA man: Bernie Casey had been Leiter in the non-Eon *Never Say Never Again*. Also ringing the changes is the testicle-torture scene, and not just because Craig is shown naked. When Le Chiffre sets to work (with a knotted rope rather than a carpet beater), Craig screams and whimpers in a way that the cinematic Bond never previously has. As in Fleming's template, Bond's rescue comes as a by-product of a third party's fury about Le Chiffre's financial recklessness. In this case Le Chiffre is killed by an associate named Mr White (Jesper Christensen).

Bond is interested in only married women. 'It keeps things simple,' Craig explains to Dimitrios's wife Solange, whom he beds. Many had condemned Bond films for their immorality, but up to this point the series had steered clear of the contempt for the institution of marriage evident in some parts of the Fleming canon, with the exception of Bond reigniting a relationship with his married old flame in *Tomorrow Never Dies*. However, Bond does fall in love with Vesper, even if the example of personal growth is spoiled a little by the fact that it comes too quickly after their daggers-drawn scenes to be convincing. Perhaps he is confusing his feelings with a need to escape his blood-drenched job while he still has a 'soul left to salvage'. Bond resigns by email to go aimlessly wandering the world with Vesper. When M calls him to ask why his casino winnings haven't been deposited in the required bank account, Bond realises Vesper is in league with the enemy. She ends up killing herself in front of his eyes in a collapsing Venice building. Craig uses Fleming's 'bitch is dead' line, but M points out that Vesper had evidently done a deal to spare his life on the day Le Chiffre was executed.

In Vesper's mobile phone, Bond finds the name of Mr White and sets off in pursuit. Bond shoots the man in the leg and, standing over him, provides for the first time the signature rendering of his name. Campbell: 'We thought we'd never get away with that but Paul and I said, "He can't possibly be Bond until the end of the movie, the Bond that we know and love." He's got to go through this learning curve and make his mistakes and his fuck-ups and everything else, and then the last line of the movie is, "The name's Bond, James Bond."'

At that last line, the closing credits start to the accompaniment – finally – of 'The James Bond Theme', the belated introduction of which is clearly another example of Bond motifs being held back until such time as the character has formed himself into the one we know. That, for the first time, plot threads are left dangling makes the 'James Bond Will Return' declaration not so much presumptuous as necessary.

Casino Royale was premiered on 14 November 2006, almost precisely four years after the release of *Die Another Day*. During that interregnum, not only had the Bourne films been received by some critics as a rebuke of the fantastical timbre of the Bond franchise, but a corollary of their success was that some started suggesting that the long absence of 007 was irrelevant because he was a throwback that was no longer needed.

Some proffered similar sentiments about *24*. Television had never previously been able to offer competition to the ultimate cinema spectacle that was a Bond movie, but with both adult content and high budgets now enabled by subscription-funded broadcasting, the Fox network series was giving Bond a run for his money. Eon had heard this sort of stuff before, of course, and many times. However, this time there was the additional issue of the less-than-universal praise that had greeted their choice of new Bond actor. Moreover, as with *On Her Majesty's Secret Service* – coincidentally, the last Bond picture wherein Bond's lover had died – cinemas were restricted in the number of showings possible: at 144 minutes, *Casino Royale* was the longest Bond film yet. (Campbell says he was put under no pressure to cut the running time: 'It was just the length it should have been.')

Eon were at least thrown an unexpected lifeline by the film censors. *Casino Royale* features violence that is brutal and vindictive rather than, as so often is the case in the series, stylish and glib. Moreover, it contains a torture scene of which Campbell admits, 'Nothing had been seen like that in a Bond film ever before.' He says it made him worried about the certifications, but says, 'The irony was the British censors made me cut one tiny bit, which is where Le Chiffre walks round and he puts the rope over Daniel's shoulder, which they took as some sort of sexual thing. It was just ridiculous. The Americans didn't worry about it at all. I didn't lose a frame for them.' He admits of the classifications – '12A' in the UK, 'PG13' in the US – 'They are lenient, there's no question.'

In reality, though, the film probably didn't need any form of providence. Bond films had a dedicated fanbase; a new instalment in history's most successful franchise was an event by default; the studio put everything into publicising the return of their franchise; Craig enjoyed the honeymoon period/curiosity status of all new Bonds and (intentionally or not) the new Bond possessed the grim timbre made fashionable by Bourne pictures and *24*. Then there was the fact that Eon's recent determination not to offend China had been rewarded by their being granted access to their cinemas. All of these things gave rise to worldwide box-office grosses of $594.2 million. *Casino Royale* entered the top ten of biggest-grossing Bond films even after inflation adjustment.

In July 2007, Ian Fleming Publications announced the name of the author they had chosen to resurrect adult James Bond continuation novels.

Kingsley Amis excepted, Sebastian Faulks was the most prestigious writer ever asked to carry on Ian Fleming's literary legacy. His acclaimed works, such as *A Fool's Alphabet*, *Birdsong* and *Charlotte Gray*, had garnered him a CBE for services to literature. A book by such a writer was certainly destined to be taken more seriously – and therefore attract more reviews in the literary pages – than the works of John Gardner or Raymond Benson. Moreover, such a writer was destined to take *himself* more seriously. Faulks initially turned down IFP's overture, then agreed to it as long as he could make his effort a historical novel. That IFP acquiesced is an indication of the greater power that such name authors possess.

Devil May Care by 'Sebastian Faulks writing as Ian Fleming' was published on 28 May 2008, the one hundredth anniversary of Ian Fleming's birth. Faulks's narrative takes place in 1967, so is effectively the successor to *The Man with the Golden Gun*. (He ignores *Colonel Sun,* as well as all the other continuation novels, something standard with new Bond writers.) Bond is tasked with dealing with the heroin flooding his home country courtesy of Dr Julius Gorner, a man with such a loathing for Britain that he plans a terrorist attack on Russia for which the UK will get the blame.

Faulks skimps on sex and brand names and the tone of Bond's exchanges with Moneypenny is from the movies, not the books. He also makes a couple of Fleming-continuity mistakes, portraying SMERSH as still operating and stating that Bond has never encountered a female SIS agent (Mary Ann Russell would hardly have been forgotten by Bond when she had saved his life in 'From a View to a Kill'). Elsewhere, though, some of the content is so Fleming-esque while simultaneously avoiding being generic as to be uncanny, among it leisurely scene-setting, colourful supporting characters, digressions (a waffling speech by the villain about the mathematics of tennis), discretion with profanity and banter about spanking. Also Fleming-like is that his villain has both a 'congenital deformity' – in this case a monkey's hand – and accidie (although Faulks confuses it with anomie).

Faulks's scene-setting is, in a way, actually more impressive than Fleming's. The latter was merely writing in his time, whereas Faulks had to research details of cars, customs, political situations, etc. Anachronisms are few.

It's such a shame, then, that, when it comes to action sequences, Faulks's descriptive powers prove inadequate. Some of them are pulpy, but mostly they sin by being ludicrously sketchy. Faulks says of a vehicle in which Felix Leiter is riding, '. . . the car flipped over on its side, slewing hard across the road on its doors' and goes no further. Fleming would have made sure to describe every chaotic, cacophonous moment of the experience of the car's passengers.

Reviews of *Devil May Care* (whose title is not explained within its pages) were generally good and sales were exceptional, with only the latest Harry Potter moving more quickly. Literary Bond was back.

After the triumph of the *Casino Royale* remake came the irritating letdown that was *Quantum of Solace*, premiered on 29 October 2008.

Martin Campbell again declined to further the adventures of a Bond he had reinvented. 'Now he's back on the trail again, hunting down the villain,' he explains. 'The fundamentals have gone back to being the same.'

The Purvis & Wade/Paul Haggis combination that worked so brilliantly on the previous movie was officially credited with the screenplay of the follow-up. However, a Writers' Guild strike came into effect partway through the process, compounding the problems created by the picture being rushed into production. In

February 2012, Craig told Dave Calhoun of *Time Out*, 'We couldn't employ a writer to finish it . . . There was me trying to rewrite scenes – and a writer I am not . . . Me and the director were the ones allowed to do it . . . We were stuffed.' The result seems to be a decision to obviate the need for plot and dialogue by filling up the screentime with action sequences.

Moreover, whoever the writers were, they had a harder task than last time out. As the quirky Fleming short story from which the movie takes its title would hardly have made for an enthralling adventure, the screenwriters were once again working from scratch. (In keeping with the general air of half-bakedness, although the organisation Bond has been pursuing since the last movie is revealed herein to be called Quantum, the 'Solace' bit is meaningless.)

Marc Forster doesn't help. Once again, Eon went for a director known more for arthouse pictures than action-oriented flicks, in this case the likes of *Monster's Ball* and *The Kite Runner*. (The Swiss Forster was the first non-Commonwealth Eon Bond director.) Forster's work here is bewildering and sometimes infuriating. His endless fast-cutting – like a parody of Peter Hunt's get-rid-of-that-pause style – often makes it difficult to understand what's happening. His determination to keep up the pace leads to an extraordinarily short Bond feature, at 106 minutes the briefest of all 007 movies.

Where he isn't being frenetic, Forster throws in the sort of arty-farty stuff never before seen in Bond. When at an Austrian opera house Bond gatecrashes a public meeting of Quantum, it leads to a pursuit that Forster juxtaposes with the graceful happenings in *Tosca*. He alternates the opera's music with dead silence.

Whether it be Forster's or the scriptwriters' fault, the action itself is substandard. One Bond signature that has remained constant throughout all of the series' wild fluctuations in tone is that its violent scenes have an unforeseeable but appropriate payoff: Dr No falling into the reactor pool because his steel hands can't grasp the girder, Oddjob being fried when reaching for his hat, Jaws being lifted by his teeth with a giant magnet and dropped into a shark pool, Renard being impaled on the plutonium rod with which he plans to commit mass murder, etc., etc. The violent scenes in *Quantum of Solace* suggest a lack of understanding of the Bond franchise: too often they end not in a stylish crescendo but utterly prosaically – such as in the pre-title sequence, where Bond, at the end of a car chase, picks up a machine gun from the seat beside him and lets rip.

That pre-title sequence ends with Bond opening the boot of his car and saying to Mr White, trussed up inside, 'It's time to get out.' In other words, the narrative is one that continues almost directly from the close of *Casino Royale*, making this a proper sequel in a way no other Bond film has been. Yet, while only hours have passed since the action in that picture, the two years that have elapsed in real life are etched into Craig's face.

Bond, of course, is insane with grief after what happened in *Casino Royale*, but that doesn't mean he can kill people rather than take them in for questioning about Quantum, especially with so many other lives at stake. Accordingly, M suspends him, leading Bond to go rogue, something that – notwithstanding that the series has been rebooted – has happened a little too often in the franchise lately.

Bolivian secret agent Camille Montes (Olga Kurylenko) assists Bond in his objective of crushing Quantum, an organisation so insidious that one of its agents was M's personal bodyguard for five years. Camille is motivated by the fact that her family was murdered by main villain Medrano (Joaquín Cosío). It seems she is being set up to be 007's love interest, but the agent's only conquest in the film is 'Fields', an MI6 office worker stationed in Bolivia. His seduction method is cringeworthy: when they check into their hotel suite, Bond calls from the bedroom, 'I can't find the . . . the stationery. Will you come and help me look?' Other throwbacks to a more flippant Bond-movie era are the fact that Bond shows himself able to pilot a plane and that he is rescued by a girl screeching up in a car.

Bond gets revenge for Vesper. However, he does this not by killing the Quantum man who betrayed her but by handing him over to MI6. He is growing.

It is then that we get Craig's first formal gun-barrel sequence. It's a little peculiar: he seems to walk too fast and appears rather hunched and almost squat. Despite the return of this tradition, albeit in an irregular place, *Quantum of Solace* is the first Bond film since 1967 without that famous line, 'The name's Bond, James Bond' or a variation thereof.

Capping an annoying cinema experience is the opening music. Eon tried to be trendy by commissioning Jack White of the White Stripes as composer. White is an indie rocker with no history of glossy anthems. As well as being completely inappropriate, his staccato 'Another Way to Die' (sung by White and Alicia Keyes in the series' first duet) is risibly American (we are told that Bond is using his 'slick trigger finger' for 'Her Majesteee' and looking out for his 'bruthaaa').

Quantum of Solace was a letdown in every area except receipts: box-office grosses were $575.4 million.

A function of IFP's acquiring a prestigious author for a continuation 007 novel was that it was destined to be a one-off: while Sebastian Faulks was genuinely delighted and intrigued to write a Bond tale, there was no way that such a cultured and independently successful wordsmith was going to want to work within those restrictive parameters for an extended period. Accordingly, he declined an invitation to write a follow-up.

IFP turned instead to Jeffery Deaver. Although, unlike Faulks, a genre writer, Deaver is considered a class act. His award-strewn crime-writing career is marked by fearsome research, gruesome forensic detail, fast pacing and trick endings.

In *Carte Blanche*, published in May 2011, Deaver went in completely the opposite direction to Faulks. In going contemporary, Deaver at least rid himself of the burden of aligning his story with Fleming's Bond chronology.

In a narrative that covers only a week, Bond travels from the Balkans to Dubai and then to South Africa in order to thwart a terrorist atrocity orchestrated by the decay-obsessed Severan Hydt. In a final section where twist is piled upon twist, Hydt turns out to be a secondary figure and Bond's love interest the real baddie.

Deaver's exposition is stiff and his descriptive passages functional. The 400-page book is much longer than it needs to be, cluttered with the viewpoints of supporting characters. Although Deaver's action sequences are better than Faulks's, they are nothing special. Deaver is strongest when it comes to procedural detail, research (he purveys interesting facts about both spy technology and recycling) and travelogue (he is quite evocative on South Africa and Dubai).

His Bond, though, feels unrelated to Fleming's. Although the likes of M, Felix Leiter, René Mathis, Bill Tanner and Mary

Goodnight all put in appearances, everything else in the 007 universe is rejigged. Bond – a former smoker – cut his chops in the war in Afghanistan. He is an employee within the 00 Section of the Operations Branch of covert British security unit the Overseas Development Group. (Their mission is to 'protect the Realm . . . by any means necessary' – the carte blanche of the title, which itself is a more modern and nuanced variant of the status Licence to Kill.)

Bond is also painfully, pointedly upright. He declines the opportunity to seduce one woman because he adjudges her to be too vulnerable in the wake of a romantic split, and another for no comprehensible reason whatsoever. His sole conquest in the book is one Deaver deliberately does not put in those terms, talking of 'mutual surrender, mutual victory'. Bond's gender-biased assumption that his father was a spy is mocked by turn of events as it is revealed that the secret agent in the family was his mother. At one point, Bond upbraids himself for being impatient with a South African police officer who resents his carte blanche: '. . . hard-working law enforcers of the world were one hundred per cent right in respecting the rules. It was *he* who was the outlier.'

Deaver's decision to make his Bond one with PC sensibilities might have felt the right and modern thing to do, but the fact that 007 narratives are nothing if they are not narratives about an alpha male is proven by this book, and especially a passage where some skilful driving cooed over by the book's villains turns out not to be by Bond, as we and they had assumed, but Ophelia Maidenstone, a female colleague acting as a decoy. The point of Bond is that he can do stuff other people can't. Making him a bog-standard operative whose place in the story could be occupied by any agent raises the awkward question of how this character is in any way interesting.

Despite all this meticulous political correctness, incidentally, the book accepts unquestioningly the concept of extraordinary rendition and the torture methods that go with it.

Although the book has clearly been carefully gone through by a British editor, Deaver's American nationality is ultimately betrayed by his lack of understanding of the English class system. Bond identifies by their driving licences some hoodies who are harassing the son of a friend. In fact, English teenage delinquents would be unlikely to have the wherewithal for wheels. Meanwhile, although villain Hydt has managed to work himself up from binman to wealthy businessman, nobody remarks on his incongruous working-class tones (or, alternatively, muses that he must have changed his accent).

On 27 July 2012, Queen Elizabeth II opened the London Olympics. Her appearance in Britain's capital city's Olympic Stadium was preceded by a short film in which a tuxedo-clad Daniel Craig in the role of James Bond went to collect Her Majesty from Buckingham Palace and accompanied her into a helicopter. Through the deployment of clever camera angles, the impression was given that the two figures who jumped from the chopper and sailed into the stadium via the use of Union Jack parachutes were Craig and the monarch.

The four-hour opening ceremony designed by film director Danny Boyle highlighted what was proposed as the very best of the host culture: James Bond had effectively been put up on a pedestal with the Industrial Revolution, the National Health Service and Shakespeare. It wasn't a bad advertisement for the next James Bond picture, which premiered in the UK on 23 October 2012.

It had taken four years for *Skyfall* to make it to the screens. The reason for the lag inevitably revolved around the financial problems of Metro-Goldwyn-Mayer. The famous movie studio whose production logo of an unconvincingly furious lion had been a part of the cinema experience of several generations of moviegoers had become another famous casualty of the 2007 credit crunch and had gone in and out of bankruptcy. Bond got back to the screen only via the fact of Eon/Sony entering into a questionable financial deal. In *Skyfall*, Bond is not seen drinking Dom Perignon '54 or a 'Vesper' but rather Heineken lager. He was also shown consuming the latter in a tie-in TV commercial. Craig candidly said to Tom Brook of the BBC News Channel, 'I whore myself out a little bit for that and we get the movie made.' That said, the interregnum resulted in a leisurely development period, which benefited the script.

It was Craig who persuaded Eon to recruit Sam Mendes. Unusually for a mainstream film director, Mendes has extensive experience in theatre. However, that did not mean he was a slouch film-wise. His cinematic CV up to that point was breathtaking in its quality, success and variety: *American Beauty*, *Road to Perdition*, *Jarhead*, *Revolutionary Road* and *Away We Go*. His debut film had won him a Best Director Oscar.

His class is often prominent in *Skyfall*, particularly in a remarkable scene in which villain Raoul Silva (Javier Bardem) approaches a bound Bond down a long room all the while orating an instructional speech about rats. Not once does Bardem stumble over his soliloquy, but not once over the course of this minute-and-a-half does Mendes cut away from his angle behind Craig's chair, revealing it to be a single take. It's not clear whether it's this that is more impressive, or the fact of this extraordinary oasis of calm in the midst of the action. Elsewhere, there is a poignant long shot of Judi Dench standing at the end of a line of Union Jack-draped coffins containing slain MI6 operatives. There are also some beautiful pieces of cinematography when the action moves to a rural setting.

Because the Secret Service/SIS/MI6 does not operate domestically, Bond films have always been set outside the borders of the UK. *Skyfall* is for the first time a very British Bond movie, much of its action taking place in London streets, the capital's underground system and (albeit with Surrey substituting) the wilds of Scotland.

The main story of screenwriters Purvis & Wade and John Logan revolves around the fact that Silva – an ex-MI6 agent with a grudge against M – has stolen a hard drive containing the names of undercover NATO agents embedded in terrorist organisations, a matter so serious that M is given notice to retire. As well as compromising agents' safety by releasing their names on YouTube, Silva remotely causes an explosion at MI6 headquarters – the second time since its mid-nineties completion that the modernistic and vaguely sinister-looking building on London's South Bank has been the subject in this franchise of a disfiguring attack.

It is this attack that causes Bond to come back from unofficial gardening leave: he had disappeared after hearing in his earpiece M instruct a female colleague to disregard danger to him and take a shot at an enemy, this not long after M had forced Bond to leave for dead a wounded fellow agent. Later in the film, Bond takes it upon himself to whisk the imperilled M to a place of safety known not even to her colleagues or superiors, albeit with M's complicity. Not only is this going-rogue thing getting overdone, it does not fit in with the idea of a top-drawer agent.

It's notable that, with Bluetooth connections and distress-signal transmitters, Bond is rarely truly alone in the field now. This may reflect real-life espionage but it could mean – what with advice and even backup never too far away – having to create a new paradigm for a Bond movie. This particular film gets around that undermining of the lone-wolf template by being to a large extent a siege picture. Much of the last half-hour is set in the place of safety to which Bond takes M. This turns out to be Skyfall, Bond's gothic ancestral home in Scotland, now falling into ruin. Bond's fondly remembered mentor, gamekeeper Kincade, is played by Albert Finney. (The writers had Sean Connery in mind for the role before it was nixed by Mendes as something that was in danger of breaching the fourth wall.) The house occasions discussion about Bond's orphan status, although the facts are kept vague. (We see the gravestone of Bond's parents, which dutifully feature the names Fleming gave them.)

The music is provided by long-term Mendes film scorer Thomas Newman, although the title song is the work of Paul Epworth and Adele. The latter chanteuse sings in her usual mangled-but-sultry style over opening titles designed by Daniel Kleinman (returning after the MK12 studio handled the *Quantum of Solace* titles) that are a dream sequence following Bond's pre-titles tumble into a river. As well as being a transatlantic top ten, Adele's song acquired an Academy Award for Best Original Song. The other Oscar garnered by the film was for Best Sound Editing (Per Hallberg and Karen Baker Landers).

The new Quartermaster is Ben Whishaw, a veritable child, apparently created to chime with the fact that technological savvy is no longer associated with sophistication and age but young geekdom. Q issues Bond a Walther PPK/S, which has a micro-sensor in the grip coded to his palm print so that only he can fire it, something in line with the recent trend in Bond films to provide Bond gadgetry only slightly ahead of what the mass of the public already have access to. Q says, 'Were you expecting an exploding pen? We don't really go in for that any more.' However, later on there is a return to classic Bond gadgetry when Bond gets out of storage the Aston Martin DB5. He jokingly threatens to propel the carping M through the ejector seat. It's a nice in-joke, of course, but doesn't fit in with the way he was depicted acquiring the car in *Casino Royale*.

Such is the air of realism granted by spurning of gadgetry and the overall grim tone that it disguises the fact that *Skyfall* is in some ways as illogical and over-the-top as a Roger Moore Bond film. Why, for example, would Silva try to kill M at the inquiry to which she is summoned rather than somewhere to which gaining access doesn't necessitate his having to derail tube trains and slaughter multiple people?

That Silva is homosexual is, unlike with Mr Wint and Mr Kidd in *Diamonds Are Forever*, not played for laughs or ridicule. However, the non-judgemental attitude tips too far the other way when Silva starts caressing the bound Bond, who comments, 'What makes you think this is my first time?' It seems a capitulation to we're-all-a-little-bit-gay PC rhetoric. Unless we are to read something into the way, after jumping for his life onto a train carriage, Bond fussily adjusts his cuffs – Craig's trademark, à la Brosnan's tie adjustment.

The film contains the series' first f-word. However, M's 'I fucked this up, didn't I?' is not in any way ostentatious, being almost muttered. Somewhat more shocking is that M succumbs to a gunshot wound, dying in Bond's arms.

There is an additional surprise in the closing stages. Bond has been working, and possibly sleeping, with a young black female agent (played by Naomie Harris, who, like all MI6 operatives ever depicted in Bond films, has received pronunciation). She has now opted to come out of the field for secretarial duties in the organisation. Although it's a little implausible that Bond has not yet been formally introduced to her, it enables the bombshell line, 'My name's Eve. Eve Moneypenny.'

The battle-hardened, anti-bureaucracy Gareth Mallory (Ralph Fiennes) becomes the new M. 'So, 007,' says Mallory when Bond walks into his office through an upholstered door (another reintroduction of a lately absent Bond motif). 'Lots to be done. Are you ready to get back to work?' 'With pleasure, M,' says Bond. 'With pleasure.'

Once again, the gun-barrel sequence is at the end of the proceedings. It's a new one, much more stylish than the quick-stepping, hunchbacked version of the previous film. It morphs into the words '50 years'.

Although the half-centenary is treated here with less fanfare than had been the fortieth anniversary within *Die Another Day*, the film's success could be said to constitute the celebration. Even at 143 minutes and without even the bait of M's death – most reviewers were considerably circumspect about that plot twist – the picture proceeded to do unprecedented business.

The James Bond series had over the decades regularly broken box-office records, but, while such figures looked good in publicity-generating headlines, they were semi-meaningless, the result of cinema prices, like everything else, costing more than they did in years previous. The Holy Grail for Eon had always been taking grosses greater than those of *Thunderball* after adjustment for inflation. That *Thunderball*'s record had stood for almost as long as the franchise's fifty-year existence was something that may even have been a point of irritation with Eon, considering that that project was as much Kevin McClory's as Broccoli–Saltzman's. *Thunderball*'s position had long seemed inviolable. However, when, in December 2012, *Skyfall*'s $950 million-plus box-office takings saw it overhaul *Goldfinger* as the second all-time most successful 007 movie even after inflation had been taken into account, something was clearly afoot. With the film still to open in the highly populous country of China, record-busting was almost guaranteed.

The release of *Skyfall* was delayed in that country by two months so that censors could remove material felt to be derogatory to the nation. Four days after *Skyfall*'s Chinese opening on 25 January came the news that the magic barrier had been breached: *Skyfall*'s overall grosses of $1,077.8 million meant it had overhauled *Thunderball*'s inflation-adjusted $1,037.3 million. It was a jaw-dropping achievement in an age of reduced cinema attendances, and was made all the more so by the prospect of the income from revenue streams such as cable showings and DVD sales from which *Thunderball* did not immediately benefit.

Since failing to entice back Sebastian Faulks, the impression given by Ian Fleming Publications is that they are themselves happy to recruit a new name author for every Bond book. This is understandable. An annual by-numbers Bond book from a second-tier author is hardly an event. An author both fresh and prestigious applying himself to a famous brand is newsworthy each time out.

IFP's next choice to be a Bond novelist was the most surprising so far. William Boyd may have been winning awards for his novels right from his 1981 debut *A Good Man in Africa*, but his work tended to describe interior landscapes and to veer towards gentle comedy, his 2006 historical spy novel *Restless* notwithstanding. Moreover, writing British-flavoured books was a relatively new thing for Boyd, a man far more familiar with African and French society.

Boyd returns 007 to Fleming's timeframe, setting *Solo* – published in September 2013 – in 1969. Perhaps predictably, the Ghana-born Boyd locates his tale in Africa, specifically the fictional newly independent state of Zanzarim. This is a tale from the days of colonialism: Bond is instructed by M to make the country's military leader Solomon Adeka 'a less efficient soldier' on the grounds that he is jeopardising Britain's oil interests in the region.

Like Faulks before him, Boyd has Bond observing youth fashions, in this case crushed velvet and Afghan coats. Unlike Fleming, he has him *au fait* with television (007 whimsically toys with the idea of getting his hair cut like David Frost, although his perception of the latter's hairstyle seems frozen in the first half of the sixties). Another example of the fun Boyd is having with the character is a footnote for Bond's salad-dressing recipe.

Boyd goes other places Fleming never did. He has the presumption to depict Bond – for the very first time in print – dropping the f-bomb without decorous dashes. Meanwhile, the anti-big-business tenor is something that it would never have occurred to Fleming to inject, even if he was a small-c conservative.

When Bond is in 'civilisation', Boyd's writing is gauche and off-key. Perhaps significantly, the book picks up in Africa: a scene where a lost Bond wanders the jungle for a couple of days drips with authenticity. In Africa, Bond meets a reasonably intriguing villain: mercenary Jakobus Breed, who has a caved-in face and a physical dysfunction that sees his eyes continually weep. The book sags again, though, when Bond goes 'solo'. Having single-handedly brought down the state of Zanzarim, he sets off to America on an unofficial mission, seeking answers from Breed to questions that still plague him about what he saw in the 'Dark Continent'. Unfortunately, Boyd has him largely do this via dialogue: the end section contains page after page of boring exposition.

Following Charlie Higson's departure, IFP decided to continue the Young Bond series.

The man who ultimately transpired to be prepared to wade into the murky area of the timeframe of the nascent agent's sexual awakening was Steve Cole, an author known for his Astrosaurs children's books but with some experience of continuing franchises through penning Doctor Who novels.

Shoot to Kill, published in November 2014, saw Bond both grappling with a new progressive school following his expulsion from Eton and uncovering some distasteful goings-on in thirties Hollywood. There were probably few children who were contrasting and comparing Higson and Cole: the series' demographic had grown up in the six years since *By Royal Command*. However, the adult Bond fans were pleasantly surprised at how Cole had kept up the quality and Fleming-faithfulness established by his predecessor even as he incrementally deepened the implausibility of James having such an eventful teenage.

Heads You Die – book two of a projected quartet – was scheduled for 2016.

Meanwhile, September 2015 saw publication of a new adult James Bond novel, *Trigger Mortis*.

Although immensely successful in young fiction and television, its author Anthony Horowitz was not quite as prestigious a name as the three previous non-children's Bond novelists. However – shades of John Gardner – one of his adult novels was *The House of Silk*, a Sherlock Holmes novel. And then there was his sequence of books about teenage MI6 operative Alex Rider, the vast success of which it seems inconceivable IFP were unaware of when they instigated the Young Bond series.

Horowitz was allowed by IFP to flesh out 'Murder on Wheels', one of the plot outlines of the aborted fifties James Bond television series. Fleming's gimmicky and cartoonish treatment involved Bond entering a Grand Prix event to thwart a Russian plot to cause then-current racing driver Stirling Moss to crash his car. Yet Horowitz does well with his flimsy base, making the racetrack scheming part of a continuum culminating in the sabotaging of a US rocket launch and planting of a bomb in New York. The race itself is convincing and exciting. In fact, Horowitz's action sequences are better than those of any previous Bond continuation novelist. Particularly thrillingly drawn are a section where Bond makes an escape after being buried alive and a denouement wherein, to defuse the bomb, he has to climb along the roof of a speeding New York subway train.

It's in other areas that Horowitz fails. His exposition and insertion of research is clumsy. His non-action prose is often utilitarian. He also fails to distinguish between sprinkling in classic ingredients and shovelling in cliché. The reader wants to groan when the villain says to 007, 'I am going to tell you the story of my life, Mr Bond . . . in a short while you will be dead.'

The villain is a SMERSH-affiliated Korean with a superbly Bondian name: Sin Jai-Seong has been Westernised against his will to Jason Sin. Chief love interest Jeopardy Lane also has a wonderfully Fleming-esque handle. However, the title of the book – an American rocket-base staff nickname for a self-destruct mechanism – is more appropriate to the juvenile territory of Alex Rider.

Moreover, Horowitz contradicts facts established by Fleming, such as Bond's having been a 'chocolate sailor' pre-*Thunderball*, gives Pussy Galore a purposeless cameo, and retro-projects modern, liberal sensibilities on the 1957 time period.

The only time Horowitz does trump Fleming is by giving Bond a fatalism about his cigarette consumption logical in the context of his perilous job: '. . . if cancer had any fancy ideas about killing him, it would just have to take its place in the queue.'

On 20 November 2006, Kevin McClory died in Dublin, aged eighty.

Although McClory acquired some kudos for writing and directing the quirky 1959 film *The Boy and the Bridge*, that he was of limited talent seems proven by the fact that, outside Bond, he did nothing else of note cinematically.

With *Thunderball*, he had a 20 per cent profit share of one of the most viewed motion pictures of all time. Yet not only did he not get off the ground any other movie projects – aside from its remake – but he did not live the lifestyle of splendour one would assume. According to Robert Sellers, in 1987 – only four years after *Never Say Never Again* – McClory was on the run from debtors, his palatial Bahamas property locked up and decaying, his gardener unpaid and his cheques to hotels and travel agents bouncing. Raymond Benson, who got to know McClory a little, says, 'I respected him but he was quite colourful, to put it mildly. He was very eccentric.'

McClory never really stopped trying to pursue what he felt were his rights to make Bond films. 'He claimed he was the father of the cinematic James Bond,' says Benson. 'He kept wanting to do more James Bond. He felt like he owned it. He felt like he was the one who should have been in Broccoli and Saltzman's shoes. He was obsessed with it. To his dying day, he was fighting it.'

In November 2013, McClory's heirs decided to stop the fight he had waged for decades. In selling to Danjaq and MGM the rights once held by McClory in the James Bond character, they brought to an end what Sellers termed 'the Battle for Bond'. In so doing, they paved the way for the return in official Bond films of SPECTRE and Ernst Stavro Blofeld.

Eon decided to make a big deal of the development even though, courtesy of constant TV screenings of classic Bonds, much of the public had no idea SPECTRE and Blofeld had ever departed from the cinematic Bond universe. In December 2014, a media conference was held on the 007 Stage in Pinewood Studios to announce the title of the new Bond picture: *Spectre*. (Almost predictably, that had been the proposed title of one of the endless Bond projects floated by McClory.) The gloss was somewhat taken off the film later that month by an Internet leak of its script. Also leaked were internal Sony communications, which revealed disquiet at the studio about the quality of that script. When the film shortly began shooting, it was widely believed that the screenplay was still being worked on, which was somewhat worrying in the wake of the ad hoc nature of much of *Quantum of Solace*.

Another strand of the leaked communications revealed that black English actor Idris Elba was the preferred choice of Sony co-chairman Amy Pascal to play Bond at whatever point in the future Daniel Craig decided to leave the role. Elba had previously been asked by the website *Reddit* whether he would take the part.

He replied, 'Yes. If it was offered to me, absolutely.' The idea of a black man playing Bond would have once been unthinkable: large-scale Afro-Caribbean immigration to the UK had begun only around five years before the first Bond book was published. Roger Moore was subsequently criticised for remarking of the Elba proposal to *Paris Match*, 'Although James may have been played by a Scot, a Welshman and an Irishman, I think he should be "English-English". Nevertheless, it's an interesting idea, but unrealistic.' However, black South African comedian Trevor Noah had in 2013 on UK comedy show *8 Out of 10 Cats* expressed similar scepticism about a black Bond when he said, 'You can't blend in in Moscow when you're black.'

Spectre – premiered on 26 October 2015 – has a new gun-barrel sequence. In two firsts for Craig movies, it's in the conventional place and the actor looks comfortable: loose-limbed and stylish. Unfortunately, the film deteriorates from that point on.

Sam Smith's 'Writing's on the Wall', co-written with Jimmy Napes, continues the Craig era's tradition of a theme song that doesn't mention the title. It's operatically sung but ordinary, while Thomas Newman provides a score that lazily cannibalises that of *Skyfall*. Daniel Kleinman's opening titles show a bare-chested Craig being caressed by nubile lovelies while tentacles alluding to Spectre's octopus logo dance in the background. It's either sensual or creepy.

Craig is by now powerful enough – and interested enough – to be co-producer. He is also, of course, primarily responsible for Sam Mendes – unusually for latter-day Bond directors – returning for an encore.

The spectacular pre-title sequence set among the Day of the

Dead festival in Mexico includes a jaw-doppingly long tracking shot. However, not even the visual splendour created by Mendes can quell the unease about the fact that Bond is extravagantly, ludicrously insubordinate from the get-go. For the fourth movie in a row – a grand slam of Craig Bonds – 007 has gone rogue. This irresponsibility inimical to secret services goes down even worse with M than it normally would: Max Denbigh, a.k.a. 'C' (Andrew Scott) is bent on disbanding the 'double-O programme' to instigate the less labour-intensive Nine Eyes, a digitally based international surveillance setup. (The phrase 'licence to kill' is revived, despite *Casino Royale*'s two-kills-to-join edict having made it contradictory.)

Bond proceeds to go even roguer from there, ignoring his suspension from duty to continue the pursuit of baddies on which he has been set by a DVD from Judi Dench's M that mysteriously arrived after she died. Scriptwriters Logan, Purvis & Wade and Jez Butterworth don't bother exploring where in the timeline she would have had the premonition of death that motivated her to pop it in the post but instead concentrate on whisking us across the globe. Italy, Austria and Morocco provide spectacular landscapes in which to set Bond's mayhem. The $300 million this all cost makes this one of the most expensive movies ever filmed. One section, incidentally, emanates from Kingsley Amis: a torture scene broadly reproduces a passage in *Colonel Sun* and is the first time that any part of a Bond continuation novel has been adapted to the screen.

The fact that Spectre no longer has a comic-book meaning – it's a name, rather than an acronym (hence the lower-case lettering) – is one of the few examples here of the Craig era's relative realism. Another is the fact that Ralph Fiennes's M is a civil-libertarian worried about the intrusion into personal privacy of the surveillance organisations. Otherwise, the picture is an awkward mixture of later Connery Bonds and the more knowing Craig brand. Its swaggering, pleased-with-itself tenor is reminiscent of *Thunderball*, while its outlandish villain's lair – a spectacular building located in a desert crater and populated by inexplicably unquestioning staff – puts one in mind of the volcano HQ in *You Only Live Twice*.

The film constitutes the origin story of Ernst Stavro Blofeld. Rather improbably, it is one that bisects with part of Bond's origin story: after gatecrashing a Spectre meeting, Bond recognises the organisation's chief as Franz Oberhauser (double Oscar-winner Christoph Waltz). It turns out that Oberhauser was so resentful of the way his father Hannes treated Bond as a surrogate son following the death of his own parents that he both killed Pater and dissociated himself from him by adopting a name from his mother's Blofeld lineage. His fate as a bad man was thus sealed, and his villainous activities have always been intertwined with an obsession with his former foster brother. This is irritating on many levels: it pointlessly messes with the facts established in Fleming's 'Octopussy' short story; it is psychologically unconvincing; it displays a self-indulgence on the part of Eon about the 007 mythos; and, most of all, it diminishes Bond's cause: 'This time it's personal' does not chime with a man so dedicated to Queen and country that his flat (shown here) is a soulless shell.

An origin is also provided for the disfiguring facial scar that Donald Pleasance memorably bore when providing the first image of Blofeld: Bond causes it when demolishing the villain's desert hideout. Despite this, a Nehru suit and the brief throwing-in of a white cat, it all feels false: Waltz comes across like an accountant, not a megalomaniac.

Spectre is revealed to be the umbrella organisation to which

Quantum and its associates have been answering all along. Perhaps it's another example of Craig-era realism that Spectre is not bent on world domination or extorting vast sums of money for the return of warheads, but the nature of its wickedness seems inchoate, even pathetic. Its plans merely revolve around organising terrorist atrocities so as to panic governments into draconian surveillance methods to which it will have access via Denbigh, who turns out to be its man on the inside of MI6. M, Q and Moneypenny race to stop Nine Eyes going live, while Bond has a showdown with Blofeld in and around the MI6 building, which for some reason the writers have decided to pretend has remained a wreck in real life following the fictional damage done to it in *Skyfall*. This can perhaps be excused as alternate reality, but it's difficult to come up with a rationale for the film's multiple discrepancies with logic, such as how Bond had a bug in the room of villain Marco Sciarra when his mission was unofficial, or how Blofeld was running the patently free agent Silva in *Skyfall*, or even why nobody bats an eyelid when Bond demolishes a train in a fight, leaving him free afterwards to engage in a bout of lovemaking.

In line with their current tendency to practically apologise for Bond and what he supposedly stands for, Eon made great play of the advanced age (fifty) of Monica Bellucci, but in fact her character Lucia Sciarra is only one of the 'Bond girls' (as they're increasingly not called) herein. The main one is Madeleine Swann (Léa Seydoux), the doctor daughter of Mr White, who is reliably young. Mr White has been exiled from Spectre and consigned to death for expressing distaste at its methods – this despite his having been happy in *Casino Royale* to work for a group behind 9/11. No more comprehensible is why the hostile Madeleine whimpers to Bond, 'I love you' after one sex session. This sort of stuff is strung out over 148 minutes, the longest ever instalment in the series.

If Eon are inclined to apologise for anything, it should be the sickening scene in which villain Hinx (Dave Bautista) sticks his steel thumbnails into a rival's eyes.

Blofeld is alive, if captured, at movie's end, leaving the way open for his return. Not necessarily the case with Daniel Craig: he is shown throwing his gun away, while Q pointedly says, 'I thought you'd gone,' before Bond and Madeleine ride off in the old Aston Martin DB5. It all gives credence to the rumour that *Spectre* is Craig's farewell. If true, it's an unfortunate and puzzling swansong, paving the way for a successor not to make more naturalistic Bond movies like his first three but to return to Connery and Moore kitsch.

Daniel Craig commented to journalist Bill Deskowitz of *Casino Royale*, 'I wouldn't have touched this movie if I didn't see an element of where we saw him change.' He told *Rolling Stone* in 2012, 'I've been trying to get out of this from the very moment I got into it, but they won't let me go, and I've agreed to do a couple more . . .' He told *Time Out* after the completion of *Spectre* that he would rather 'slash my wrists' than do another Bond and that 'All I want to do is move on.'

Some might view Craig's comments as ungrateful and graceless, notwithstanding shooting schedules that oblige him to be away from his family for eight-month stretches and the multiple operations on his body the rigours of the part have necessitated. Sony seem to think so. It was reported that he had been reprimanded by the studio after the *Time Out* comments.

Nonetheless, it's difficult to dislike Craig. Whatever his luvvie pretensions, his Scouse background has given him a candour (he cheerfully admits to accessing Internet porn), an earthy sense of humour (a joke he tells about his grandmother's private parts and five oysters is not for the faint-hearted) and directness (when in 2011 Alex Bilmes of *Esquire* asked him what his new film *Cowboys & Aliens* was about, he responded, 'It's about cowboys and fucking aliens, what do you think it's about?').

His directness extends to 007. Speaking about his Bond tenure to Bilmes a couple of months before *Spectre*'s release, he said, 'No disrespect to what happened before but this is completely different. It's got weight and meaning.'

When Fleming created Bond, divorce was so difficult to obtain that marriage was for many synonymous with lifelong burden, while casual sex had a corresponding air of freedom and glamour. Now that marriages are as easy to exit as enter, making companionship less fraught with peril, middle-aged bachelorhood like Bond's seems not so much enviable as immature. Craig seemed to be reflecting this when he opined of 007, 'He's very fucking lonely. There's a great sadness. He's fucking these beautiful women but then they leave and it's . . . sad. And as a man gets older it's not a good look. It might be a nice fantasy – that's debatable – but the reality, after a couple of months . . . Hopefully, my Bond is not as sexist and misogynistic as [earlier incarnations]. The world has changed. I am certainly not that person.' One can't imagine any previous Bond actor coming out with such comments. They certainly have more truth than the metronomic insistence of the actresses playing Bond girls from at least the late 1980s that their character is different from all the previous ones as they unconvincingly throw around phrases such as 'strong woman' and 'more than a match for . . .'

After all the hoo-hah first surrounding the engagement of his services, Craig has made the Bond role his. In doing so, he has redrawn definitions of male beauty. He has also, of course, redrawn definitions of 007. Like all serving Bonds, he has a gravitas and authority by default (one that, by the same token, can be whisked away in a heartbeat upon replacement: many now can't believe Roger Moore and Timothy Dalton were ever allowed to play Bond). Yet his aura comes from something more than incumbency. His thoughtfulness and dedication – which feed into the quality of his films – make us forget for the duration of the viewing experience that there were other, very different 007s. Such has been the overhaul to the character his tenure had brought that's it's difficult to imagine where the series will go once he leaves. Will it carry on the Craig films' grim timbre and self-contained continuity or will it rewrite the rules and the facts again?

Craig and his cohorts have confirmed that Bond can be updated and reordered almost beyond recognition while maintaining brand loyalty. His portrayal of the character bears no relation to the *ding-dong!* quality of the longest-serving Bond but has actually widened the profit-making abilities of what was already history's pre-eminent movie series.

JAMES BOND
WILL RETURN

Although much media fuss was made about the Sony Internet leak, the problems it allegedly revealed about *Spectre* were doubtlessly viewed by James Bond cognoscenti as an inconsequential blip destined to be forgotten as soon as the first grosses came in.

The simple fact is that there has never been a flop James Bond movie. Eon and/or their distributors may have been slightly disappointed by the respective box-office performances of *On Her Majesty's Secret Service*, *The Man with the Golden Gun* and *Licence to Kill*, but all of those films took money hand over fist and were failures only when compared with the fiscal standards set by other Bond movies. Even when 007 pictures have been terrible (the 1967 *Casino Royale*) or quasi-illegitimate (*Never Say Never Again*), they have brought punters into cinemas.

Bond's allure remains consistent on the printed page as well. Not only are all of Ian Fleming's works still in print, they now enjoy the status of Modern Classics. Additionally, the publishing schedules will continue to play host to writers authorised to rearrange and reinterpret the fixtures of the universe first established for Bond by Fleming more than sixty years ago.

Whereas the respective media presences of once-prominent twentieth-century action heroes have often been reduced to zero, James Bond remains one of the most famous fictional characters in the world, despite that world having shifted and metamorphosed around him. The reasons can be debated: Bulldog Drummond was too brutish to sustain a long-term appeal; Biggles too rooted in a precise point in history; Tarzan too limited to a specific geographical terrain; Richard Hannay too lacking in distinct characteristics; Simon Templar too freelance and piecemeal in his mission. The main reason, of course, is that James Bond was with spectacular success transplanted to the medium of the motion picture, and that that series of motion pictures – and its signature catchphrases and set pieces – have been carefully cultivated each and every outing for purposes of optimum effect and continued relevance.

Today is possibly the most exciting of all times for Bond fans. The films have been transformed from something approaching, in the arch Roger Moore era, a joke to something in the Daniel Craig era that Academy Award winners are pleased to direct and appear in. They please the intelligentsia while packing fleapits with those of less sophisticated palates. Meanwhile, the curators of the Bond book rights have alighted on a commissioning policy that has hauled 007 back to a position where he can hold his own with his cinematic incarnation. New Bond novels are once again both events and bestsellers. Bond is even a cultural presence for those people interested in neither films nor books: he stands on equal footing with titans of video gaming like *Grand Theft Auto*, *Call of Duty* and *World of Warcraft*.

The most prominent manifestation of Bond will, of course, continue to be the motion-picture one. Roger Moore is impressed by the way the latest generation of Broccolis guide their birthright. 'Michael and Barbara are very clever in that they keep one step ahead of public tastes and changes, and adapt,' he says. 'They lead and others follow. Jim will be around for a long time to come as a result.'

But will he? Every dog has its day. Can David V. Picker – so instrumental in guiding 007's transition from book to screen, as well as a man who knows of the fluctuating fortunes of motion-picture properties – see a point where Bond pictures will cease being successful? Where they will dribble away in a manner once considered unthinkable for other colossally successful, long-running film series such as Sherlock Holmes, Andy Hardy and Tarzan? 'No,' he says simply. 'There are just some things that work. Bond worked and I'm sure will continue to work. It may vary a little bit one way or the other, but the fact is that you can't destroy a unique aspect of the film industry.'

Summing up, he says, 'Tarzan had his time. Andy Hardy had his time. James Bond seems to me for all time.'

THE END. NOT QUITE THE END . . .

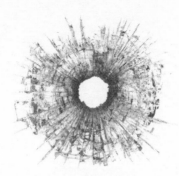

ACKNOWLEDGEMENTS

My grateful thanks to the following people for granting me interviews: Raymond Benson, Martin Campbell, Jeremy Duns, Sir Roger Moore, Monty Norman, John Pearson, David V. Picker and Norman Wanstall.

Additional thanks to Jeremy Duns for providing valuable advice and insight and to Fionn Morgan, who read through parts of the manuscript directly concerned with Ian Fleming's life and family.

SELECTED
BIBLIOGRAPHY

BOOKS

Amis, Kingsley, *The James Bond Dossier* (Pan, 1966)

Broccoli; Albert R., and Zec, Donald, *When The Snow Melts: The Autobiography of Cubby Broccoli* (Boxtree, 1998)

Bryce, Ivar, *You Only Live Once: Memories of Ian Fleming* (Weidenfeld & Nicolson, 1975)

Burlingame, Jon, *The Music of James Bond* (Oxford University Press, USA, 2012)

Chancellor, Henry, *James Bond: The Man and His World* (John Murray, 2005)

Chapman, James, *Licence To Thrill: A Cultural History of the James Bond Films* (Tauris, 2007)

Christie, Thomas A., *The James Bond Movies of the 1980s* (Crescent Moon, 2013)

O'Connell, Mark, *Catching Bullets* (Splendid, 2012)

Cork, John, and Scivally, Bruce, *James Bond – The Legacy* (Boxtree, 2002)

Mankiewicz, Tom, and Crane, Robert, *My Life as a Mankiewicz: An Insider's Journey Through Hollywood* (University Press of Kentucky, 2012)

Desowitz, Bill, *James Bond Unmasked* (Spies LLC, 2012)

Duns, Jeremy, *Rogue Royale: The Lost Bond Film By The 'Shakespeare of Hollywood'* (Kindle, 2014)

Fiegel, Eddi, *John Barry: A Sixties Theme: From James Bond to Midnight Cowboy* (Faber & Faber, 2012)

Field, Matthew, and Chowdhury, Ajay, *Some Kind of Hero: The Remarkable Story of the James Bond Films* (History Press, 2015)

Fleming, Fergus, *The Man with the Golden Typewriter: Ian Fleming's James Bond Letters* (Bloomsbury Publishing, 2015)

Fleming, Ian, Hern, Anthony, Gammidge, Henry, and McLusky, John, *James Bond: Casino Royale* (Titan, 2005)

Griswold, John, *Ian Fleming's James Bond: Annotations and Chronologies for Ian Fleming's Bond Stories* (new edn) (AuthorHouse, 2006)

Lane, Andy, and Simpson, Paul, *The Bond Files: The Unofficial Guide to the World's Greatest Secret Agent* (Virgin, 2002)

Lindner, Christoph, *The James Bond Phenomenon* (2nd edn) (Manchester University Press, 2006)

Lycett, Andrew, *Ian Fleming* (Orion, 2009)

Macintyre, Ben, *For Your Eyes Only: Ian Fleming and James Bond* (Bloomsbury, 2008)

Mills, Alec, *Shooting 007: And Other Celluloid Adventures* (The History Press, 2014)

Moore, Roger, *My Word Is My Bond* (Michael O'Mara, 2009)

Morecambe, Gary, and Sterling, Martin. *Cary Grant: In Name Only* (Robson, 2003)

Pearson, John, *The Life Of Ian Fleming: The Man Who Created James Bond* (Aurum, 2003)

Pfeiffer, Lee, and Worrall, Dave, *The Essential James Bond* (Boxtree, 2003)

Rosenberg, Bruce A., and Stewart, Ann H., *Ian Fleming* (Twayne Publishers, 1989)

Sellers, Robert, *The Battle for Bond* (2nd edn) (Tomahawk, 2008)

Simmons, Bob, *Nobody Does it Better* (Javelin, 1987)

Simpson, Paul, *The Rough Guide To James Bond* (Rough Guides, 2002)

Stein, Ellin, *That's Not Funny, That's Sick: The National Lampoon and the Comedy Insurgents Who Captured the Mainstream* (W. W. Norton & Company, 2013)

Wood, Christopher, *James Bond, The Spy I Loved* (Twenty First Century, 2006)

Yeffeth, Glenn, *James Bond In The 21st Century: Why We Still Need 007* (Benbella, 2006)

WEBSITES

http://007today.blogspot.co.uk
http://archive.today
http://classicbond.com
http://commanderbond.net
http://dochermes.livejournal.com
http://edition.cnn.com
http://eustonfilms.blogspot.co.uk
http://fivedials.com
http://jamesbond.wikia.com
http://jamesbondmemes.blogspot.co.uk
http://literary007.com

http://shatterhand007.com

the007dossier.com

http://thebondbulletin.blogspot.co.uk

http://thebondologistblog.blogspot.co.uk

http://www.007james.com

http://www.007magazine.co.uk

http://www.007museum.com

http://www.afi.com

http://www.bbc.co.uk

http://www.bbfc.co.uk

http://www.boxofficemojo.com

http://www.bucksherald.co.uk

http://www.cinemaretro.com

http://www.corgi.free.fr

http://www.dailymail.co.uk

http://www.democracynow.org

http://www.ianfleming.com

http://www.interviewmagazine.com

http://www.jamesbondfirsteditions.com

http://www.jeremy-duns.com

http://www.john-gardner.com

http://www.mi6-hq.com

http://www.oscars.org

http://www.piercebrosnan.com

http://www.raymondbenson.com

http://www.readthespirit.com

http://www.scotsman.com

http://www.script-o-rama.com

http://www.sylvanmason.com

http://www.thebookbond.com

http://www.universalexports.net
http://youngbonddossier.com
https://archive.org
https://en.wikipedia.org
www.007forever.com
www.allmusic.com
www.oxforddictionaries.com

MAGAZINE ARTICLES

'Richard Maibaum 007's Puppetmaster' by Lee Goldberg, *Starlog*, March 1983
'Gardner's World' by Raymond Benson, *007* magazine, #28, October 1995 (as reproduced on http://www.john-gardner.com)

MISCELLANEOUS

History of James Bond Games (1983–2014) by Fat Mad (YouTube compilation)
Never To Be Disclosed: Government Secrecy in Britain 1945–1975 (thesis) by Christopher R. Moran BA, MA